Social Work with
Children and Families

of related interest

Divorcing Children
Children's Experiences of their Parents' Divorce
Ian Butler, Lesley Scanlan, Margaret Robinson, Gillian Douglas and Mervyn Munch
ISBN 1 84310 103 3

The Developing World of the Child
Edited by Jane Aldgate, David Jones, Wendy Rose and Carole Jeffery
ISBN 1 84310 244 7

The Child's World
Assessing Children in Need
Edited by Jan Horwath
ISBN 1 85302 957 2

Supporting Parents
Messages from Research
David Quinton
Department of Health
ISBN 1 84310 210 2

Child Development for Child Care and Protection Workers
Brigid Daniel, Sally Wassel & Robbie Gilligan
ISBN 1 85302 633 6

Making an Impact
Children and Domestic Violence
A Reader
Marianne Hester, Chris Pearson and Nicola Harwin
ISBN 1 85302 844 4

Competence in Social Work Practice
A Practical Guide for Professionals
Edited by Kieran O'Hagan
ISBN 1 85302 332 9

Handbook of Theory for Practice Teachers in Social Work
Edited by Joyce Lishman
ISBN 1 85302 098 2

Social Work with Children and Families

Getting into Practice

Second Edition

Ian Butler and Gwenda Roberts

Jessica Kingsley Publishers
London and Phildaelphia

Contents

List of Figures

List of Tables

Dedication

Daniel, Elin, Ffion, Madlen, Mark, Matthew, Richard,
and to Holly Welch

Acknowledgements

Everything we know someone else taught us, although our teachers can take no responsibility for our errors and omissions; those really are all our own work. In the case of the material presented here, we acknowledge our debt to all of those colleagues with whom we worked when we were practitioners ourselves. More immediately, we acknowledge the enormous contribution made by fellow teachers on the qualifying social work course at the University of Wales, Cardiff, where most of the exercises and other teaching materials were first tried and tested. In particular, we would like to thank Dolores Davey, Penny Lloyd, Richard Hibbs, Geoff Waites and Tony Bloore. Thanks are due also to the many students who took part in our experiments. We probably learned more from them than from anyone else, except perhaps those children and families for whom we did our best (and worst) when we were social workers.

Our own children and families are probably used to being left until last: we are grateful for your patience and support and promise not to do this sort of thing again (until the next time). A special thanks to Pat Smail for proofreading the manuscript and the typescript and the printer's proofs.

Ian Butler and Gwenda Roberts

Preface to the Second Edition

The first chapter of this book begins with an account of a cricket match being played in the garden. By the time it came to write the preface to this, second edition, the batsman had finished his first year at secondary school. He has spiked his hair and wears a studded dog collar. His big brother is now a medical student. Neither has touched a cricket bat for years. Their middle brother (who was up in his bedroom playing his guitar when the other two were playing cricket) is the one who has turned out to be the serious sportsman in the family. How times change!

On the other hand, the England side has had another disappointing winter and their father is still at his desk, still writing and still thinking he would rather be outside in the sunshine. Some things never change. So, too, with the task in hand. In preparing a second edition of this book, we were struck by how much we had to do to bring the text up to date. Social work education has been transformed and entirely new regulatory structures have come into being. There is another Green Paper out for consultation that may usher in widespread changes in the local delivery of services to children. There is new legislation to consider, both general and specific. There have been new policy initiatives, new inquiries into child deaths, new regulations, new guidance, new jargon, new Jerusalems. But still, much remains the same. There are still a great many children and their families in the UK who are denied the opportunities in life that others are afforded. There are still far too many social workers who think that they can know and understand others without knowing or understanding themselves. There are too many people who think that there are easy solutions to complex problems (there are, of course, but they are almost always the wrong answers!).

In revising this book, we have updated and considerably expanded the 'hard knowledge' we include, reflecting changes in the law and incorporating evidence from research published in the period since the first edition of this book went to press. In particular, we have taken much fuller account of the policy context in which contemporary forms of practice are set. This means that we have included detailed reference to a number of central government initiatives (such as 'Quality Protects') and to the relevant 'standard forms' of practice that have developed over recent years (such as the Framework for Assessment of Children in Need). We do not do so uncritically and we make some reference to the controversies that surround the new orthodoxy of evidence-based practice and 'third way welfare'. We have also taken account of the new regulatory framework that surrounds contemporary practice and included sections on, for example, the National Care Standards Commission and various National Minimum Standards.

There is always more that one could add and so, in order to extend the scope of what can be included within the covers of a single book, we have added to each Unit a section providing access to resources available via the internet. We have however retained the form of the book (how to use this book is explained a little later) and we have not altered in our belief that it is through a process of 'study, reflection and application' that we can best 'get into practice'.

We would very much like to acknowledge the additional help we have received in preparing this edition of the book. In particular, we want to thank Graham Allan (Keele University) for his help in revising certain sections of Unit 2 and Alison Brammer (also of Keele University) for her meticulous review of those sections of the book that deal with the law. We are also enormously grateful to artist and therapist Elaine Holliday for the drawings that bring the text to life.

We would also like to note, with sadness, the death of a former colleague of ours, Tony Bloore, who was a leading light in the delivery of the lectures and seminars around which the original book was written. He was the most conscientious of social workers and one of the kindest.

Ian would also like to acknowledge the part played by the Calshot Bankers (The Daddy, Prince Marco, The Captain, Three-Piece, American

Dave, Rocco and Stevo), not the best but certainly the coolest cycling team in the UK, for providing so many insights into how to live with personal problems!

Ian Butler and Gwenda Roberts
July 2003

Introduction

Any teacher will tell you that it is often the simplest questions that require the most complicated answers. What kind of work do social workers and other professionals undertake with children and families? Where does such work take place? What do you need to know in order to begin work with young people and their carers? Even the terms of the questions defy easy definitions. What exactly do you mean by 'children'? What precisely is a 'family'? This book is offered in response to such deceptively simple enquiries.

It has its origins in a series of seminars for first- and second-year students following a basic social work qualifying course. The seminars were intended to introduce participants to the nature and range of child and family social work, to provide them with opportunities to apply their broader appreciation and knowledge of social work theory and practice to work in this area and to encourage them to reflect on what they brought to the helping process. The first part of this book is intended to fulfil the same ambitions. It is aimed at those who have recently begun or who are intending to work with children and families and who recognize the need to start from first principles. The second part of the book is aimed more directly at supporting the development of specialist knowledge and skills, or rather the application of generic skills in particular settings.

Of course, if we really could fully answer the questions that we began with, then this book would probably be a great deal longer than it is. It would also be the only one of its kind on the shelves. The fact that it is neither is proof enough that we do not make any exaggerated claims for it. What we aim to do in this book is to ask what are, in fact, fiendishly complex questions in such a way that the reader can provide the answers for him- or herself using all the means at his or her disposal, including his or her own experience and knowledge drawn from elsewhere. The structure of the book reflects this aim in that each Unit is predicated on the active involvement of the reader, who will ideally have the opportunity to compare his or her developing understanding with others in the same position. Although it is perfectly possible to use this book as a self-contained introduction to child and family social work, in neither situation could it be considered a passive read. In this way it is different to other textbooks in this area.

This book is different also in that it contains sufficient 'hard knowledge' to enable serious engagement with the key themes of social work practice with children and families but without pretensions to exhaustiveness. As such, we hope we have provided a framework through which knowledge derived elsewhere, possibly as part of a broader-based social work or specific child care training, can be extended and applied.

We firmly believe that whatever interventive technologies or fashions currently exist, or are likely to emerge in future years, ultimately it is only people who change people. In the classroom, and in this book, our aim has been to encourage social workers to know themselves better: their prejudices, strengths and limitations and what they bring to the helping process. Practitioners must be able to reflect on what they do and be able to articulate and defend their motivations, theoretical perspectives and beliefs. We hope that the process of study, reflection and application – the pattern for each Unit in this book – will impress itself upon the reader, who will then be able to 'get into practice' with children and families in both senses of the term.

How to Use This Book

The material in each Unit is arranged under headings as follows:

Course Text – this stands in lieu of the trainer or teacher. The 'Course Text' introduces and links the themes and issues that are the focus of each Unit.

Exercises – at the core of each Unit are a number of exercises for you to complete. In the second part of the book, most of the exercises are based on an extended case study.

Study Texts – these are intended to provide you with sufficient factual information and background knowledge to complete the exercises and extend your specialist knowledge of the field.

Points to Consider – these are prompts to reflect more broadly on key issues that should occur to you as you complete the exercises.

Notes and Self-Assessment – these, which come at the end of each Unit, will provide you with an opportunity to think back over all that you have read in the Unit and to locate what you have learned in a wider professional and personal context.

Recommended Reading – this is a list of two books that we think will help you to extend and develop your understanding of the material presented in the Unit. We have decided to recommend books rather than journal articles, simply on the grounds that many readers may not have easy access to the kind of libraries that will carry professional or academic journals. All of the books that we have recommended are in print and can be ordered from any local authority or university library.

Trainer's Notes – these are suggestions of how to adapt the exercise material contained in the Unit for use as a basis for working in groups.

Web Resources – these are websites that provide access to e-resources and documentary material that we think you will find helpful, not only for the purposes of working your way through this book but also when you are actually 'in practice'. We have tried to include a range of resources, from government department sites that contain information on developments in top-level policy to sites offering material for use in direct work. Because individual 'pages' on websites are frequently moved or re-designed, we have tried to give the URL ('address') of more 'stable' home pages. This may mean that you will have to use the webpage's 'sitemap' or search facility to find the exact source that we have identified.

Many of the sites, especially government ones, offer the facility to download documents in 'portable document format' (pdf). This will require you to have particular software on your computer (Adobe Acrobat). Most sites will help you with acquiring this free software. If in doubt, visit http://www.adobe.co.uk/main.html.

PART I

Developing Basic Knowledge and Skills

UNIT I

Children and Childhood

OBJECTIVES

In this unit you will:

- Reflect on your own and others' experience of childhood.
- Examine how childhood is socially constructed.
- Review the needs and rights of children.
- Explore the principle of welfare paramountcy.

 PLAYING CHILDREN

As these words are being written, there is a game of cricket in progress outside. The batsman is aged six and the bowler thirteen. The six-year-old is taking the game very seriously. In between balls, he is practising shots, examining the pitch and checking for any changes to the field settings. The thirteen-year-old is messing about, running up to bowl on 'wobbly legs' and broadcasting a much exaggerated, and very loud, commentary on the game. From his desk, their father is watching the game. He is caught between knowing that he has to finish this chapter and desperately wanting to go out and play. By staring out of the window, he manages to do neither and, out of frustration, shouts at the players to take their game elsewhere. Which one of these three could best be described as being a child or as behaving like one?

It seems entirely appropriate that we should begin this book with a question about children. We suspect that everyone would claim to know something already about the subject and it is a sound educational principle to ask questions only when one has a reasonable expectation of receiving an answer. It's obvious who the children are, isn't it? Possibly, but on what basis do we decide? Age doesn't seem to be the determining factor. The six-year-old is the one behaving most sensibly. Physical ability doesn't seem to be decisive in that each one of them can do some things to the envy of the others. The possession of particular skills and knowledge does not seem to be helping either the thirteen-year-old or the forty-year-old. Nor do the activities in which they are engaged seem to be the deciding factors. Children and adults both write and play cricket. If we were to ask these three characters themselves how they might respond to being likened to children, the thirteen-year-old, despite his behaviour, is the one most likely to object and the forty-year-old, within reason, is the one most likely to be pleased at being mistaken for someone younger. The six-year-old wouldn't expect to be referred to as anything else. Perhaps the answer to our question is not quite so obvious after all.

Few of the everyday terms and 'common-sense' ideas encountered in social work with children and families, such as 'childhood', 'family' or 'parenthood', are as straightforward as they first appear. It is central to the purpose of this book to explore the meaning of such terms and to recognize how our understanding of them might affect our practice. If we were to look at childhood beyond this trivial example, across generations and geographical boundaries, then our sense of what the term means would become much less obvious. What are the similarities and differences between these three lives and those of the thousands of young people who, in the thirteenth century, went off to fight in the Children's Crusade? Or with the daily lives of those children press-ganged into the eighteenth-century Navy or who, not much more than a century ago, pulled wagons of coal to the earth's surface just a few miles from where these words were written? What links the experiences of these children with the 40,000 others who will die today and every day from malnutrition or the 150 million more who live on in poor health across the world?

This Unit is about children or, more accurately, social work in relation to our understanding of children. The first exercise in this Unit and the study text that follows it are intended to widen your appreciation of the variability of childhood and encourage you to question some of the assumptions you and others may make about it.

Exercise 1.1: Images of Childhood

Assemble a selection of recent newspapers and general interest magazines. Look through them for pictures of children. All kinds of images (not just news photographs) should be included. Once you have collected about twenty images, spread them out so that you can see all of them at once.

TASKS

1. 'Quickthink[1]' a few words that you associate with each image.

2. Write down for what purpose you think each image is being used.

3. Write down what each image reminds you of about your own childhood or those of children for whom you are personally or professionally responsible.

Then complete the following sentence with at least ten different answers:
   Childhood is...

Points to Consider

1. Does your collection of images suggest that childhood is experienced or represented differently depending on gender or race, for example? If so, how?

---

1   'Quickthinking' is a little like word association. All you have to do is write down, without 'editing', as many words as you can think of that you associate with the particular stimulus or prompt.

2.   Would you say that there are there any universal components to the experience of childhood? If so, what are they?

3.   Overall, do the images suggest that children are highly valued in contemporary society? What qualities/attributes seem particularly valued?

4.   Do you detect any differences between how you, as an adult, and the children in the images might describe what each image contains?

5.   How much of what you understand by childhood is determined by your own experience of it?

6.   Would you like to be a child again? What is attractive/unattractive about the idea?

Study Text 1.1: The Myths of Childhood

In broad terms, the history of childhood has been described as a gradual process whereby the 'distance in behaviour and whole psychological structure between children and adults increases in the course of the civilizing process' (Elias 1939, p.xiii). This particular view of the history of childhood, developed in quite different ways by Aries (1960), de Mause (1976), Shorter (1976) and Stone (1977), and subsequently criticized, not least on historical grounds, by Pollock (1983) and MacFarlane (1986), now constitutes something of an orthodoxy (see, for example, Hayden and others 1999). Aries' central thesis, to take perhaps the best-known example, was that, in early-medieval European society, childhood as a recognizable set of social roles and expectations did not exist and that the transition from the physical dependency of infancy to the social maturity of adulthood was unbroken. Young people quite literally occupied the same social, economic and psychological space as older people, playing, working and sharing relationships on much the same terms. According to Aries, 'childhood', as a distinct set of social roles and expectations, was 'discovered' in the fifteenth century, slowly diffusing throughout European society over the next three hundred years or so.

Whatever the historical accuracy of such accounts as Aries', their importance for our purposes lies in the contribution they made to the development of what has been called the 'theoretically plausible space called the social construction of childhood' (James and Prout 1997, p.27). Put simply, this idea, which stems from a tradition in sociology that is concerned with the meaning rather than the function of social events and processes, implies that very little of what we associate with children or the kind of childhood that they experience is universal, fixed or certain. Rather, childhood is built up, or 'constructed', in society and is occupied by young people in much the same way that adults occupy the various social roles available to them; for example, 'parent', 'worker', 'middle-aged'. Hence, the meaning, social significance and experience of childhood will vary across time, even within generations and between cultures, as the society in which it is embedded changes and develops. An appreciation of childhood as a social artefact like many others allows social scientists to ask interesting questions about why it should take a particular form at any given time and what social processes shape the social realities that young people have to face. It also allows questions to be asked about whose interests are best served by any particular construction of childhood. More important, understanding childhood as a social construction requires us, as adult professionals or simply as professional adults, to recognize that our account of children and childhood is not the only one possible and that our understanding of childhood may say more about us and the society we live in than it does about the real lives of the children we encounter.

While it may not be the case that adults wholly determine the social facts of childhood, it is adults who write about them. Indeed, much has been written about the way in which adults invest childhood with all kinds of meanings according to their purpose at the time (see Butler 1996a). It might even be argued that the history of childhood is the history of adult myth-making about childhood and that, in popular as well as social scientific terms, childhood is what adults say it is. For example, there is a strong tradition of presenting childhood as a kind of idealized age of innocence, almost as a state of grace. The French author Antoine de Saint-Exupéry's *The Little Prince* exemplifies this tradition. The story tells of how a pilot makes a forced landing in the desert. Here he meets the Little Prince who tells him stories of the planet where he lives and of his various adventures and companions and, in so doing, points the difference between the world of possibilities and the world of sordid realities and, indirectly, between the worlds of adulthood experience and childhood innocence. The Little Prince points out how adults and children see and experience quite different worlds to one another even in respect of the most mundane and commonplace objects. When the Little Prince (or any child) sees a house, for example, he or she, according to de Saint-Exupéry, might notice the rosy colour of the brick, the flowers in the window and the birds in the roof. The adult, looking at the same house, sees only its market value. The story of the Little Prince is a story about childhood written for adults. It is a useful reminder that children see the world differently to adults but you must judge for yourself whether, on the basis of stories such as this, you consider that adults are always reliable witnesses to the experience of childhood.

A sharply contrasting account to de Saint-Exupéry's vision can be found in the writings of the child liberationists and radical feminists of the early 1970s. John Holt's child liberationist 'manifesto' *Escape from Childhood – The Needs and Rights of Children* describes the state of childhood as 'being wholly subservient and dependent, being seen by others as a mixture of expensive nuisance, slave and super-pet' (1975, p.15). In Holt's view, even parental love is fuelled by less than disinterested motives. Children are, to their parents, no more than 'love objects' – in the same way that women have been treated by men as sex objects.

The association of the emancipatory progress of women and other subordinated groups with the experience of childhood has produced some striking rhetoric around the nature of modern childhood. The feminist writer Shulamith Firestone (1979, p.50) saw in the 'myth of childhood' a way for adults to compensate for all the things that are missing in their lives:

> it is every parent's duty to give his child a childhood to remember (swing sets, inflated swimming pools, toys and games, camping trips, birthday parties, etc.). This is the Golden Age that the child will remember when he grows up to become a robot like his father... Young adults dream of having their own children in a desperate attempt to fill up the void produced by the artificial cut-off from the young...

Consequently, according to Firestone, children are:

> burdened with a wish fantasy in direct proportion to the restraints of
> their narrow lives; with an unpleasant sense of their own physical
> inadequacy and ridiculousness; with constant shame about their
> dependence, economic and otherwise ('Mother, may I?'); and humilia-
> tion concerning their natural ignorance of practical affairs. Children
> are repressed at every waking minute. Childhood is hell.

Despite their obvious differences, what all three of these romantic and
radical accounts of childhood have in common is the recognition that contemporary childhood is clearly separated from adulthood emotionally,
economically and culturally. The radical accounts also seem to attest to the
relative powerlessness of children. It should not be assumed that this is an
inevitable consequence of children's apparently limited capacities and
competences. There is a growing body of evidence (e.g. Jensen and McKee
2003; Butler and others 2003) that children have the potential to be (and
actually are) much more significant authors of their own biographies, both
literally and figuratively, than many adults might assume. The limitations
placed on children are also intrinsic to the way in which childhood is constructed in many contemporary Western societies.

Many social work constructions of childhood reflect particular views
of this 'otherness' of children. For example, many social workers, particularly those steeped in the developmental psychologies of Freud, Jung and
Adler, understand childhood almost exclusively as a state of becoming, not
one of being. The primary value of childhood in such accounts lies in its
use as a preparation for adulthood simultaneous with its capacity to ensure
the stability of social and cultural norms. Childhood is understood merely
as a transitional process driven by a fury of evolutionary, biological and
hormonal imperatives until the advent of the staid, middle-aged individual
of modest, moderate and settled needs. Some accounts of childhood
acknowledge the influence of other children in the socialization process
and focus on the peer group as a factor in the production and maintenance
of (usually deviant) behaviour. Other accounts reflect the relative powerlessness of children to prevent their victimization by adults. But a common
thread running through many such accounts of the 'otherness' of childhood is the way in which the experience of children is presented and
largely understood in terms of their incapacities and *naïveté* rather than in

terms of their strengths and experiences. Such deficit models of childhood can imply that childhood is less subtle, complex and meaningful than adulthood and consequently less interesting, valuable and important.

It is not our purpose to persuade you to any particular understanding or view of childhood. Our aim is to encourage you to reflect on what images of childhood you carry around with you and to question the attitudes, values and knowledge that inform your particular view. By being aware of the presumptions that you bring to your understanding of the circumstances of specific children, we hope that you will meet each individual child on his or her own terms without imposing your meanings on their lives.

 NEEDS AND RIGHTS

We can see how the contested nature of childhood has a direct bearing on social work practice by exploring the apparent opposition that is sometimes established between children's needs and children's rights. At a general level, the proponents of a rights-based model for practice might argue that an emphasis on children's particular needs tends to infantilize them well beyond the period of their infancy. It might also be the case that talk of 'needs' sometimes derives from a desire to impose adult constructions upon children's lives, such as when adults say that a child 'needs' a 'highly structured and controlling environment' when what they mean is that *they* want the child to be locked up; or when a child is said to 'need' 'clear boundaries and explicit means of discipline' when what is intended is that the child should be subjected to corporal punishment. One commentator has advised children that whenever 'they hear the word "need", [they should] reach for their solicitor' (Shaw 1989, p.2). On the other hand, an advocate of a needs-based approach might acknowledge that, while it is perfectly possible to use the rhetoric of rights to protect the integrity of individual children and to encourage them to play their full part in civil society, it is also the case that 'rights-speak' can look suspiciously like neglect when it leaves eight-year-olds 'free' to carry automatic weapons or to be exploited and sexually abused in brothels and back streets.

The social work task is located right at the centre of such apparent contradictions. How you resolve them in practice will depend on the particular image or construction of childhood that you bring to your work as much as on the particular theoretical frameworks that you bring from your knowledge of the social sciences or elsewhere. The following exercise is intended to sensitize you to your understanding of children's needs and rights and to explore further the particular model of childhood to which you currently subscribe.

	Needs	*Rights*
Person aged 0–5	1.	1.
	2.	2.
	3.	3.
	4.	4.
	5.	5.
Person aged 5–10	1.	1.
	2.	2.
	3.	3.
	4.	4.
	5.	5.
Person aged 10–18	1.	1.
	2.	2.
	3.	3.
	4.	4.
	5.	5.
Person aged over 18	1.	1.
	2.	2.
	3.	3.
	4.	4.
	5.	5.

Figure 1.1 Needs/rights grid

Exercise 1.2: Needs and Rights

Using the grid (Figure 1.1), write down what you consider to be the most important needs and rights of the individuals concerned.

Points to Consider

1. How important is the age of the individual to any consideration of his or her needs or rights?

2. Would your account of needs or rights be different if the individuals were differentiated by race, gender or disability? If so, how?

3. Does an individual have a right to have all of his or her needs met?

4. How far does an individual have a need to be able to exercise his or her rights?

5. Compare the words that you have used to describe rights and those you have used to describe needs. What does the difference tell you about how you regard the two concepts?

6. What does your understanding of needs and rights tell you about your own construction of childhood? Where would you stand on a continuum that ran from maternalism/paternalism at one end to radical liberationist at the other?

Study Text 1.2: The Needs and Rights of Children

CHILDREN'S NEEDS

Discussion of children's needs tends to be associated with ideas about children's development. The subject of child development is a broad and a dynamic one and is not without its controversies. It is also too large a subject for a single chapter such as this. Even if we thought we could, we do not intend to provide you with a comprehensive check-list of the needs of a child, appropriate to its every age and stage of development (but see, for example, Kellmer Pringle 1974; Cooper 1985; Bryer 1988 for historical examples). To do so would suggest that such needs inventories or maps are more fixed and consensual than they are. Nor would we wish to imply that social work could be done 'by numbers' or entirely on the basis of received wisdom.

We think it is important to introduce you to one specific formulation or 'mapping' of children's developmental needs, however, as it is one that has particular currency in contemporary social work practice. It is the model of child development that informs the inter-departmental *Framework for the Assessment of Children in Need and their Families* (Department of Health and others 2000). (You should note that 'in need' is being used here in a 'technical' sense, which is explained in Study Text 4.1. You can take the term at face value for our present purposes.) The *Framework* takes into account a much broader range of factors that workers will need actively to consider when undertaking assessments, and we will discuss these in more detail in Units 4 and 7. Our interest in the *Framework* at this point is in seeing how it describes the nature and scope of children's developmental needs. Figure 1.2 describes the seven dimensions of a child's developmental needs contained in the *Framework*.

Health

Includes growth and development as well as physical and mental well-being. Genetic factors may also need to be considered. Involves receiving appropriate health care when ill, an adequate and nutritious diet, exercise, immunizations where appropriate and developmental checks, dental and optical care and, for older children, appropriate advice and information on issues that have an impact on health, including sex education and substance misuse.

Education

Covers all areas of a child's cognitive development, which begins from birth. Includes opportunities to play and interact with other children, to access books, to acquire a range of skills and interests and to experience success and achievement. Involves an adult interested in educational activities, progress and achievements, who takes account of the child's starting point and any special educational needs.

Emotional and Behavioural Development

Concerns the appropriateness of response demonstrated in feelings and actions by a child, initially to parents and caregivers and then, as the child grows older, to others beyond the family. Includes the nature and quality of early attachments, characteristics of temperament, adaptation to change, response to stress and degree of appropriate self-control.

Identity

Concerns the child's growing sense of self as a separate and valued person. Includes how a child views him- or herself and his or her abilities, feelings of belonging and acceptance by the family and wider society, and the strength of his or her positive sense of individuality.

Family and Social Relationships

Concerns the child's development of empathy and the capacity to place oneself in someone else's shoes. Includes a stable and affectionate relationship with parents or caregivers, good relationships with siblings, increasing importance of age-appropriate friendships with peers and other significant persons in the child's life and the response of family to these relationships.

Social Presentation

Concerns the child's growing understanding of the way in which appearance and behaviour are perceived by the outside world and the impression being created. Includes appropriateness of dress for age, gender, culture and religion; cleanliness and personal hygiene and availability of advice from parents or caregivers about presentation in different settings.

Self-Care Skills

Concerns the acquisition by the child of both practical and emotional competencies required for increasing independence. Includes early practical skills of dressing and feeding, opportunities to gain confidence and practical skills to undertake activities away from the family and independent living skills as older children. Includes encouragement to acquire social problem solving approaches. Special attention should be given to the impact of disability and other vulnerabilities on the development of self-care skills.

Figure 1.2 A child's developmental needs
Source: Department of Health and others (2000), p.19 (Crown copyright).

You may find it helpful to compare the list of needs that you produced for the last exercise with the categories provided in Figure 1.2. You will certainly need to refine and develop your understanding of children's needs and general development through further reading and direct observation of children but, as you do so, you should also consider some general points about the maturational process and the needs of children.

First, the speed of development, particularly of very young children, is one of the real wonders of the natural world. The proverbial cry of 'My, hasn't s/he grown!' from friends or relatives who have only occasional contact with a child has a real basis in fact. If you consider that in a little over four years most of those snuffling new-born bundles of sensation and smells are transformed into neat rows of schoolchildren making their first attempts to put their 'news' down on paper, then you would probably agree that the rate of change is breathtaking. In focusing on any child's needs, at any age, be aware of the amazing pace of change and do not 'trap' a child into a pattern of needs that he or she has long outgrown.

Always be mindful of the complexity of all human beings. There is infinite variety in the interaction of all human needs and no-one, at any age, should be reduced to only one or two dimensions of their personalities or attributes. It is never appropriate to focus all our effort on meeting the physical needs of a child if we fail to meet its social or emotional needs, to take an obvious example. Children, just like everyone else, have to be considered holistically and their needs should be understood as dynamic rather than fixed and enduring. We will see later how the *Framework* attempts to take such a holistic view of children and includes a detailed consideration of their social, economic and cultural contexts. One of the enduring and fascinating controversies to occupy social scientists still is the way in which extrinsic factors, such as economic disadvantage and/or parental inadequacies, interact with intrinsic factors, such as temperament or personal resilience; and how these impact on a child's development (see Daniel, Wassell and Gilligan 1999).

Finally, whatever our views on the determining influence of genetic inheritance or environmental influence (nature versus nurture), we would all probably agree that each human being is unique and individual. All babies do not look the same! Nor do all five-year-olds act or think in the same way or have identical needs, any more than all forty-year-olds do.

There are consistencies, of course; but there are differences too and they are often the more important considerations.

CHILDREN'S RIGHTS

The enfranchisement of any subordinated group is always a slow and halting process and the contemporary debate on children's rights is of surprisingly recent origin. It wasn't until 1993 that Peter Newell was able to declare that children's rights had 'come of age' (Newell 1993, p.xi). The legitimacy of children's claims to rights, and indirectly the occasion of Newell's remarks, was the adoption by the United Nations General Assembly in November 1989 of the Convention on the Rights of the Child. You might usefully compare the list of rights that you have devised with those established by the Convention (see Figure 1.3).

As well as establishing some important general principles, the Convention establishes the following rights for children:

- The inherent right to life (Article 6)
- The right to have a name from birth and to be granted nationality (Article 7)
- The right to live with parents (unless incompatible with best interests), the right to maintain contact with parents if separated (Article 9)
- The right to leave the country and to enter their own in order to be reunited with parents or to maintain the child–parent relationship (Article 10)
- The right to express an opinion and to have that opinion taken into account in matters affecting the child (Article 12)
- The right to freedom of expression (Article 13)
- The right to freedom of thought, conscience and religion (Article 14)
- The right to freedom of association (Article 15)
- The right to protection from interference with privacy, family, home and correspondence (Article 16)

- The right of access to appropriate information that promotes social, spiritual and moral well-being (Article 17)
- The right to be protected from abuse and neglect (Article 19)
- The right to special protection for those children deprived of a family environment (Article 20)
- The right to special protection for refugee children (Article 22)
- The right of children with disabilities to special care, education and training (Article 23)
- The right to the highest level of health possible and to health and medical services (Article 24)
- The right to periodic review of placement for children placed by the State for reasons of care, protection or treatment (Article 25)
- The right of children to benefit from social security including social insurance (Article 26)
- The right to an adequate standard of living (Article 27)
- The right to education (Article 28)
- The right of children of minority communities and indigenous peoples to enjoy their own culture and to practise their own religion and language (Article 30)
- The right to leisure, play and participation in cultural and artistic activities (Article 31)
- The right to be protected from the exploitation of their labour (Article 32)
- The right to be protected from drug abuse (Article 33)
- The right to be protected from sexual exploitation (Article 34)
- The right to be protected from sale, trafficking and abduction (Article 35)
- The right to respect for human and civil rights in relation to the administration of justice (Article 40)

Figure 1.3 The UN Convention on the Rights of the Child

Although the Government ratified the Convention in 1992, it does not have legal force in the UK. While the UK Government must seek to observe its provisions and publish reports accordingly, the Convention cannot be relied upon in any legal proceedings in the courts of England and Wales, although it can be taken into account in the interpretation of domestic law. This is not the case in respect of another potentially important source of authority in establishing children's rights, the Human Rights Act 1998 (HRA). This Act, essentially the European Convention on Human Rights, which the UK signed in 1950, came into force in October 2000. Under the Act, courts can make a judgment in response to a case made by an individual that their rights under the Act have been infringed. Figure 1.4 describes some of the rights established by the Act. The Act also requires public authorities (such as local authority social services departments) to uphold a person's rights, not just to avoid infringing them. It is too early to say at this stage what impact the Act will have on the lives of children and young people although it may have an important part to play in improving standards of public services to children (see Schwehr 2001).

The following are the individual citizen's rights set down in Schedule 1 of the Act. In our view, all of them are relevant for children.

Article 2   Everyone's right to life shall be protected by law

Article 3   No one shall be subjected to...inhuman or degrading treatment or punishment

Article 4   No one shall be held in slavery or servitude. No one shall be required to perform forced or compulsory labour

Article 5   Everyone has the right to liberty and security of person. No one shall be deprived of his liberty save in the following cases...[amongst others] the detention of a minor by lawful order for the purposes of educational supervision or his lawful detention for the purposes of bringing him before the competent legal authority

Article 6   In determination of his civil rights and obligations or of any criminal charge against him, everyone is entitled to a fair and public hearing within a reasonable time by an independent and impartial tribunal

Article 7   No one shall be held guilty of any criminal offence...
which did not constitute a criminal offence...at the time it
was committed

Article 8   Everyone has the right to respect for his private and family
life, his home and his correspondence

Article 9   Everyone has the right to freedom of thought, conscience
and religion

Article 10   Everyone has the right to freedom of expression

Article 11   Everyone has the right to freedom of peaceful assembly
and to freedom of association with others

Article 12   Men and women of marriageable age have the right to
marry and to found a family, according to the national laws
governing the exercise of this right

Article 14   The enjoyment of the rights and freedoms set forth [here]
shall be secured without discrimination on any grounds
such as sex, race, colour, language, religion, political or
other opinion, national or social origin, association with a
national minority, property, birth or other status

Under Part II of the First Protocol of the Act, the following rights are
also listed:

Article 1   Every natural or legal person is entitled to the peaceful
enjoyment of his possessions...

Article 2   No person shall be denied the right to education...the
State shall respect the rights of parents to ensure such
education is in conformity with their own religious and
philosophical convictions.

Figure 1.4 The Human Rights Act 1998

It is possible, with only a little distortion (see Archard 1993, 2001; Van Beuren 1995; Fortin 1998 for more detailed accounts), to group those rights defined by the Convention and the Human Rights Act into four categories:

- Survival rights (e.g. Art. 6 of the Convention and Art. 2 of the HRA).
- Development rights (e.g. Art. 28 of the Convention and Art. 2 of Part II of The First Protocol of the HRA).
- Protection rights (e.g. Art. 34 of the Convention and Art. 5 of the HRA).
- Participation rights (e.g. Art. 13 of the Convention and Art. 14 of the HRA).

Specific formulations of the first three groups of rights – which we might describe together as 'nurturance rights' (see Rogers and Wrightsman 1978) – might command wide acceptance (although you should note that many countries, including the UK, have entered specific reservations concerning the Convention and do not accept all of its provisions). It is probably the case that many of the rights that you described in Exercise 1.2 were broadly of this type. In practice, such rights may, at worst, represent little more than good intentions and, at best, be no more than a reflection of current ideas of what constitutes children's needs. For the most part, rights of this type, even where they are enforceable in law (e.g. the right to education), are defined and enforced by adults on the child's behalf. The fourth group of rights, participation rights, are of a different order in that they have 'self determination orientations' (Rogers and Wrightsman 1978) and so make a case not for 'welfare' but for 'liberty' (Franklin 1995). It is rights of this sort that pose the greatest challenge to the dominant deficit models of childhood that we described in Study Text 1.1 and which provide the liveliest debates in social work with children and their families.

There are a number of arguments and counter-arguments that are routinely made concerning the exercise of children's participation rights. For example:

- *Children are not sufficiently rational or intellectually capable to make competent choices.* In the case of infants this will be true but it does seem that children's capacity for rational thought is considerably greater than most adults are prepared to credit.

We know of no research findings that suggest that the social world of children is less subtle, complex and nuanced than that of adults (see Butler and others 2003). Also, if reason and intellectual capacity rather than age are the criteria, then many adults should be denied their rights too.

- *Children lack sufficient experience on which to base their decisions, which can only develop with maturity.* This might be considered a self-fulfilling prophecy in the light of the previous argument and does seem to rest on a touching faith in the capacity of humans to learn from their mistakes. This argument usually rests on a confusion between 'the right to do something [and] doing the right thing' (Franklin 1995, p.11) and if the ill-judged consequences of the exercise of certain rights are sufficient to deny those rights then a similar argument should, logically, apply to many adults too.

- *Children are not self-sufficient and, as dependent individuals, do not qualify as full stakeholders in civil society.* On this basis, almost everyone might be denied their rights to some degree but certainly those who are ill, elderly or with a disability would be denied theirs.

- *Children's rights can only be achieved at the expense of the inalienable rights of parents.* We explore the changing balance of power between parents and children in Unit 3, although this argument is usually only a thinly disguised attempt to protect the institution of the family from the inquisitorial attentions of the State. This, in turn, is sometimes only a thinly disguised argument for the dismantling of welfare provision of all sorts and contains echoes of the 'no such thing as society' point of view that makes all talk of civil rights redundant.

NEEDS VERSUS RIGHTS?

Underlying the debate about needs versus rights we see a glimpse of the central dynamic of childhood itself, the progress from dependency to autonomy; which, as we have indicated, is a matter of debate. In reality it is neither necessary nor helpful to think of 'needs' and 'rights' as opposites or as mutually exclusive concepts. Both 'needs-speak' and 'rights-speak' are useful correctives to one another. The biological dependency of infants, for example, calls forth a primal and beneficial concern for the nurture and protection of children. Similarly, in a society in which children are exploited and abused it is important that children possess a civil and legal status from which they can defend their interests.

The progress from dependency to autonomy is not the only dynamic along which childhood operates. It moves also between powerlessness and the possession of power, between innocence and experience and between a state of nature and a state of grace. The precise point at which you locate the circumstances and experiences of each child whom you encounter will be a function not just of the characteristics of the child him- or herself but of the image of childhood that you bring to the encounter. If you believe that children should be seen much more than heard, if you think that *Lord of the Flies* rather than *Swallows and Amazons* captures the true essence of childhood experience or if you believe that children are more Bonnie and Clyde than 'bonny and blithe' then you will, in all likelihood, find a plausible justification for your views in the conduct or circumstances of the child concerned.

It is axiomatic in social work practice generally that the attitudes and values that you bring to your work are critical to the process and outcome of any intervention. *The National Occupational Standards for Social Work* (NOS) requires social workers to demonstrate that they are able to 'evaluate their own values and principles and identify any conflicts and tensions that may arise' (TOPSS 2002, Unit 9). In working with children in particular, it is just as important that you are aware of your particular construction of childhood and that you are able to explain and defend it when required.

To return to the central dynamic of dependency/autonomy, the next exercise will help you to determine your current position and how well you can articulate it.

 Exercise 1.3: Needs and Rights in Action

Read the text of Article 16 of the UN Convention on the Rights of the Child and think how you might apply its provisions in the situations described below. You should supply whatever additional material you need in order to determine your response.

No child shall be subjected to arbitrary or unlawful interference with his or her privacy, family, home or correspondence, nor to unlawful attacks on his or her honour or reputation. (Article 16 (part))

1.   You are the responsible social worker and a young person asks you if he or she can make a private phone call to his or her father who is accused of abusing him or her.

2.   You are visiting a children's home and the young person you are seeing tells you that another young person is in possession of stolen goods.

3.   While on duty in your agency you overhear a conversation between two young people in which one tells the other that she thinks she is pregnant and is too scared to tell anyone else.

4.   On a holiday you are planning for children known to your agency, you are asked to keep a covert watch on one young person's contact with another as it is believed that they are planning to commit a serious crime together.

5.   The head teacher of a young person for whom you are responsible asks you for a copy of previous case conference minutes 'for the records'.

6.   After a series of attacks on residents, your agency wants to install closed-circuit TV in a children's home. One of the cameras will unavoidably overlook the residents' recreational space.

7.   You believe that a young person for whom you are responsible is injecting proscribed drugs. During a visit to the young person you have the opportunity to search his or her room without permission but with no risk of being observed.

8.   A colleague has written a damning court report on a family based on what you know to be inaccurate information. A member of the family concerned asks you what the report says.

9.   The parent of a teenager for whom you are responsible tells you that their son or daughter is enuretic and would you 'have a word' with them.

10. A child that you are working with is described as an abuser in a local newspaper. The opposite is in fact the case. You are asked by a reporter for your comments.

Points to Consider

1. Do children need privacy?

2. Are the limits on a child's right to privacy any different to those you would tolerate for yourself?

3. What, if any, needs have priority over a child's right to privacy?

4. Is your professional obligation to maintain confidentiality helped or hindered by a child's right to privacy?

5. In whose interests are you working when/if you decide to set limits on a child's right to privacy?

6. How would you integrate Article 16 into your own practice?

THE BEST INTERESTS OF THE CHILD

However one might describe or categorize any particular construction of childhood, it seems likely that its proponents hold the views that they do out of a sincere commitment to do what is 'best for the child'. The UN Convention on the Rights of the Child 1989 is premised on such a belief:

> In all actions concerning children, whether undertaken by public or private social welfare institutions, courts of law, administrative authorities or legislative bodies, the best interests of the child shall be a primary consideration. (Article 3)

Inevitably, perhaps, the 'best interests of the child' is yet another of those terms that defies a simple or consensual definition. The term is somewhat vague and thus amenable to being used as a justification for any outcome that the decision-maker might prefer. It too is dependent on how one understands the nature and the experience of childhood as much as it depends on a particular set of life circumstances. However, in social work terms, determining the best interests of the child cannot remain simply a matter of philosophical or sociological speculation. It is a professional imperative and, in some cases, a statutory requirement. The Children Act 1989 provides an important account of what is meant by 'the best interests of the child'. The relationship between social work practice and the law (Braye and Preston-Shoot 1997) is a complex one and needs to be understood in a broader context than this book allows. A standard textbook on social work and the law (Brayne, Martin and Carr 2001, p.1) takes the view that:

> [social workers] were created to perform – and only to perform – the jobs that Parliament has given you. Although there is plenty of room for good intentions, these do not define your job; the statutes do. The statutes tell you who you have responsibilities towards, and how they shall be exercised.

It is certainly true that there is an ever-increasing wealth of legislation that defines areas of social work practice in terms of duties and powers. Brammer (2003, p.5) notes, however, that 'to be legally competent a social worker must be able to apply relevant law to factual situations and not simply regurgitate its provisions in abstract'. An appropriate understanding of the social work task therefore needs to acknowledge the relevance and application of law set against a context of social work values and practice skills. Even so, it is unarguably the case that the provisions of the Children Act 1989 significantly determine contemporary child care practice. A brief discussion of the Children Act 1989 as a political Act, like any other, is given in Study Text 3.4. At this stage, however, we require only that you regard the provisions of the Act as an important reference point and not necessarily as the final arbiter of good practice. The Act, like all of its predecessors, will one day have to be re-written. In reading the final study text of this Unit, which describes the model of 'best interests' that governs decision-making in the courts, you should consider what image of childhood lies beneath the text of the Act and in the decisions of courts and reflect on how closely it approximates to your own.

Study Text 1.3: The Welfare Principle

The Children Act 1989 refers not to the 'best interests of the child' but to the 'welfare of the child', which shall be the court's 'paramount consideration'[2] when it determines any question concerning the upbringing of a child or the administration of his/her property (The Children Act 1989, s. 1(1)). This is essentially a re-enactment of a principle established in English law by the Guardianship of Infants Act 1925 (and incorporated into the now repealed Guardianship of Minors Act 1971). Lord MacDermott's interpretation, made under the old law, still provides an authoritative gloss on what is usually referred to as the welfare principle, which he described as:

> a process whereby, when all the relevant facts, relationships, claims and wishes of parents, risks, choices and other circumstances are taken into account and weighed, the course to be followed will be that which is most in the interests of the child's welfare as that term is now understood. (*J* v *C* [1969] 1 All ER 788 at 820–821[3])

The welfare of the child is to be considered 'before and above' any other consideration (Lord Chancellor, *Hansard*, HL vol. 502, col. 1167), even the

---

2   Note that this duty applies to courts only. It does not apply to parents or to the actions of local authorities. Unit 3 explores the duties that attach to a child's parents and Unit 5 describes the lesser duty on the local authorities to 'safeguard and promote' the child's welfare. The Children's Act 1989, s. 17.

3   References to particular cases are given in the form that lawyers conventionally adopt when citing cases. The first element refers to the parties to the case, then the year and then the paragraphs or page numbers of the particular series of law reports where the case is described. There are several different series of law reports. For our purposes, the most frequently cited are the Family Law Report (FLR) and the All England Law Report (All ER).

essential justice of the case. The same welfare principle has been introduced to adoption through the Adoption and Children Act 2002.

The Act itself contains no definition of 'welfare'. It does, however, provide a check-list of factors which courts are required to consider in particular circumstances; namely, when the court is considering making an order under Part IV of the Act (care and supervision orders) or when it is determining a contested application under s. 8. The check-list may be used in other circumstances of course, and provides a useful framework for the preparation of reports. The items on the check-list are not presented in any particular order and none is automatically any more important than the other. As Lord Justice Dunn has observed: '…the circumstances of each individual case are so infinitely varied that it would be unwise to rely on any rule of thumb, or any formula, to try and resolve the difficult problem which arises on the facts of each individual case' (*Pountney* v *Morris* [1984] FLR 381 at 384D). Neither is the check-list exhaustive and it should best be regarded as a minimum range of issues to be considered.

The check-list comprises seven items, as follows (s. 1(4)):

- *The ascertainable wishes and feelings of the child concerned* (considered in the light of his or her age and understanding): the court retains its discretion as to how much weight it should attach to the wishes and feelings of the child, which will vary according to the nature of the subject matter of the application but it does have to consider them and can promote a child-centred approach. This means that social workers and others, including Children's Guardians and Children and Family Reporters will have first to obtain them. (Unit 10 contains a detailed description of the role and tasks of Children's Guardians and Reporters – see Study Text 10.1.) The question of the child's age and understanding (also discussed in Study Text 3.4) is to be understood as a developing one whereby with increasing competence comes increasing influence. The Court of Appeal has held (in *M* v *M* (Removal from Jurisdiction) [1993] 1 FCR 5) that the wishes and feelings of a 10- and 11-year-old, both intelligent and articulate, should have had considerable weight attached to them.

- *The child's physical, emotional and educational needs*: the court will expect to be informed of the day-to-day arrangements in place to secure the basic physical care of the child. Courts have shown a preference for stability in a child's daily routine (*Re B (A Minor) (interim Custody)* [1983] FLR 683). In terms of meeting a child's emotional needs, courts have shown a strong preference for keeping brothers and sisters together, for maintaining an enduring relationship with both parents and for placement with family members rather than non-relatives where that is possible. As Lord Scarman has observed (*Re (SA) (A Minor)* [1984] 1 All ER 289 at 292): 'A home with his natural parents, if circumstances are right and a loving relationship exists, must be best.' However, the 'if' is a significant one: '…of course there is a strong supposition that, other things being equal, it is in the interests of the child that it shall remain with its natural parents. But that has to give way to particular needs in particular situations' (Lord Donaldson in *Re H (A Minor) (Custody: Interim Care and Control)* [1991] 2 FLR 109). Courts may interpret educational needs broadly and may consider the arrangements made by carers to promote the child's education, including, for example, the capacity of a parent to balance the competing demands of homework and television (*May v May* [1986] 1 FLR 325).

- *The effect of any change*: courts have shown a marked preference for the status quo, especially in relation to younger children, provided that the status quo is satisfactory. In *Re B (Residence Order: Status Quo)* [1998] 1 FLR 368, the Court of Appeal overturned a decision to give a residence order to the mother of an eight-year-old child who had lived with his father since the age of two. The provisions of s. 1(5) of the Act, the 'non-intervention principle', strengthen this preference for the status quo considerably. This prohibits the court from making any order in a case unless it considers doing so 'would be better for the child than making no order at all'. The delay principle (s. 1(2)) is also relevant and it is essential that delaying tactics are not employed to strengthen the status quo argument of one party.

- *The child's characteristics*: subject to the overriding commitment to the paramountcy of the child's welfare, courts have shown a preference for placing younger children, particularly girls, with their mothers. It has also been held that a girl approaching puberty would be better placed with her mother and that a boy aged eight, as a general rule, would be better placed with his father. Each case must be considered on its own facts, however; and there is no presumption in law that a child of any age should be placed with one parent or the other (*Re W (A Minor)* [1992] 2 FLR 332). Courts have also had regard to racial and cultural factors in determining where the child's welfare will best be served.

- *Harm*: 'harm' in this context, and elsewhere in the Act, means 'ill-treatment or the impairment of health or development' (s. 31 (9). See Study Text 10.1). Courts are able to consider any harm done to the child and, in determining the likelihood of harm, may take into account the harm done by a proposed carer to any other child or adult. In private law proceedings, e.g. a residence application, if the court has concerns about harm it may direct the local authority to carry out an investigation with a view to commencing care proceedings (s. 37).

- *The capacity of parents and others*: in the course of proceedings, parties may wish to parade every piece of evidence relating to the alleged past incapacities of other parties, whereas courts will primarily be concerned with the carer's capacity to care for the child in the future. The question of capacity is not the same as intention and courts do not have to have regard to the 'best interests' of parents in determining their capacity to care for a child. The financial circumstances of carers, while a consideration, is not usually a determining factor. The word 'others' in the text of this subsection invites the court to consider the capability of relatives or new partners. The sexuality of new partners may also be considered relevant. Early caselaw suggested that the stigma of being brought up in a gay or lesbian household could outweigh the benefit to the child (*S v S (Custody of Children)* [1980] 1 FLR 143). More enlightened thinking is evident in the more recent decision of *Re W (Adoption: Homosexual Adopter)* 1997 2 FLR 406, in which the court stated that there was nothing in law to prevent a man in a homosexual couple from adopting a child.

- *The powers of the court*: in effect, any court may make any order under the Act – although not all orders may be made simply by the court's own motion; some may only be made on the application of an interested party. This provision ensures that the court is best able to tailor its decision to the particular circumstances of the child, although the provisions of the 'non-intervention principle' apply to all proceedings under the Act. It also enables the court to exercise its powers to require further information, possibly in the form of reports, in order to reach a decision (s. 7).

The Act makes one further specific provision concerning the welfare of the child and the court process, namely that delay in proceedings is likely to 'prejudice the welfare of the child' (s. 1(2)). A distinction is to be made between purposeful delay where time may be taken in order to resolve a particular problem or to determine the effect of particular circumstances and damaging drift (Butler and others 1993; *C* v *Solihull MBC* [1993] 1 FLR 290). It is essential that cases are allocated to the appropriate court at an early stage, as transfer between courts has been identified as a significant cause of delay (see Brophy and others 1999).

 CONCLUSION

The history of the study of childhood is the history of *adults'* study of childhood and adults' accounts may be different from those of children themselves. The adult world, including the social work world, is littered with the never-consulted casualties of the social worker who 'knew best' or 'knew already'. Recognizing the 'otherness' of childhood, expecting and respecting difference, and accepting the limits of one's own experience and understanding of the process are absolute prerequisites to working in the child's best interests.

The images of childhood that you bring to your work exert a powerful influence on the kind of social worker you are and the kind of work that you do. Since you will frequently find what you are looking for, we hope that you will make a strenuous and conscious effort to meet each child that you encounter as they really are and not as you remember, imagine or would like them to be.

NOTES AND SELF-ASSESSMENT

1. When does childhood begin and end? When did you stop being a child?

2. What does it mean to be treated like a child?

3. In what ways do you treat children differently to adults?

4. What potential for oppressive practice does your own construction of childhood have?

5. What do you think you have to learn from the children with whom you work?

6. How does your image of childhood help you to help children?

RECOMMENDED READING

James, A. and James, A. (2003) *Childhood: Theory, Policy and Practice.* Basingstoke: Palgrave/Macmillan.

Foley, P., Roche, J. and Tucker, S. (2001) *Children in Society.* Basingstoke: Palgrave (in association with the Open University).

TRAINER'S NOTES

Exercise 1.1: Images of Childhood

As well as newspapers and magazines, film and TV programmes are other sources of images for this exercise – although the very best source is the family photograph album. This exercise works equally well if participants are asked to provide written accounts of childhood from their own reading, especially their childhood reading. Similarly, any book of quotations will provide a list of concise and challenging accounts of childhood. Whatever the graphic or written stimulus, however, the liveliest discussion and the clearest reminiscences of childhood are produced by the purchase and consumption of the participant's favourite childhood sweets!

Exercise 1.2: Needs and Rights

This exercise can be started as a large group and with some quickthinking of both needs and rights. These needs and rights can then be attributed to various categories of individuals distinguished by age, gender, race, etc., either in a large group or in smaller groups. Alternatively, a wide range of needs and rights can be written onto cards beforehand and, either as a large group or a series of smaller groups, they can be attributed to various categories. Discussion can be encouraged if there is a lack of consensus over any particular attribution.

Exercise 1.3: Needs and Rights in Action

A large group can be split into three smaller groups, one representing the child concerned, one the parent or carer of the child and the other the social worker. The several groups could then negotiate a consensus on the application of the right to privacy in each mini-scenario. This exercise works particularly well if tailored to the particular work or placement setting of group members. Participants can be encouraged to develop

'Practice Guidelines' for their particular work or practice learning context and to bring the views of colleagues back to the group for discussion.

 WEB RESOURCES

http://www.unicef.org This is the home page of the United Nation's Children's Fund. UNICEF declares that its work is guided by the Convention on the Rights of the Child and strives to establish children's rights as enduring ethical principles and international standards of behaviour towards children. UNICEF insists that the survival, protection and development of children are universal development imperatives that are integral to human progress.

http://crights.org.uk This is the website for the Children's Rights Alliance (CRAE), an alliance of over 180 organizations committed to children's human rights. CRAE publishes on-line *Children's Rights Bulletins* that provide up-to-date information on government policy, legislation, and human rights cases. It also provides access (via its 'publications' page) to the full, downloadable text of *State of Children's Rights in England: A Report on the Implementation of the Rights of the Child*, published in 2002.

http://www.article12.com/ Article 12 is a children's rights organization run by young people. Its name derives from Article 12 of the UN Convention of the Rights of the Child, which states that a 'child who is capable of forming his or her own views [has] the right to express those views freely in all matters affecting the child, the views of the child being given due weight in accordance with the age and maturity of the child'. It contains links to child-friendly versions of the UN Convention and to the Human Rights Act.

You should note that almost all of the 'official documents' referred to in this book, including Acts of Parliament and publications by government departments, are available 'on-line' as part of a national 'open government' strategy. We have found the following to be amongst the most useful sites:

http://www.official-documents.co.uk This website contains a wide selection of papers, reports and other documents covering a broad range of topics including the economy, work, health and welfare, transport and the environment. There are two main categories of documents stored, Command Papers (White or Green Papers) and House of Commons Papers (Departmental and other reports of official bodies).

http://www.hmso.gov.uk/legis.htm This site provides access to UK legislation (downloadable in many cases).

http://www.doh.gov.uk This is the Department of Health's website. Despite its size (it is vast!), it is very easily navigable and has a sophisticated 'search' facility that you will soon get used to.

Other government sites that you may find useful are:

The Home Office **http://www.homeoffice.gov.uk**

The Department for Education and Skills **http://www.dfes.gov.uk**

The Welsh Assembly Government **http://www.wales.gov.uk**

The Northern Ireland Assembly **http://www.ni-assembly.gov.uk**

The Scottish Parliament **http://www.scottish.parliament.uk**

The Cabinet Office **http://www.cabinet-office.gov.uk**

Social Exclusion Unit **http://www.socialexclusionunit.gov.uk**

UNIT 2

The Family

OBJECTIVES

In this Unit you will:

- Consider the variety of family forms and household structures to be found in contemporary Britain.

- Explore your personal construction of the family.

- Consider the experience of family life from a gendered perspective.

- Explore critical issues in working with Black families.

 MEET THE FAMILY

Consider these two appreciations of the family:

1. At the risk of stating the obvious, may I start by saying what I mean by the family? I mean by a family a couple, consisting of a husband and wife, with or without children, living together throughout their lives. I include, too, the extended family; that is grandparents and other relatives. And, throughout our history this has been the accepted meaning of the word 'family'. It is a public commitment to marriage by both parties to a lasting relationship. That is what the marriage service, and indeed the civil ceremony in a Registry Office, is all about. It is not about

anyone's rights. It is entirely about the duties and responsibilities of both parties. As the Prayer Book says, 'for richer, for poorer, in sickness and in health, till death us do part'; an awesome promise.

It clearly means an absolute responsibility and commitment by both husband and wife to the upbringing of children. I begin as I have because this definition of the family is now widely questioned, and the term 'family' is used to cover all types of co-habitation, single parents (the single-parent 'family') and single-sex relationships. The British are, I believe, a very tolerant people. It is one of their great strengths. But by their very tolerance they have succeeded in, I believe, an unintended way of downgrading marriage to one of a series of equally valid alternative lifestyles. There is now a real possibility that marriage may at some date in the future, and the not-too-distant future at that, disappear altogether. The number of marriages has fallen each year. By 2020 it is estimated that married couples will be in the minority of the population for the first time ever. I am told that for an anthropologist the widespread unwillingness to marry is a sign of impending disaster.

2.   Family life, family values, decent normal family fun, family shopping, family leisure. The word is used these days as the word 'Aryan' was used in Germany during the 1930s. Anything that isn't Family is 'unfamily', and anything that is unfamily is unrepresentative of the joyful majority. Obedience, compulsion, tyranny and repression are family words as much as love, compassion and mutual trust. It rather depends on the family.

The first quotation is from a speech made by the Rt. Hon. The Baroness Young DL, at the Centre for Policy Studies Lecture at the Conservative Party Conference on 4 October 2000, and the words of the second were written by actor and broadcaster Stephen Fry (1993) in his regular column in *The Listener*. Many of the issues that arise for social workers when thinking about the family are to be found in these two short extracts.

First, there is the recognition that the family as an idea, as well as a set of social roles and expectations, can mean very different things to different people. Second, it is clear that the family as a set of social realities is likely to vary. Third, the family can be an aspect of ideology and can be used to further particular socio-political ends. Finally, the experience of family life, as well as being widely variable, is also more equivocal and ambiguous than is immediately apparent. Like 'childhood', the 'family' is another of those central but elusive terms that are the common currency of social work but which are rarely tested either for their meaning or their value. Also, like childhood, the family is both a social and a personal construction rather than a fixed set of relationships or some aspect of a 'natural order' of things. Understanding your own construction of the family and being sensitive to the myriad other ways in which the term can be meaningful is an important part of understanding the families with whom you intend to work.

Before we explore our own ideas of what constitutes a family, we should, perhaps, take some account of what household structures and family forms exist in the UK today and how these are changing. The next exercise is intended to alert you to some of the assumptions that you might hold concerning family formation and household structure. You are not expected to know the right answers! You will find these in the trainer's notes for this Unit and in the study text that follows Exercise 2.1. The point of the exercise is for you to find out what assumptions you make about contemporary family forms and household structures.

 Exercise 2.1: Family Fortunes

Make the best estimate that you can in answer to each of the following questions and note any pattern that emerges in the way that you have either under- or over-estimated the statistically correct answer:

1.   What proportion of households are one-person households?

2.   Is the average size of households today greater or smaller than 30 years ago?

3.   Is size of household the same across all ethnic groupings?

4.   Which is the most common form of household in Great Britain?

5.   What proportion of households consists of lone-parent families?

6.   What proportion of the population lives in couple-family households (i.e. a household headed by a couple)?

7. What percentage of children live in families with two parents?

8. Is the proportion of children in the population rising or falling?

9. Are women having more or fewer children?

10. What proportion of children are born outside marriage?

11. What proportion of births outside marriage are registered in the names of both parents in the UK?

12. Are more or fewer people marrying?

13. What proportion of marriages are remarriages?

14. How many children per week are involved in divorce?

15. What percentage of all families with dependent children are stepfamilies?

 Points to Consider

1. On what sources of knowledge/information did you base your answers to these questions?

2. What are the usual sources of information about household structure and family formation to which the general public have access?

3. Would you say that you have tended to over- or under-estimate the variations that exist in family form? Why might this be?

4. Do you regard any of the rates or proportions that you have noted as actually *too* high or *too* low? Which one(s) and why?

5. Which, if any, of the rates or proportions that you have identified do you regard as problematic? Should anything be done about the state of affairs described?

6. How far can statistics help you to decide what is a 'typical' family? What is the difference between a 'typical' family and a 'normal' one?

Study Text 2.1: The Facts of Family Life

This study text provides a digest of statistics drawn from government sources that bear on the social realities of household structure and family form in the UK. It is highly selective and is intended to illustrate patterns of continuity as well as change, although it does focus particularly on emerging demographic trends and phenomena. Before reading on you may want to find out the answers to Exercise 2.1 directly from the National Statistics website – see the web resources listed at the end of this Unit.

HOUSEHOLDS

More people are living alone. In 2001, almost three in ten of all households in Great Britain were one-person households, a proportion that has more than doubled since 1961. Households are also getting smaller; the average household size has decreased over the same period from 3.1 persons to 2.4 (ONS 2002, Table 2.1). The size of household can also vary substantially depending on the ethnic origin of the head of the household. For example, the average size of a household headed by someone of Bangladeshi origin is almost twice the overall mean at 4.6 persons (ONS 2002). Average household size also varies regionally.

The two most common types of households in the UK are single-person households and couples without children (each amounting to 29% of all households). The next most common is the couple with either one or two children (19%). Lone-parent households (with dependent children) make up 6 per cent of households (ONS 2002). Taken together, families with children (however many) outnumber families without children.

FAMILIES

For statistical purposes, a family is a married or cohabiting couple, with or without children, or a lone parent with children. The 12 per cent of people who lived alone in 2001 are not defined as a family for statistical purposes. (You may wish to ask yourself why.) Almost three-quarters of the population live in a couple-family household but the proportion of people living in lone-parent families has trebled since 1961 with as many as one in ten people in Great Britain and one in six in Northern Ireland now living in lone-parent families (ONS 2002). The majority of children live in two-parent families (79% in 2001) with 20 per cent in one-parent families. Compare this with 1972 when the proportions were 92 per cent and 7 per cent respectively (ONS 2002).

As with household size, the proportion of families with children varies according to the ethnic grouping of the head of the household. Over 80 per cent of Bangladeshi and Pakistani families and over 90 per cent of Indian families include children.

CHILDREN

Of the 59 million people living in the UK, one in five is under 16 years old compared to almost one in four who were under 16 in 1961 (NCH 1999). There are marked differences in the age structure of the population according to ethnic origin. In the Bangladeshi community, for example, 39 per cent are under 16 while 23 per cent of Black Caribbean and 20 per cent of White communities are under 16 (ONS 2002, Table 1.4).

FAMILY-BUILDING

Women are having fewer children. Women born in 1937 had an average of 1.9 children compared to 1.3 children for women born in 1967 (NCH 1999). The proportion of children born outside marriage has increased to almost 40 per cent of all births – four times more than in 1975 (ONS 2002). The proportion of children born outside marriage is rising throughout Europe but Britain has the highest rate of teenage births in Western Europe. It is an indication of the growth in the number of cohabiting couples (particularly since the 1970s) that 80 per cent of all births occurring outside marriage in the UK were registered in the names of both parents (ONS 2002).

As well as having fewer children, women are having them later in life. The average age at which women are giving birth has risen to 29 years in 1999 compared to 26 years in 1971.

MARRIAGE AND DIVORCE

Fewer people are marrying and they are marrying later. The average age at first marriage in England and Wales is 29 years for men and 27 years for women compared to 26 years and 23 years respectively in 1961 (ONS 2002). Forty per cent of all marriages are remarriages (NCH 1999) and stepfamilies accounted for 6 per cent of all families with dependent children (ONS 2002). In 1999, a quarter of all single women under 60 were cohabiting, double the rate for 1986. The 159,000 divorces in 1999 involved 148,000 children, compared to 176,000 children in 1993 (ONS 2002) but that still amounts to over 2800 children per week experiencing the breakdown of their parents' marriage.

 ## WHAT'S IN A NAME?

The demographic variability of family form and the degree to which patterns of change and continuity are evident in family formation and dissolution across time and between cultures, even within one set of national boundaries, ensure that any definition of the 'family' is likely to be partial, in both senses of the word. One commentator has noted that:

> if not only family form, family activity, family functioning but also the emotional interior of the family is highly variable, then it is questionable whether the term 'family' should be dispensed with...'family' would appear to refer neither to a specific empirical type nor to a theoretical type...(Harris 1984, p.246)

The almost infinite range of relationships, domestic arrangements, social circumstances and personal networks to which the term 'family' has been applied means that it can be used in the service of almost any political ideology. That is not to say that some legislators do not prefer certain family forms. For example, a local authority is forbidden by law in England and Wales (but not in Scotland which repealed the relevant legislation in June 2000) to: 'promote the teaching in any maintained school of the acceptability of homosexuality as a pretended family relationship' (Local Government Act 1988, s. 28). While no one has been prosecuted for breaking this law, one might easily argue that the legislation is discriminatory and encourages prejudice (see the web resources at the end of this

Unit). An attempt to repeal Section 28 in England and Wales was defeated in the House of Lords in February 2000, despite attempts to engender support for the Government's position by the introduction of new Guidance on sex and personal relationship education. The Guidance issued by government states:

> As part of sex and relationship education, pupils should be taught about the nature and importance of marriage for family life and bringing up children. But the Government recognises...that there are strong and mutually supportive relationships outside marriage. There-fore, pupils should learn the significance of marriage and stable rela-tionships as key building blocks of community and society. (Depart-ment for Education and Employment 2000a, p.4)

The vilification of lone parents by certain politicians over recent years has been a recurrent strand to a variety of 'back to basics' crusades. It is not our intention to debate the social policy response to the changing fortunes of the family (but see Van Every 1992) or to characterize particular ideologi-cal orientations to the family (but see Study Text 3.4) or even to explore the sociological analyses that inform and illumine them (but see Cheal 1991). Our point is that, just as we saw in relation to defining children and child-hood, as well as a wide variety of social 'facts' that need to be accommo-dated in our understanding of the term 'family', there are a wide range of deeply held beliefs about the family that we need to appreciate as a prelude to working effectively in this field. The next exercise will begin to sensitize you to some of the attitudes you have towards the family.

 Exercise 2.2: Is this a Family?

Decide which of these households is a family and why. You may find the following criteria useful in determining family status:

- the degree of emotional commitment
- the degree of commitment to the future of the arrangements
- the degree of emotional interdependence

- the degree to which social and domestic life is interwoven
- the degree of financial interdependence
- the intimacy of the relationship(s)
- the duration of relationship(s)
- the exclusivity of relationship(s).

Note any other criteria that occur to you as you complete the exercise.

1. John and Jane are both students in their early twenties. They have shared a flat for nearly three years and divide all the household bills between them. They have bought some furniture and household items together. They eat together, spend a lot of time in each other's company, and frequently go out with each other socially. Over the last few months, they have slept together but both have had intimate relationships with others at the same time. When they leave college, John plans to return to his home area. Jane is thinking of travelling abroad for a year or two.

2. Betty and George have been married for eight years. They hardly speak to one another except to argue or to 'sort out' practical matters to do with the children, Jo aged four and Chris aged six. Betty has a long-standing relationship with another man. Both pay their wages into separate accounts, although each pays half of the household bills. Betty does most of the necessary child care during the week and George takes over at weekends.

3. Surinder is a lone parent. She cares for her daughter, Shama, aged ten. Shama's father does not support the family financially. He is married and has three other children of his own. He regularly brings the children to play with Shama and will sometimes baby-sit so that Surinder can go out by herself. Surinder receives a lot of practical help from her mother, with whom Shama spends a great deal of time. During long school holidays, Shama's grandmother moves into Surinder's house so that Surinder can carry on going to work.

4. Jason and Justin have lived together for nearly twelve years. They jointly own their own home, its contents and a car, and have left everything to each other in their wills. Theirs has been a monogamous relationship and they are deeply committed to each other. They have separate careers but spend all their free time together. They have a number of shared interests and hobbies.

5. Jean and Eric, both divorced, have lived together for three months. Eric's children, Sara aged 17 and Paul aged 15, together with Sara's baby, Amanda, and Jean's children, Thomas, James and Edward (all under five), live with Jean and Eric. Sara's boyfriend sleeps in the house most nights. The children, because of their ages, have little to do with one another. Jean 'will not get involved' with the care of Amanda and Eric disapproves of Sara's boyfriend. Bills are paid by whoever has the means at the time and are a cause of friction between Jean and Eric. The tenancy of the house is in Jean's name. The current arrangements were undertaken on a 'trial basis', the terms of which are not clear.

6. Glyn and Rita have been married for 18 years. They have no children. Rita has never worked outside the home. Glyn has a good job that more than covers their regular outgoings. They own their own home, run a car and have regular holidays abroad. Glyn and Rita describe themselves as 'soul mates' although they do not spend as much time in each other's company as they used to do.

Points to Consider

1. Which criteria did you regard as the most useful in determining whether these households could be called a family?

2. Are there any criteria that you would regard as critical in determining whether any particular household could be called a family?

3. On the basis of the choices you have made, how would you now define what you mean by the term 'family'?

4. How much does your definition of the 'family' originate in your own experience of family life?

5. Which of the households described in Exercise 2.2 comes closest to your ideal of family life?

6. Which of the households described in Exercise 2.2 is the most likely to come to the attention of social workers and why?

FAMILY INTERESTS

Expectations of what constitutes a family are not to be found only in the minds of social workers or the mouths of politicians. Every fast-food restaurant, railway carriage and tour operator in Britain seems to proceed on the assumption that we eat, sleep and move around in groups or multiples of four! Just as we need to differentiate between, and respond to, families on the basis of how they are actually constituted (rather than on how we imagine they are or think they should be), so too do we need to differentiate between the interests and experiences of different family members. For example, as one of us has noted elsewhere:

> developments in our knowledge and understanding of child abuse, particularly sexual abuse, over recent years ensure that we recognise with renewed clarity the truism that not all families share the same unconditional commitment to family health and harmony as the family. That a family can be an oppressive, cruel and hopeless environment for some children…should be sufficient to remind us that it is a dangerous assumption to leave entirely undifferentiated the interests of children and their parents… (Butler and Williamson 1994, p.9)

As well as differentiating between the interests and experiences of parents and children, it is important to differentiate the experience of family life according to gender. The following exercise, and the study text which follows, will clarify what we mean.

Exercise 2.3: A Day in the Life

Consider the following descriptions of a day in the life of the Smith family, provided by Doreen and John Smith, then compare their accounts against the criteria you developed for the purposes of Exercise 2.2. You may wish to add to that list these additional measures:

- the degree of personal autonomy that each has
- the nature and extent of social networks to which each has access
- the relative social status that each might have in the eyes of others
- the degree of control over their time and labour that each has.

The Smiths have been married for 25 years. They have four children, three of whom are still living at home. John Smith is 47 and works at a local factory. Doreen is 41 and works part-time. They live on a large housing estate in a home they are buying through a housing association.

John: I get up every morning at six and take a cup of tea to Doreen. If she's been at work the previous night, I'll leave her to lie in till I leave for work at quarter to seven and I'll wake the two youngest for school. I don't usually bother with breakfast. I drive to work, which takes me about an hour through the traffic. I've been doing this for years but I still hate the journey. It's all stop, start, stop, start. I have to be in work by 8 a.m. I don't enjoy my job but I don't hate it either, like some of the lads at work do. It can be a laugh sometimes and I have got some good mates at work. We usually get out for half an hour at lunchtime and have a bit of a kick-around with a ball or read the paper. I finish at 4.30. You might not think so but it's hard work and by knocking-off time, I've had enough. Then I have to drive home, have a wash and I'm ready for something to eat. Doreen either makes me something if she's in or she leaves me something in the microwave. If she's working that's me sorted. I can't go out and I watch the box. Work, TV, bed, work. The kids more or less look after themselves until bedtime and, if Doreen's not in, I pack them off for the night. Whenever I do get the chance to get out I do. I think that is not much to ask in return for the years I've put in at work. I need something to take my mind off the bills, the job, the journey. My marriage is like everybody else's, more habit than anything, but I have done my best for them and I won't let them down.

Doreen: If it needs doing in our house, I have to do it. John's out all day and would be every evening if he could be. I do get a cup of tea in the mornings but I've yet to come in to a hot meal. I work three mornings a week on the tills at the local supermarket and three nights a week stacking shelves at a big chemists. I have to fit everything around my work, including the kids. They're very good but they don't get much of a look in, even at weekends. I'm not interested in going out in the evenings. I'm usually too tired to care! I work because we need the money. Every penny I earn is spent before I get it. I'm not interested in what passes for entertainment around here – clubs, pubs, bingo – plus the fact that I haven't really got anyone I could go out with. I don't know many of the people on the estate. The housework doesn't do itself in this house and I don't think I could tell you what 'free time' means. I like to listen to the radio when I'm ironing. I worry about the kids and what they'll do for a living when the time comes. As for me, I have no choice but to carry on carrying on. I do sometimes think of just walking away from it all and, when the kids have gone, I might. If there was ever any love in our marriage, it's gone now. I need more than this.

Points to Consider

1.   On the information that you have before you, who do you think derives most benefit from family life, John or Doreen?

2.   How fairly do you think the household chores are distributed between John and Doreen?

3.   Who contributes most to the 'maintenance work' that keeps this family going?

4.   Would you regard this as a 'successful' family? Why/not?

5.   With which aspects of John and Doreen's attitudes and behaviours would you most like to take issue? Why?

6.   Do you think this family offers an appropriate environment for bringing up children? Why/not?

Study Text 2.2: Women and the Family

As in the Smith family, it would appear that women have always taken the main responsibility for child-rearing and domestic tasks. It has been suggested (Elliot 1986) that their burden increased after the Industrial Revolution but that even in agrarian societies women had/have a far greater degree of responsibility for running the home than men. In the UK at present, despite women's greater participation in the labour market, the sexual division of labour in the home shows only slight evidence of resolving itself more equitably. Table 2.1 shows how little appears to be changing in relation to whether household chores are undertaken mainly by men, mainly by women or are shared equally.

Table 2.1 Division of household tasks by gender, May 1999			
Minutes per person per day	*Males*	*Females*	*All*
Cooking, baking, washing up	30	74	53
Cleaning house, tidying	13	58	36
Gardening, pet care	48	21	34
Care of own children and play	20	45	33
Maintenance, odd jobs, DIY	26	9	17
Clothes, washing, ironing, sewing	2	25	14
Care of adults	4	3	4
All	*142*	*235*	*191*

Source: ONS (2001), p.224 (Crown copyright).

It could be argued, because of structural factors within the UK labour market such as the fact that men with children under ten years old work longer hours than any of their European counterparts (European Network on Childcare 1996), that there is a limit to any more equitable sharing of domestic work. However, patterns of family life, typified by the Smiths, reflect a more traditional attitude to women's work and the sexism that sustains such attitudes. The roots of sexism extend well beyond the scope of this study text, although its consequences for practice in this field are important. Sexism has been defined as 'the belief in the inherent superiority of one sex over another and thereby the right to dominance' (Lorde 1984, p.115) and as part of a 'cultural value system which perceives men as more valuable than women' (Burden and Gottlieb 1987, p.2). As such, sexism disadvantages women more than men, although Phillipson (1992) and others have drawn attention to how sexism discriminates against both men and women in families by preventing each of them from achieving their full potential. Sexist stereotyping can prevent a man from showing the caring part of his nature, for example, as well as condemn a woman for not appearing caring enough. However, the systematic undervaluing of women's labour is reflected not only in the disadvantageous distribution of domestic chores but also quite literally in their opportunities in the wider labour market. In 1994, women's full time gross weekly pay was only 72 per cent of men's and it is almost the same, today. Moreover, 64 per cent of those at or below the Council of Europe's decency threshold in terms of wages were women. One might note that it has been estimated (Joshi 1992) that a mother with two children would lose an average of £202,500 in potential earnings over a lifetime, without taking into account the loss of pension rights. Besides economic determinants, other factors (such as traditional patterns of sex-role socialization) tend to operate to 'make males more focused on gaining independence through the outside world of work and correspondingly to make females more focused on accepting dependence in the inside world of the family' (Burden and Gottlieb 1987, p.26). But, as well as being unpaid and undervalued, housework and child care, especially the care of very young children, can be incredibly boring, lonely and depressing for some women:

> Women have the main burden of children and they often carry it in isolation. The realities of the experience are often very different from the idealized picture of women as gaining satisfaction from their maternal role... Women often feel trapped and frustrated by their roles as housewives and mothers, even if they love their children and husbands. (Abbott 1989, p.83)

For example, while it is known that women are more likely than men to refer themselves to their general practitioner when they are depressed, more women than men suffer from depression (see Davis, Llewellyn and Parry 1985; Burden and Gottlieb 1987; Corob 1987); particularly married women and those from working class backgrounds. As social workers, you may not regard it as your role to begin to tackle systemic sexism or to stand in opposition to the larger economic currents at work beneath the surface of our society, but you need to recognize how they bear directly on your own work. For example, understanding that the social exclusion and isolation of many women is as much a function of structural factors as personal pathology may help you to address the problems that can arise:

> When I read a study of baby battering I can't help thinking, 'there but for the grace of God go I'... If all mothers who have ever shaken a screaming baby, or slapped it, or thrown it roughly into its cot, stood up, we would make a startling total. (Oakley 1982, p.223)

The emergence of feminist social work in the 1980s (Brook and Davis 1985; Wise 1985; Dominelli and Mcleod 1989; Hanmer and Statham 1988) encouraged practitioners to recognize how social work itself can continue the oppression of women in families. Social workers must resist any temptation to look at women to fulfil their own stereotypical and sexist expectations. For example, they must not take advantage of women's ability or of their willingness to care. It is tempting for a social worker with perhaps a number of pressing cases, but too few resources, to take advantage of mothers – '*cherchez la femme*' (Hale 1983) has been a recurring theme whatever the nature of the referral. More recent commentators (e.g. O'Hagan and Dillenburger 1995; Scourfield 2003) have noted how the over-dependence on women in child care work originates in child care law and child care training.

The phrase 'good enough *parenting*' (see Unit 3) may well have replaced the 'fit *mother*' but, on the whole, it is still mothers who are taught parenting skills by social workers, not fathers. Ideas of who does what and why in a 'proper family' are more open to scrutiny than many would like to admit. As well as a haven and a place of joy, it can be a place of drudgery and unfulfilled ambition. As Stephen Fry indicated at the beginning of this Unit, it rather depends on the family. We would add that it also depends on which of its members you ask.

 ## BLACK FAMILIES

Just as with children, so families come in all shapes and sizes. Also, the idea of 'the family' carries a burden of meaning that may have as much to do with the observer as with the experiences of those being observed. Clearly, the lived experience of family life is as varied as the range of domestic arrangements that bear the name, and needs to be differentiated according to age and gender. There is one further dimension of social work with children and families that we wish to consider in this Unit: the position of Black families and social work approaches to work with Black families.

STUDY TEXT 2.3: SOCIAL WORK WITH BLACK FAMILIES

The failure of social work to address the needs of Black families is comprehensive and continuing. The Social Services Inspectorate, in a study of eight authorities' services to ethnic minority children and their families (Department of Health 2000, p.1), found that:

> most councils did not have strategies in place to deliver appropriate services to ethnic minorities and that families were often offered services that were not appropriate or sensitive to their needs.

These finding echo those made much earlier by Cheetham (1986) that, whether in terms of antenatal care, day care for pre-school children, support services to families in need or arrangements for children looked after by the local authority, the sensitivity, effectiveness and relevance of social work services are too often found wanting (see also Richards and Ince 2000). Yet, ethnic minority communities remain specifically vulnerable in some respects, not least in terms of economic deprivation. Berthoud (1998) found that:

- Pakistani and Bangladeshi communities constitute the poorest groups in the UK. High unemployment among men, low levels of economic activity among women, low pay and large family sizes all contribute to a situation in which 60 per cent of Pakistanis and Bangladeshis are poor.

- Indian and Chinese people have high levels of employment, and their earnings are on a par with those of White workers. On these measures, they can be seen to be prospering. But overall, their rates of poverty are higher than for White households.

- A disproportionally high number of people of Caribbean origin are unemployed, and there is a high rate of lone parenthood in this community but, overall, the rate of poverty among people of Caribbean origin is only slightly higher than that among White households.

- The social security system, and especially means-tested benefits, contributes a large proportion of the incomes of some minority groups, especially Pakistanis and Bangladeshis.

There is insufficient opportunity in a book such as this to explore the causes of the economic and social oppression of Black people in the UK. The history of Black people in Britain goes back many generations. Dominelli (1997) is unequivocal in her analysis of racism as fundamental to the processes of social exclusion and subordination: 'British racism is about the social construction of social relationships on the basis of an assumed inferiority of non-Anglo Saxon ethnic minority groups and flowing from this, their exploitation and oppression' (p.6). Racism, as a 'socially constructed and reproduced historically specific phenomenon' (Dominelli 1997, p.11), adapts to suit prevailing economic circumstances in order to ensure the economic and cultural domination of White interests. Accordingly: 'With racism as the subtle playing out of relations of subordination and domination in respect of "race" in everyday routines and the minutiae of life, no aspect of social work is free from it' (Dominelli 1997, p.22).

Hence, structurally, and at the level of individual interactions, Black children and families live with the consequences of racism. This will be true in relation to their contacts with social workers too. As MacPherson noted (1999, p.3 – see the web resources at the end of this Unit for the text of the Stephen Lawrence Inquiry):

> Racism, institutional or otherwise, is not the prerogative of the police force. It is clear that other agencies…also suffer from the same disease. (p.3)

As White writers, we cannot and would not presume to write from anything other than a White perspective. We can only write with any authority of the demonstrable insufficiencies of past social work practice. In particular, this study text will examine how social work has tended to pathologize Black families, refused fully to recognize the position of Black people as service users and failed to monitor and evaluate services to Black people.

We recognize that a study text that focuses specifically on Black families runs the risk of maintaining a tendency 'to keep social work with Black families outside the mainstream framework of social work theory and practice' (Ahmad 1992, p.4).

> Perception and assumption that perpetuate this tendency usually stem from a notion that 'special' needs of Black families are so alien that they can not relate to the mainstream social work. (p.4)

We might also be charged with mere tokenism where 'the experiences of black families are simply added as an afterthought, without leading to a questioning of the central elements of the framework [of the whole text]' (Gambe and others 1992, p.22). In either event, we feel it is important to reserve some space in this book to focus attention on some of the more obvious weaknesses of past approaches to practice in this area.

At the heart of the failure of social work to address the needs of Black families (which are as ethnically, culturally and individually diverse as any other grouping of families) lies the persistent tendency to pathologize Black families based on crude racial stereotypes. It is rare still to find in the social work literature or in practice a clear focus on:

> the strengths of black families, strengths rooted in cultural traditions, in the survival of generations in spite of discrimination and the disadvantages of the stresses of migration and sometimes persecution. (Cheetham 1986, p.3)

Rather more commonly, one finds crude stereotypes (e.g. 'Asian families have a strong work ethic and Asian women are deferential'; 'Afro-Caribbean families are female-dominated as the men shirk their familial responsibilities'; 'Travellers aren't interested in education') substituting for culturally informed, objective and professionally accomplished assessments. In this way:

> complex family situations tend to be reduced to simplistic, catch all, explanations, such as 'endemic culture conflict' which offer no real understanding and fail to confer any positive regard for the client's cultural roots. (Gambe and others 1992, p.26)

For example, Qureshi, Berridge and Wenman (2000), in their study of
South Asian families living in Luton, reported:

- South Asian parents expressed the view that family stress and
  breakdown were more common in their communities than was
  often perceived by professionals and the wider public.

- Although there were specific cultural and religious issues,
  comments from South Asian parents about family support were
  similar to findings from other research involving White
  families.

- Social services employed very few Asian staff and no South
  Asian managers: there were no specific policies concerning
  services for South Asian families, nor had any specific training
  been provided for staff.

- Most social workers had tried to provide culturally appropriate
  services but felt that they lacked confidence and skills in this
  area.

- Professionals' misunderstanding about family circumstances
  had sometimes led to negative assumptions about parenting.

Such pathologizing, however unwitting, is ethnocentric (and racist) in so
far as it gives 'privileged status to the world view or experience of the
dominant ethnic group at the expense of other ethnic groups' (Gambe and
others 1992, p.22). In contrast to such deficit models of Black family functioning, Ratna Dutt (in Macdonald 1991, p.77ff.) has developed a model
of practice which:

- recognizes and values the real life experiences of Black people
- recognizes what is implied in surviving racism
- is sensitive to cultural pride
- encourages and promotes the development of positive
  self-images for Black children and families
- is based on a holistic approach to the family and their support
  systems.

It is perfectly possible to offer an account of the potential strengths of
some Black families, although one might be reluctant to for fear of substituting one set of stereotypes for another. Such an account would include
the fact that some families will include kinship ties that are much more

extensive than in traditional White families. Such ties may extend across continents and time and be an invaluable source of support in times of stress. A Black family's sense of community may be much more positive and one's sense of personal identity may owe more to family and community than to the Western idea of 'rugged individualism'. Family patterns and the importance of blood ties, rather than, in some instances, marriage ties, may elevate the importance of inter-generational relationships above those more commonly found in White families and provide additional sources of support. There may be greater respect for the wisdom of elders and so on (see Grant 1997).

We repeat that we do not wish to imply a set of all-embracing Black cultural norms. Our purpose is to encourage you to reflect on your own potential to see Black families in pathological, deficit and racist terms and to:

> build in a recognition of cultures of strength and resistance to racism into the mainstream of [your] social work theories and models. This is a necessary first step in the development of antiracist social work practice in the area of child and families. (Gambe and others 1992, p.27)

A second major strand in the failure of social work to respond to the needs of Black families has been a reluctance to acknowledge the inadequacy of existing models of service delivery. Typically, practitioners and planners have adopted a 'colour blind' approach, where Black service users are treated the same as White service users. Not only does this fail to recognize the specific experience of racism, it fails to take account of cultural and ethnic differences and strengths. In order to take account fully of the value of different cultures, histories and traditions, it may be necessary to treat people differently. For example, in relation to Black children who have to live away from home and be looked after by the local authority, the child's particular needs in relation to food, clothing, personal care, sense of cultural identity and sense of self as a Black child need to be taken fully into account.

Another familiar strategy for refusing to amend existing models and modes of practice is to place all of the responsibility for Black children and families on Black workers. This neatly makes Black people responsible for the consequences of racism and allows White workers to consider the needs of Black service users as someone else's problem.

Such techniques of avoidance are both cause and effect of the lack of strategic monitoring by the providers of social work services of the appropriateness, take-up and usefulness of their services to Black children and families. Richards and Ince (2000), in their survey of 157 local authorities, did find some examples of good practice, however, on which progress might be built. Services were considered to be of better quality where

- provision for Black families was seen as the responsibility of the social services department as a whole with ownership by the director, senior management and political members

- anti-racist practice and culturally sensitive service provision was kept consistently on the agenda, with rolling programmes of training, use of team meetings to keep issues alive, and responsibility on team managers to ensure that culturally sensitive services were not seen as an 'add-on'

- proactive outreach work was done with the Black community, consulting with service users and community groups about what needed to change and how

- proper translation and interpreter services for family members with appropriately disseminated information were available

- recognition and value was given to the role of Black staff, by supporting Black staff in meeting together to consider policy proposals; following those through wherever possible and actively recruiting, supporting and retaining Black staff at all levels of the organization.

Consultation with actual or potential Black service users remains the exception rather than the rule, however; and the active engagement of Black people in the management, planning and delivery of such services, rarer still. Beginning to see social work as part of the problem is the first step to making it part of the solution. It needs to be if we are to ensure that Black families' needs are better met and their legitimate entitlements are more fully secured in future years than they have been hitherto.

CONCLUSION

Both as an idea and as a particular set of personal and social relationships, the family is a major organizing principle in our lives. But, just as much as our lives are infinite variations on a single theme, so too are our ideas and experiences of the 'family'. The family is all of the things that this Unit has described and much more besides. In this richness and variety lies the family's capacity to respond and adapt to the changing social context in which it continues to evolve. The death of the family has been much exaggerated. Because of its richness, variety and adaptability, the family satisfies many individual and societal needs. The only thing that the family is not is a fixed set of expectations and common experiences. It isn't even a demographic fact! As a social worker you will encounter the family in all its many and varied forms. You should celebrate its diversity rather than condemn its deviations from what you may have experienced, were expecting or might prefer to find.

NOTES AND SELF-ASSESSMENT

1. Where do you set the limits on whom you count as 'family'?

2. Do you think that others might define your family differently? Who and why?

3. Are your relationships with members of your family fundamentally different to your relationships with other people?

4. Is your family a 'typical' family? Why/not?

5. What does the phrase 'to start a family' mean to you? Have you or do you intend to do so? Why/not?

6. What does the phrase 'family values' mean to you?

RECOMMENDED READING

Allan, G. and Crow, G. (2001) *Families, Households and Society*. Basingstoke: Palgrave/Macmillan.

Solomos, J. (2003) *Race and Racism in Britain*. Third edition. Basingstoke: Palgrave/Macmillan.

TRAINER'S NOTES

Exercise 2.1: Family Fortunes

In a group setting, the questions can be put in the form of a quiz, following the pattern of any one of a number of TV game shows. Plotting individual answers on a chalkboard or flip chart can provide a graphic account of the range of answers that will be provided. Reviewing the results in this way (as though they were obtained by some kind of survey) is useful in encouraging a debate on the sources of people's (mis)perceptions without participants having to defend their own position or particular guesstimate. All of the answers are in the study text so we will not reproduce them here!

Exercise 2.2: Is this a Family?

A larger group can be broken down into smaller groups and answers compared in the usual way. A much more challenging (but safe) discussion can be engendered by having pairs take the position of the various putative families and argue their case with the larger group for their being accorded 'family' status. Some 'families' have an 'easier' case to argue so the larger group may need to be encouraged to range more widely in their reasons for denying such status; for example, by considering communal forms of child care, such as kibbutzim, as more appropriate to true family life. At the end of the 'debate' the whole group should consider what difference it would make to the 'families' concerned whether they were accorded family status or not. Practical consequences, such as entitlement to state support, should be considered as well as more personal considerations, such as one's sense of identity and the degree of social in/exclusion that follows from recognition as a family.

Exercise 2.3: A Day in the Life

A similar approach to that used in Exercise 2.2 can be adopted here with group members 'taking sides' in a debate. However, it is important that the group should focus on the inter-relatedness of the conditions that impinge upon both John and Doreen and how adjustments in one area imply consequences in others.

 WEB RESOURCES

http://www.homeoffice.gov.uk/inside/org/dob/direct/reu.html The Race Equality Unit of the Home Office is a good source of research studies on the circumstances and experiences of Black communities in Britain.

http://www.archive.official-documents.co.uk/document/cm42/4262/4 262.htm This is the text of the Stephen Lawrence Inquiry.

http://www.myweb.lsbu.ac.uk/~stafflag/lawsection28.html This is an account (with useful links) of the current state of Section 28 of the Local Government Act, 1988.

In Unit I we identified some useful government websites. Another extremely useful source of information to help you locate your practice in a broader context is the Office for National Statistics ('National Statistics Online'). This website provides easy access to a staggeringly broad range of statistical data, often accompanied by well-written and informative commentaries. Start your search at:

http://www.statistics.gov.uk The National Statistics Online website provides helpful commentaries on UK and local statistics covering a wide range of topics including crime, health and population change. The website includes information from the 2001 Census.

Individual statistics on different nations and regions can be found at:

http://www.wales.gov.uk/keypubstatisticsforwales (for Wales)

http://www.scotland.gov.uk/stats (for Scotland)

http://www.nics.gov.uk/index.htm (for Northern Ireland).

Parenting

OBJECTIVES

In this Unit you will:

- Explore the nature of parenting and examine the core skills and tasks of parenting.

- Explore personal models of what constitutes 'good enough parenting' in the context of the Children Act 1989.

- Develop an understanding of the model of parental responsibility established by the Children Act 1989.

 PARENTING

Unit 1 explored the needs and rights of children and concluded that children both have needs to be met *and* have rights to be honoured. They certainly have a need and a right to have someone around to look after them – someone to care for them during the period when they are unable to care entirely for themselves. In this Unit we will focus on parenting and explore what it involves and what it means to be a 'good enough' parent.

The following study text illustrates how elusive any fixed sense of what we mean by parenting can be and begins with a consideration of what motivates people to become parents in the first place.

Study Text 3.1: Defining Parenting

It is not always clear what it is that motivates people to become parents. You may wish to speculate on why your parents had you. The sort of reasons which are usually advanced include:

- personal fulfilment
- to please a partner
- for immortality
- failed contraception
- to secure housing
- to complete a family.

It is important to realize that parenting can be begun for largely selfish reasons but, even if people choose to have children with the noblest of intentions, parenting is something that parents have an interest in too. Parenting is not something 'given' to children disinterestedly. The frustration of parental expectation can, in itself, sometimes be the cause of family dysfunction. Parents have needs and rights too, as well as an emotional stake in the relationship. We make this point to remind ourselves that parenting needs to be understood more broadly than as a straightforward response to the needs and rights of the child. We have seen how childhood can be socially constructed (Unit 1). It is useful to consider parenting in a similar way and as equally problematic. What passes for appropriate parenting varies over time, and according to social structure, just as fascinatingly as does childhood. Before the Industrial Revolution in Britain, for example, parenting was more evenly shared amongst the wider family, along with much economic activity. Later, when paid labour was organized outside the home, women increasingly became the primary caregivers (see Table 2.1).

A good illustration of how ideas about parenting can change even over a relatively short time can be found in a comparison of the advice given in parent manuals and baby-care books. In 1946, for example, mothers were advised that:

> Babies and children are all the better for a little 'wholesome neglect'. From the beginning an infant should be trained to spend most of his time lying alone... Do not point things out to him. (Frankenburg 1946, p.171)

Little more than a generation later, parents were instructed:

> After love the next most important thing that you can give your child is stimulation. A small child is like a sponge soaking up practically every new idea and experience he or she comes in contact with. So, to be good parents, start introducing your child to the outside world. (Stoppard 1983, p.12)

It remains very tempting to understand parenting only in the context of our own experience and our personal construction of family life. However, there is a danger in judging parents according to only one, often very restricted, standard or set of experiences. As with childhood, the nature of parenting varies across cultures, as well as over time. Indeed, Rashid (1996, p.75) has argued for a degree of 'cultural humility' when it comes to thinking about parenting. This is not to argue for a crude cultural relativism, such that all forms of parenting are equally acceptable. In Quinton's (1994) review of 'cultural and community influences' on development, while he makes the case that different developmental outcomes or features need to be located in their appropriate cultural context if their meaning is to be fully understood, he goes on to note that (p.178):

> it seems clear that many features of parent–child relationships have similar outcomes in widely different cultural settings and that within-culture variation on these features can be as great, if not greater, than cross cultural variations.

Research would suggest (see Quinton 1994) that there may be more than one way of parenting effectively but that these variations are around a common theme, namely meeting a child's developmental needs. In establishing the principles of good practice that underpin the Children Act 1989, the Department of Health made the point forcefully (Department of Health 1990, p.7):

Although some basic needs are universal, there can be a variety of ways of meeting them. Patterns of family life differ according to culture, class and community and these differences should be respected and accepted. There is no one perfect way to bring up children and care must be taken to avoid value judgements and stereotyping.

One useful way of thinking of parenting that does not imply a particular household structure, class or cultural origin but which still provides for the care of children is to deconstruct it into its constituent parts and imagine it as a job like any other. That is the function of the next exercise.

 ### Exercise 3.1: The Job of Parenting

TASKS

1.   Using Figure 3.1, devise a job description for a parent.

2.   Design a simple advertisement for the job.

3.   Design a selection process so that the right person gets the job.

 ### Points to Consider

1.   Is this a 'post' that is best job-shared? If so, how?

2.   What working environment would best suit this job?

3.   What prospects of career development are attached to this post?

4.   What training is most appropriate for this job?

5.   Are the rewards commensurate with the duties?

6.   Is it a job that you would ever consider taking on? Why/not?

JOB DESCRIPTION and PERSON SPECIFICATION

Post: Parent

Hours: ....p.w.   **Salary:** £ ....p.a.
Annual leave entitlement:

Responsible to:

Responsible for:

Main areas of activity:

Qualifications required:

Previous experience required:

Personal qualities required:

Figure 3.1 Parenting job description

PARENTING SKILLS

While it might be amusing to think of parenting in the way that you might think of paid employment, the comparison is an instructive one. In terms of the commitment of time and effort, parenting would stand comparison with almost any job, of course. But thinking of it in this way might also have prompted you to consider how, like many other jobs performed primarily by women, it is undervalued, exhausting and highly skilled. Just how skilled a role it is, we shall explore in the following exercise.

 Exercise 3.2: Core Skills of Parenting

TASKS

1. Make a list of skills needed to parent a child of 0–10 years.

2. Make a list of skills needed to parent a child of 10–18 years.

3. Compare both lists and underline similarities and note the differences.

4. Identify the core skills of parenting.

Make sure that you concentrate on skills, not on qualities – that is, patience may be needed, but it is a quality. The skill lies in how a parent actually copes with the behaviour of the child that requires patience; for example, by the use of non-verbal skills, listening skills, or the ability to switch off!

Points to Consider

How well does your list of parenting skills fit your map of children's needs, constructed in Exercise 1.2, or those described in the *Framework for the Assessment of Children in Need and their Families* (Department of Health and others 2000 – see Figure 1.2).

1. Which parenting skills (if any) come 'naturally'?

2. If not by nature, where or how do you think people acquire the appropriate skills for parenting?

3. Is it likely that any one individual or couple will possess *all* of the skills that you have identified as being appropriate to the tasks of parenting?

4. Is it possible to teach particular parenting skills?

5. If it were, what skills would be required by the person providing the training?

 ## GOOD ENOUGH PARENTING

We have hinted already that parenting cannot be fully understood simply as a set of motivations and particular skills. We have indicated that there are other, contextual factors to be taken into account, such as 'cultural and community influences'. Seeing parenting as a set of narrowly defined skills or behaviours also fails to recognize how little we know from research about how to relate particular aspects of parenting to particular outcomes or to weigh parenting 'strengths' against parenting 'weaknesses'. Moreover, there are some dimensions of parenting, such as emotional warmth, that are more difficult to describe or measure in the way that one might measure or describe parenting skills. Parenting is certainly a dynamic and an interactive process and will frequently be mediated by the child him- or herself. Parenting will also vary according to much more mundane considerations such as the number of children in the family and a child's position in his or her family. (Un)fortunately, there are no simple check-lists, skills inventories, or sets of core competencies available by which you can come fully to understand parenting.

Yet, examining parenting and making judgements on its adequacy in relation to particular children is a core social work activity. It is the second of the critical dimensions of the *Framework for the Assessment of Children in Need and their Families* (Department of Health and others 2000) that we introduced to you in Unit 1. The *Framework* describes six key dimensions against which parenting might be assessed (see Figure 3.2).

Basic Care

Providing for the child's physical needs, and appropriate medical and dental care. Includes provision of food, liquid, warmth, shelter, clean and appropriate clothing and adequate personal hygiene.

Ensuring Safety

Ensuring the child is adequately protected from harm or danger. Includes protection from significant harm or danger, and from contact with unsafe adults/other children and from self-harm. Recognition of hazards and danger both in the home and elsewhere.

Emotional Warmth

Ensuring the child's emotional needs are met and giving the child a sense of being specially valued. Includes ensuring the child's requirements for secure, stable and affectionate relationships with significant adults, with appropriate sensitivity and responsiveness to the child's needs. Appropriate physical contact, comfort and cuddling sufficient to demonstrate warm regard, praise and encouragement.

Stimulation

Promoting child's learning and intellectual development through encouragement and cognitive stimulation and promoting social opportunities. Includes facilitating the child's cognitive development and potential through interaction, communication, talking and responding to the child's language and questions, encouraging and joining the child's play, and promoting educational opportunities. Enabling the child to experience success and ensuring school attendance or equivalent opportunity. Facilitating child to meet challenges of life.

Guidance and Boundaries

Enabling the child to regulate his or her own emotions and behaviour. The key parental tasks are demonstrating and modelling appropriate behaviour and control of emotions and interactions with others; and guidance, which involves setting boundaries, so that the child is able to develop an internal model of moral values and conscience, and social behaviour appropriate for the society within which he or she will grow up. The aim is to enable the child to grow into an autonomous adult, holding his or her own values, and able to demonstrate appropriate behaviour with others rather than having to be dependent on rules outside him- or herself. This includes not over-protecting children from exploratory and learning experiences. Includes social problem solving, anger management, consideration for others and effective discipline and shaping of behaviour.

Stability

Providing a sufficiently stable family environment to enable the above dimensions of parenting to operate reasonably consistently. Includes responding in a similar manner to the same behaviours, providing consistency of emotional warmth over time. In addition, ensuring children keep in contact with important family members and others.

Figure 3.2 Dimensions of parenting capacity
Source: Department of Health and others (2000), p.21 (Crown copyright).

The empirical support for this particular 'map' of parenting is set out by Jones (2001) and builds on research which suggests that conflict between parents, inadequate parental monitoring and lack of positive parental involvement are very likely to be associated with behavioural and/or emotional problems in children.

Study Text 3.2: Good Enough Parenting

According to many contemporary definitions of parenting, including that on which the *Framework for the Assessment of Children in Need and their Families* (Department of Health and others 2000) is based, parents not only provide physical care but they show affection, stimulate, discipline and reward their children. They also socialize them and give them room to become independent. The hours are long and the pay can be very poor indeed. And so far we have only considered the more generic components of parenting. Some parents may need to take into account other considerations; a Black parent, for instance, will need to teach his or her child to counteract racism (Madge 2001) or the parent of a child with disabilities may need to deal with daily discrimination and denial of opportunities (Beresford 1994; Meyer 1995).

While parenting might be 'mapped' in this way, we must recognize also that certain structural conditions may prevent a parent from developing, maintaining or exercising his or her parenting capacity. Poor housing, unemployment and poverty add to the stress of child rearing and may limit a person's ability to parent adequately. Such considerations form the third and final set of factors included in the *Framework for the Assessment of Children in Need and their Families* (Department of Health and others 2000). (See Figure 3.3.)

Family History and Functioning

A child's inheritance includes both genetic and psychosocial factors. Family functioning is influenced by who is living in the household and how they are related to the child; significant changes in family/household composition; history of childhood experiences of parents; chronology of significant life events and their meaning to family members; nature of family functioning, including sibling relationships, and its impact on the child; parental strengths and difficulties, including those of an absent parent; the relationship between separated parents.

Wider Family

Who are considered to be members of the wider family by the child and the parents? This includes related and non-related persons and absent wider family. What is their role and importance to the child and parents and in precisely what way?

Housing

Does the accommodation have basic amenities and facilities appropriate to the age and development of the child and other resident members? This includes the interior and exterior of the accommodation and immediate surroundings. Basic amenities include water, heating, sanitation, cooking facilities, sleeping arrangements and cleanliness, hygiene and safety and their impact on the child's upbringing.

Employment

Who is working in the household, what is their pattern of work and are there any changes? What impact does this have on the child? How is work or absence of work viewed by family members? How does it affect their relationship with the child? Includes children's experience of work and its impact on them.

Income

Income available over a sustained period of time. Sufficiency of income to meet the family's needs. The way resources available to the family are used. Are there financial difficulties which affect the child?

Social Integration

...ation of the wider context of the local neighbourhood and community and its impact on the child and parents. Includes the degree of the family's integration or isolation, their peer groups, friendship and social networks and the importance attached to them.

Community Resources

Describes all facilities and services in a neighbourhood, including universal services of primary health care, day care and schools. Includes availability, accessibility and standard of resources and impact on the family.

Figure 3.3 Family and environmental factors
Source: Department of Health and others (2000), p.23 (Crown copyright).

We will consider how all of the various components of the *Framework* knit together in Unit 5. For our present purposes, it is important simply to note how most parents, at some time, will be too worried about making the money stretch to the end of the week to remember to praise and encourage their children, or will be too tired or too busy. There are some obvious and some unexpected delights in being a parent but it can be a difficult job, not least because it seems to demand so much commitment and emotional investment. It should not be surprising that parenting cannot always be maintained at the highest level or that it sometimes breaks down altogether. So, if perfect parenting is unachievable, what might constitute 'good enough' parenting?

D.W. Winnicott coined the phrase 'good enough parenting' in his 1965 book, *The Maturational Process and the Facilitative Environment.* For Winnicott, good enough parenting was where parents provided what he described as a 'facilitating environment' that permitted each child to have her or his needs met and potential developed. It meant parents adapting their behaviour and lifestyle as far as possible for the child's well-being rather than their own, and for parents to put their child's needs first in all major family plans and decisions. Although this account of good enough parenting might be considered to represent a counsel of perfection, the term clearly implies that there is no such thing as simple, undiluted good parenting. It implies that no parent can meet her or his child's needs all of the time and that it will be important to find a balance between parents' own needs, their circumstances and those of their children. The Children Act 1989 is said to recognize that parents are individuals with needs of their own and that social work has an important part to play in supporting parents in their care-taking role:

> parents are entitled to help and consideration in their own right. Just as some young people are more vulnerable than others, so are some mothers and fathers. Their parenting capacity may be limited temporarily or permanently by poverty, racism, poor housing or unemployment or by personal or marital problems, sensory or physical disability, mental illness or past life experiences. Lack of parenting skills or inability to provide adequate care should not be equated with lack of affection or irresponsibility. (Department of Health 1990, p.8)

'Good enough' parenting also implies that parenting is situational, that several different forms of parenting can be good and that there is no single universal model across class and cultures. Jones (2001, p.265) has suggested that the idea of 'parenting' is not especially helpful unless 'it is set within a broader ecology of the child's world'. Thus, our understanding of parenting must extend to include not just the specific motivations, skills and behaviours of parents towards their children; it must include also a consideration of the 'influences of family relationships on parenting, extended family networks and the influence of neighbourhoods on the capacity of parents to care for their children' (Jones 2001, p.265) as well as broader cultural influences. We will examine some of the implications of applying such a broad understanding of parenting to direct practice in Unit 4.

Clearly, however, the term 'good enough' also implies that the parenting still needs to be good. If a child is abused or rejected, the parenting is clearly not 'good enough'. How do you, as social workers, come to recognize and be able to articulate where your threshold of tolerance of 'good enough' parenting stands? In part, your judgement will arise from your understanding of the needs and rights of children and from a realistic assessment of what is involved in parenting. Part of your judgement, however, will be based on your own untested assumptions, attitudes and values. The next exercise is intended to provide you with the opportunity of examining the foundations of your own judgements of 'good enough' parenting.

 ### Exercise 3.3: Good Enough Parenting

TASKS

For each of the following five scenarios, rank the parenting on a scale from 1 to 5 (1 = good enough; 5 = totally unacceptable).

Identify very clearly on what basis you have reached your decision.

1. Jim and Sue have three children under five. They have just won first prize in the national lottery and decide to put their three children up for adoption, buy a boat and sail around the world. It is something that they both dreamed of doing before they had children. All three children are adopted by a childless couple who could never have had their own children.

Good enough   *1*   *2*   *3*   *4*   *5*   *Totally unacceptable*

2. Liz is a single parent living in a damp twelfth-storey flat. She has two children: Sarah, aged nine and Tom, aged five. Tom is still in nappies; even Sarah still wets the bed at night. She is rarely in school or seen out playing. Liz says that she needs to keep Sarah at home to help look after Tom and to mind the flat, especially if Liz has to go out to the shops, as she is scared that the flat would be broken into again if left unoccupied. Sarah is Liz's only company, according to Liz. She has suffered several attacks on the house.

Good enough   *1*   *2*   *3*   *4*   *5*   *Totally unacceptable*

3.   Mary had Jason, now aged two, when she was 17 years old. Alan,
      Jason's father, is 22 and lives with Mary and Jason. Mary says
      that Alan is too strict with Jason and won't let her pick him up if
      he cries at night or even play with him when Alan is around.
      Mary says that this is partly Jason's own fault as he is very
      demanding and does wear her out. 'He has never been a good
      baby, like other people's.' She has been to the doctor to get
      something to make Jason sleep at night. 'Things were OK
      between Alan and me before Jason was born.'

Good enough   1   2   3   4   5   Totally unacceptable

4.   Pete and Steph are solicitors with busy, high profile practices.
      Pete is often abroad for long periods. Steph works long hours.
      Sophie, the youngest child, aged four, is collected daily from play
      school and spends the afternoon at her childminder's house. In
      the evenings, Mrs Evans, a qualified nanny, puts Sophie to bed
      and reads her a story. Pete and Steph's other two children are at
      boarding school. During the holidays Pete and Steph take the
      children on exotic holidays. At the weekend, the children, if at
      home, go to the cottage that the family have in Norfolk, usually
      with Mrs Evans.

Good enough   1   2   3   4   5   Totally unacceptable

5.   Sian has been in prison three times for shoplifting since the birth
      of her children. Bill, her husband, takes off for long periods
      'working away'. The three children of her marriage, aged three,
      five and seven, have all been fostered on several occasions,
      separately and together. Bill's idea of helping at home is to smack
      the children if they are naughty. He says this is a hard world and
      the children have got to learn to stand on their own two feet and
      the sooner the better. Sian refuses to do all the cooking and
      washing. 'Why should I?' she says, 'Bill doesn't do anything'.
      There are lots of arguments between Sian and Bill. The children
      often have to fend for themselves.

Good enough   1   2   3   4   5   Totally unacceptable

If you find it difficult to come to a decision, you may wish to examine each scenario more closely by means of the 'Parenting profile' grid (Figure 3.4) and consider how each example of parenting meets the different needs of a child and then calculate an average score for the purposes of comparison.

Needs of child	*Good enough*			*Totally unacceptable*	
	1	*2*	*3*	*4*	*5*
Health					
Education					
Emotional and behavioural development					
Identity					
Family and social relationships					
Social presentation					
Self-care skills					

Figure 3.4 Parenting profile

 Points to Consider

1. Do parents have to be 'good enough' in all areas or is it sufficient to be only 'good enough' in most?

2. Does being 'good enough' in one area compensate for not being 'good enough' in others?

3. How might a child's view of 'good enough' parenting differ from that of an adult?

4. Is the lack of 'permitting circumstances' sufficient to excuse not 'good enough' parenting?

5.   Is your parenting or that which you received as a child 'good enough'? Why/not?

6.   Is the term 'good enough' a meaningful tool for a social worker to use when coming to a decision about the care of a child?

 RESPONSIBLE PARENTS

The research on parenting, while it may have focused more on particular family forms thought to be problematic, is nonetheless consistent in out-lining the essential features of good parenting:

> Absence of conflict, even when parents are divorced or separated, reliably providing physical care and comfort, consistently demon-strating love and affection, the ability of parents to see the child's point of view, setting clear limits but paying more attention to good behaviour than to bad and much praise and little criticism are all likely to prove beneficial to the child. Spending time with children and engaging in enjoyable activities with them is important too. (Depart-ment of Health 1996, p.6)

Several of the scenarios in Exercise 3.3 suggested that one further aspect of 'good enough' parenting is the balance struck between the needs and rights of the child and those of the parent. You probably found it fairly easy in the first scenario to recognize that the balance was far from right. In Scenario 4 the decision is a little less straightforward. If the two carers had less glamorous occupations and their economic circumstances were a little less comfortable, the balance might be said to have shifted. In Scenario 2 the situation is altogether more complicated.

Given that the Children Act 1989 (the Act) is sometimes (wrongly) referred to as the Children's Act and, like every other piece of child care legislation in modern times, is frequently described as a 'children's charter', one might anticipate that the law has come to favour the child's case over the parent's in a way that D.W. Winnicott might have warmly endorsed. In fact, the situation is much more complex. The position of parents in law has been clarified through the introduction, in the Act, of the very important concept of 'parental responsibility'. The next study text provides a technical account of what is meant by parental responsibility and the final study text in this Unit relates parental responsibility to a wider consideration of parenting and the law.

 ## Study Text 3.3: Parental Responsibility

INTRODUCTION

Somewhat illogically, the Children Act 1989 (the Act) defines the concept of parental responsibility only after it has established how it is allocated or acquired. To avoid confusion, we have chosen to do much the same. However, you may wish to note the formal definition of parental responsibility provided by the Act as a preliminary to a brief explanation of its distribution. Section 3 (1) of the Act defines parental responsibility as: 'all the rights, duties, powers, responsibilities and authority which by law a parent of a child has in relation to the child and his property'.

DISTRIBUTION AND ACQUISITION OF PARENTAL RESPONSIBILITY

Not all parents have parental responsibility, as defined by the Act, for their children. Similarly, not everyone with parental responsibility for a child will be the birth parent of that child. Certain categories of person have parental responsibility as of right and others can acquire it. Indeed, more than two people can hold parental responsibility simultaneously. This may all seem very odd at first, but if we consider parental responsibility as primarily involved with matters concerning the upbringing of a child, it will be clear that parenting can easily be shared with others besides a child's biological parents.

A child's mother always has parental responsibility for a child until the time of the child's majority, death or adoption. This applies whether the mother was married or not and even if anyone else, including a local authority, also has parental responsibility (although see below and Study

Text 10.1 for how the exercise of parental responsibility is affected by the making of certain court orders, e.g. a care order).

A child's father will have parental responsibility, as of right, only if he was married to the child's mother at the time of the birth or if he subsequently marries her or if, by other statute, the child is deemed to be legitimate. The unmarried father can acquire parental responsibility by adopting his child, by being appointed the child's guardian upon the death of the child's mother, by formal agreement with the child's mother under s. 4 (1)(b) (which can only be brought to an end by order of the court), (s. 4 (3)), or by obtaining a parental responsibility order (s. 4 (1)(a)). A test to be applied in parental responsibility applications was developed in the case of *Re H (Minors) (Local Authority: Parental Rights) (No. 3)* [1991] Fam 151. Courts should consider the degree of commitment shown by the father to the child; the degree of attachment between father and child; and the reasons for the application. If a residence order is made in favour of an unmarried father, then the court must also make a parental responsibility order which may survive the residence order.

The Adoption and Children Act 2002 makes two important amendments to the Children Act 1989 with regard to parental responsibility. In future, an unmarried father who is registered as the child's father on the birth certificate will acquire parental responsibility. In addition, a stepparent may acquire parental responsibility by agreement with the child's mother (and father if he has parental responsibility) or by court order. It continues to be possible for a stepparent (i.e. someone married to a child's parent), provided that the child was treated as a child of the family, to obtain parental responsibility by adopting the stepchild or by obtaining a residence order in respect of the child. The parental responsibility attaching to a residence order that is not in favour of a child's parent or guardian specifically excludes the right to consent (or withhold consent) to adoption or to appoint a guardian (s. 12 (3)). The parental responsibility attaching to all residence orders also excludes the right to change the child's name and the right to take the child out of the UK for more than a month unless the court or all those with parental responsibility agree (s. 13).

A local authority can obtain parental responsibility upon the making of a care order (see Study Text 10.1). The parental responsibility attaching to a care order specifically excludes the right to determine the child's religion, to appoint a guardian, to free for adoption, to change the child's surname and to arrange the child's emigration (s. 33). Although the making of a care order does not extinguish the parental responsibility of anyone else (except those who hold parental responsibility exclusively by virtue of a residence order), it does give the local authority the power to determine how far others may exercise their parental responsibility. A local authority may also acquire parental responsibility (as would any applicant) upon the making of an emergency protection order. This is a very restricted form of parental responsibility directly concerned with the emergency protection of the child.

The other category of person who can obtain parental responsibility is someone appointed to act as a child's guardian after the death of the parent(s) who made the appointment (s. 5). Rather confusingly, the Adoption and Children Act 2002 further amends the Children Act 1989 and introduces a new order known as 'special guardianship' (at s. 14). The special guardian will also acquire parental responsibility. Special guardianship is intended to provide stability for a child and may be a suitable order for foster carers who wish to care for a child on a more permanent basis or in circumstances where adoption might not be suitable. Unlike in the case of adoption, the birth parents would also retain their parental responsibility, but would have a very limited ability to exercise it.

Everyone who has parental responsibility for a child may act independently unless the consent of others with parental responsibility is specifically required or unless the court has prohibited the exercise of an aspect of parental responsibility. Consent to a child's marriage requires the consent of all of those with parental responsibility (Marriage Act 1949, s. 3). If a residence order is in force, all parental responsibility holders must agree to the child's name being changed or to the child being taken out of the UK for more than a month (s. 13). The consent to a child's adoption requires the consent only of the biological parent(s) with parental responsibility (Adoption Act 1976, s. 16). The views of the unmarried father without parental responsibility should be obtained although he does not have to give his consent to the adoption. The extent of involvement of an unmarried father may depend on whether he is considered to have 'family life' with the child under Article 8 of the European Convention of Human Rights (*Re H, Re G (Adoption: Consultation of Unmarried Fathers)* [2001] 1 FLR 646).

THE MEANING OF PARENTAL RESPONSIBILITY

The Act itself does not develop or illustrate what is meant by 'parental responsibility' beyond the rather general definition noted above. When originally formulated, the intention was to provide sufficient flexibility in the law to meet the changing needs and circumstances of children (see *Guardianship and Custody*, Law Commission 1988, No. 172, para. 2.6). However, the courts have given consideration to various aspects of parental responsibility. These include, as we might have anticipated from the foregoing, the power or duty to:

- determine a child's religion
- determine the child's education
- name the child
- appoint a Guardian for the child
- consent or withhold consent to medical treatment for the child
- consent or withhold consent to the child's marriage
- represent the child in legal matters
- consent or withhold consent to the child's adoption
- lawfully correct the child
- arrange the child's emigration
- protect and maintain the child
- administer the child's property
- have the physical possession of the child
- have contact with the child.

The legal arrangements for most of these have already been described but we would wish to comment further on three aspects in particular: the rights/powers to consent or withhold consent to medical treatment for the child, to correct lawfully the child and to protect and maintain the child.

CONSENT TO MEDICAL TREATMENT

A person obtaining the age of 16 is able to give or withhold consent to her or his own medical treatment, surgical, medical, or dental, including any diagnostic process or test. Below that age, the decision is dependent upon whether 'the doctor considers [the child] of sufficient understanding to understand the consequences of consent or refusal' (Department of Health 1991a, para. 2.32). This determination, which follows an important decision in the Gillick case (see Study Text 3.4), sets an important condition upon parental responsibility in that it clearly indicates that the exercise of parental responsibility is mediated by the child's developing competence. However, in some circumstances, despite apparent competence, the courts may still overrule the decision of a child or his or her parents where it is considered to be in the child's best interests. For example, in *Re W (A Minor) (Wardship: Medical Treatment)* [1992] 4 All ER 627 the refusal of treatment by a 16-year-old girl suffering from anorexia nervosa was overruled. The Children Act 1989 allows a child of sufficient understanding to refuse a medical or psychiatric examination or other assessment ordered under a child assessment order, emergency protection order, interim care order or supervision order.

LAWFUL CORRECTION

Section 1 of the Children and Young Persons Act of 1933 establishes that it is an offence to assault, ill-treat, neglect or abandon a child (under 16) in such a way as might cause unnecessary suffering or damage to health. However, Section 1(7) of that Act states that: 'Nothing in this section shall be construed as affecting the right of any parent…to administer punishment to him'. It is, therefore, a legitimate defence to a charge of assault upon a child to show that what was done was done by way of lawful correction. The correction must not be excessive either in kind or quantity. Corporal punishment is unlawful in children's homes, foster placements or schools, though there may be circumstances where reasonable force can be used to restrain pupils. Some would regard it as anomalous that it can continue in private homes and, in a controversial decision in 1994, the court ruled that childminders may use physical punishment (*Sutton LBC* v *Davis* [1994] 2 WLR 721).

Article 3 of The European Convention on Human Rights is relevant to the issue of corporal punishment. The Article absolutely prohibits torture or inhuman or degrading treatment or punishment. In *A* v *United Kingdom* [1998] 2 FLR 959, a nine-year-old child was beaten by his stepfather with a stick. The stepfather was acquitted of assault having argued the defence of reasonable chastisement. The European Court found that the lack of clear guidelines as to what constituted 'reasonable chastisement' and the failure to protect 'A' amounted to a breach of Article 3.

There is growing professional support for the view that any physical punishment of children should be banned (see web resources at the end of this Unit) although, following a consultation exercise, the government has, at the time of writing (July 2003), decided against legislative reform in this area. Any cases where reasonable chastisement is argued will now be considered under guidelines issued by the Court of Appeal in *R* v *H* [2001] 2 FLR 431. The judge must direct the jury to consider the nature and context of the defendant's behaviour, its duration, physical and mental consequences for the child, the child's age and characteristics, and the reasons given for administering the punishment.

PROTECTING AND MAINTAINING THE CHILD

Besides the duties imposed by the 1933 Act to do no unnecessary harm, there is a common law duty on any person who is looking after a child to protect him or her from physical harm by providing the 'necessities of life' (*R* v *Gibbins and Proctor* (1918) 13 Cr. App R 134). Given the powers held by virtue of the right to correct lawfully a child, you might be surprised to find the positive duty to look after a child expressed in such meagre terms.

IN LOCO PARENTIS

There are many occasions when a child is in the actual care of an adult who does not hold parental responsibility for that child. Teachers and foster carers are obvious examples. Parental responsibility can effectively be delegated to them and authority for that person to act in the child's best interests can be drawn from s. 3(5) of the Children Act, sometimes referred to as the '*in loco parentis*' provision. It states that a person who does not have parental responsibility for a child, but has care of the child, may do what is reasonable to safeguard or promote the child's welfare.

We will return to examine some of the broader themes that emerge from an understanding of parental responsibility in Study Text 3.4, but in order to make sure that you fully understand parental responsibility, as defined by the Children Act 1989, you should try the following exercise.

Exercise 3.4: Parental Responsibility

Answer *True* or *False*:

1. A child's birth father always has parental responsibility for his child.

2. A child's unmarried mother always has parental responsibility for her child.

3. Stepfathers, if they simply marry the child's mother, will have parental responsibility for that child.

4. Once parents are divorced, only the mother retains parental responsibility.

5. A brother or sister of a child cannot have parental responsibility for that child.

6. A specific issue order carries parental responsibility with it. (See Appendix 1 for a description of this and other orders referred to in this exercise.)

7. A residence order carries parental responsibility with it.

8. An emergency protection order does not carry parental responsibility with it.

9. A local authority can never obtain parental responsibility for a child.

10. The local authority can never interfere with the exercise of a mother's parental responsibility.

11. There is no limit to the number of people who can have parental responsibility for a child.

12. Once you have parental responsibility you can never lose it.

You can check your answers with those given in the trainer's notes at the end of the Unit.

Study Text 3.4: Children, the Law and Public Policy

At several points during this Unit, we have raised the question of the balance between the legitimate interests of parents and those of children. This study text considers that balance further and raises another important question of balance: that between the interests of the parents and the interests of the state.

In considering whether to make a care or supervision order, and in certain other circumstances (Children Act 1989, s. 1(4)), the court is required to consider 'the ascertainable wishes and feelings of the child' (s. 1(3)(a)). This reference to the wishes and feelings of the child could be construed as evidence of the way in which the Children Act (the 'Act') in particular, but also the law more generally, has moved towards an increasingly 'child-centred' approach in family matters.

We have indicated already how:

> the courts have come to regard parental responsibility as a collection of powers and duties which follow from being a parent and bringing up a child, rather than as rights which may be enforced at law...[the term parental responsibility] more accurately reflects that the true nature of most parental rights is of limited powers to carry out parental duties. (Department of Health 1989, p.9)

In this light, 'parental responsibility' can be understood as a responsibility *to* children and young people.

This point of balance can be seen to follow a series of precedents in the courts. A watershed judgment was that by Lord Denning, when he ruled in 1970 that the legal right of a parent 'is a dwindling right, which the courts will hesitate to enforce against the wishes of the child, the older he is. It starts with a right of control and ends with little more than advice' (per Lord Denning in *Hewer* v *Bryant* [1970] 1 QB 357). More frequently cited is the judgment by Lord Scarman in the 'Gillick' case, in which the principle was established that 'parental right yields to the child's right to make his own decisions when he reaches a sufficient understanding and intelligence to be capable of making up his own mind on the matter requiring decision' (per Lord Scarman in *Gillick AC* 112 at 186). We have already noted how this decision has had profound effects on a child's capacity to give or withhold consent to medical treatment. There are other ways, too, in which the Act would appear to have strengthened the position of children in relation to decisions taken about them. For example, a young person aged over 16 may consent to the provision of accommodation for him- or herself irrespective of the wishes of his or her parents (s. 20(11)) and the local authority is required to consult the child concerned when any decision is taken about him or her if s/he is looked after by the local authority (s. 22(4)).

However, it is possible to see this shift in the balance in the relative power of parents and children to make decisions as standing in direct contradiction to another central theme of the Act, namely the stress that the Act lays on the primacy of the family. The family, especially the family of origin, is central to the operation of the Act and much other social policy (see Butler and Drakeford 2003), and to any real understanding of the concept of 'parental responsibility'. The Act is officially described as resting 'on the belief that children are generally best looked after within the family with both parents playing a full part and without recourse to legal proceedings' (Department of Health 1991b, para 1.5). As Section 17 of the Act makes clear, it is the duty of every local authority towards 'children in need' 'to promote the upbringing of such children by their families' (s. 17 (1)). We will see in Units 6 and 9, in the context of child abuse and child protection, that the interests of children and their parents may not always be congruent and that too often the family's interests are seen to be expressed exclusively in the adults' actions, attitudes and interests.

The apparent conservatism of the Act in this regard would seem to reflect the particular Conservatism that produced not only this Act but which also froze Child Benefit and changed the social security rules to penalize young people living away from home during the same parliament. This is to see the Act in the context of what McCarthy has called the 'new politics of welfare' (see also Drakeford 2000). In McCarthy's account, these politics offered:

to reduce expenditure and shed responsibilities...[they] would strike a curiously populist chord, finely tuned to the Thatcherite emphasis on freedom, self help and responsibility, which would enable tens of thousands to 'give something back' to their local communities by participating in social support. (McCarthy 1989, p.43)

In this context the family would have an important role to play. It would be the family that would serve 'in the front-line of care' (McCarthy 1989, p.43), not just for children but for older people, people with disabilities and those with mental health problems. In this way, the Act is to be seen as a close ideological relative of the later NHS and Community Care Act. But we have already noted how family form is changing and that the boundaries around the legal concept of marriage are becoming less distinct (Butler and others 2003). Hence, it is *parenthood* that is increasingly being regarded as 'for life' in statutory terms:

[if] the bonds of parenthood are now assuming the degree of indissolubility once accorded to marriage, any significant readjustment in the relationship between the parents themselves and between parents and children is just as deserving of regulation as the dissolution of marriage itself. (Eekelaar 1991, p.173)

In establishing the concept of 'parental responsibility', the Children Act 1989 can be seen as doing just as Eekelaar describes. The parental responsibility of married parents can be ended only by death or adoption and the State will never assume exclusive parental responsibility for a child. The law will permit the concept of parental responsibility to extend to 'non-marriage' partners. Even where the birth father does not assume parental responsibility as defined by the Act, his role in maintaining the child financially cannot be escaped following the provisions of the Child Support Act 1992. Understood in this sense, the concept of 'parental responsibility' is not to be understood as simply implying that parents are responsible *to* their children, it implies also that parents are responsible *for* their children.

These sentiments have found strong echoes in the criminal law as it affects children over recent years. For example, Section 8 of The Crime and Disorder Act 1998 introduced the parenting order, which may consist of two elements:

- a requirement on the parent or guardian to attend counselling or guidance sessions (which can last up to three months); and

- requirements encouraging the parent/guardian to exercise a measure of control over the child.

(See Butler and Drakeford (2001) for an account of the social authoritarianism of the New Labour Government.)

There can be few who would take issue with the idea that parents have particular duties towards their children and that they should have the necessary rights to fulfil those duties. But, in any given social context, the question arises of whether the rights and duties of parents, children and the State are properly balanced. It will be interesting to see how the Human Rights Act 1998 (see Unit 1) will affect the current balance. Article 8 of the European Convention ('the right to respect for...private and family life') applies to everyone, including parents. A number of divorced fathers have attempted, so far unsuccessfully, to use Article 8 as the basis for actions in the domestic courts to prevent a mother with care of the child from, for example, taking the child permanently to live abroad (*Payne* v *Payne* [2001] EWCA Civ 166, [2001] 1 FLR 1052, CA) or from curtailing the father's contact with the child (*Re L, V, M, H (Contact: Domestic Violence)* [2001] 2 FLR 334, CA). It was suggested in such cases that s. 1(1) of the Children Act 1989, which now provides that the child's welfare is the court's 'paramount consideration' in determining questions relating to the child's upbringing, was incompatible with Article 8, since it appears to provide that the parent's right must be overridden when the child's welfare so demands. The courts in England and Wales have thus far rejected such claims.

Are we to assume that the current balance held between the interests of the child, the parents and the State implies that the family can enjoy greater security from intrusion by the State? Does it imply that families will have to rely more on their own resources to meet their children's needs? Does it imply that, in the privatized family, parental authority is strengthened? Are the interests of children as well protected in law as those of parents?

These are not simply interesting theoretical points. These are precisely the boundaries that you will negotiate, as a social worker, every day of your working life.

CONCLUSION

There can be little doubt that parenting is a demanding and highly skilled occupation. We have concentrated rather more on the 'performance' aspect of the role in order to broaden your appreciation of just what is involved in the 'flesh and snot' realities of parenting. We hope that you will appreciate more sensitively the myriad opportunities there are for parenting to go awry and that you will recognize that a parenting-skills approach can be a useful way into improving borderline or 'not good enough' parenting when it is applied with an appreciation of the wider context in which parenting takes place. Besides being a collection of skills and a range of practical tasks, parenting is also a set of affective relationships and we will explore some of the complexities and subtleties when we consider separation and loss in Unit 5.

Beyond this, parenting is also an idea and an ideology. It is an idea that is used to establish the boundaries between the social worker and the families who receive a social work service and between the interests of parents and children. These are dynamic boundaries that, by negotiating in your professional role, you will also help to shape.

NOTES AND SELF-ASSESSMENT

1. Is parenting a full-time occupation?

2. Does everyone have a right to be a parent if they choose?

3. What obligations do parents have towards their children and vice versa?

4. How would you assess the parenting that you give/have received and how does this experience affect the judgements you might make of others' parenting?

5. Are the criteria that you would apply in order to judge parenting in your own family the same as those that you would use for the families with which you will work?

6. How good a parent would/do you make?

RECOMMENDED READING

Cleaver, H., Unell, I. and Aldgate, J. (1999) *Children's Needs – Parenting Capacity: The Impact of Parental Mental Illness, Problem Alcohol and Drug Use, and Domestic Violence on Children's Development.* London: The Stationery Office.

Ghate, D. and Hazel, N. (2002) *Parenting in Poor Environments: Stress, Support and Coping.* London: Jessica Kingsley Publishers.

TRAINER'S NOTES

Exercise 3.1: The Job of Parenting

Group discussion, after comparisons of job descriptions, can focus on whether, on the basis of the advertisement, anyone present would apply for the job. This should allow a focus on the benefits as well as the disadvantages of being a parent; for example the child's first words, the first nativity play or special religious occasion. Role playing 'interviews' for the job allows participants to review the kind of reasons that people give for wanting children and can give rise to a discussion on when people 'should' have children and on who 'should not'. A lively discussion is the surest way of encouraging participants to reflect seriously on their understanding and preconceptions about parenting.

Exercise 3.2: Core Skills of Parenting

Divide participants into two groups: one to consider the skills needed to parent a child of 0–10 and the other to parent a child of 10–18 years. Make sure both groups can see each other's 'results' and go through them quickly, underlining similarities and debating differences. Then ask both groups to identify some core skills and to consider whether these are universal for every culture, country, religion, era in history, etc.

Exercise 3.3: Good Enough Parenting

Ask participants to work in pairs to rank the parenting on a scale of 1–5, identifying very clearly on what basis they have reached their decisions. Feed back by recording the range of scores for each scenario. This usually makes the point that the assessment of parenting, based on the same facts, will vary substantially from person to person (social worker to social worker).

You may wish to go a stage further and explore in more detail some of the reasons on which people based the scores they gave. This can be done in open discussion or by asking groups to reconcile widely varying scores and not to let them out until they agree!

It is also possible to explore the different scores by reference to Figure 3.4. Using a different colour for each scenario, take feedback from the participants. Discussion should centre on the value base for awarding a ranking on each of the criteria. Try and get a consensus and mark the point on the scale. When each of the aspects of the child's needs have been addressed, join up the markings, thus making a profile. Do this for each scenario. You will see different shaped profiles emerging.

Exercise 3.4: Parental Responsibility Quiz

Answers: 1. *False*. 2. *True*. 3. *False*. 4. *False*. 5. *False*. 6. *False*. 7. *True*. 8. *False*. 9. *False*. 10. *False*. 11. *True*. 12. *False*.

WEB RESOURCES

http://www.ncb.org.uk/cdc/index.htm This is the website of The Council for Disabled Children. The council provides a national forum for the discussion, development and dissemination of a wide range of policy and practice issues relating to service provision and support for children and young people with disabilities and special educational needs. The site is accessed via the National Children's Bureau website (http://ncb.org.uk), itself a valuable source of information on a wide range of subjects relevant to practice.

http://www.parentcentre.gov.uk This is the Department for Education and Skills website section for parents. It deals primarily with education information for parents but there is also a helpful area on the health and welfare problems of school-age children and young people. It has an extensive and reliable 'links' section to other sites dealing with all aspects of parenting.

http://www.childrenareunbeatable.org.uk Children Are Unbeatable is an alliance of over 350 organizations formed in 1998 which campaigns to give children the same legal protection against being hit as adults and to promote positive, non-violent discipline. It has a section offering advice on 'positive discipline' that contains an extensive directory of useful sources of advice for parents and professionals.

UNIT 4

Supporting

OBJECTIVES

In this Unit you will:

- Examine the statutory basis on which support services to children and families are provided.
- Explore the range of support services available to children in need.
- Explore what is meant by 'partnership practice'.
- Consider the application of partnership practice to the provision of support services.

 SUPPORTING CHILDREN AND FAMILIES

Unit 3 concluded with an appreciation of the demands of parenting. As a child grows, the skills required and the resources needed to parent effectively continue to change and develop. Children and parents mature and their personalities, expectations and needs alter with the passage of time. There are any number of points, especially in the changing context of child-rearing practice and family formation, where relationships can go awry. Similarly, circumstances can be such that effective parenting is made even more exacting. Racism, low income, ill health and poor housing can make an already difficult job almost impossible (Ghate and Hazel 2002). It is hardly surprising that most, if not all, parents and children need help with the business of growing up and getting on with each other at some time or other. Social work with children and families is substantially about the provision of such help (see Eekelaar and Dingwall 1990).

It is important to recognize how recently the question has arisen of how, or even if, there should be formalized and systematic services to help support families through the processes of parenting. The first half of this century bore the indelible mark of deeply humiliating and publicly shaming Poor Law provision. Writing about the state of the law in 1947, S. Clement Brown (p.iii) reminds her readers how the legacy of the preceding age found a strong echo in her own time:

> Some of our laws still express the view that our duty to the homeless child ends when we have fed and clothed him and trained him in habits of soberness and industry. The duty of the local authority in respect of destitute children, beyond giving them 'relief', is still only to set [them] to work or put [them] out as apprentices.

In truth, the specific welfare of children was not much more than a minor note in the monumental social policy shifts that took place after the Second World War (see Butler and Drakeford 2003, p.56ff) although this period did produce the first major piece of legislation for forty years that bore on the welfare of children, the Children Act 1948.

The principle on which the Children's Departments that the Act established were to carry out their duties represented a significant break with previous legislation in that s. 12 of the Act required local authorities to carry out their responsibilities to a child 'so as to further his best interests and to afford him opportunity for the proper development of his character and abilities'. The second part of s. 12 required local authorities, in providing for children in their care, to 'make use of facilities and services available to children in the care of their parents'. It has been argued that any commitment of the 1948 Act to family preservation and to preventive work was more implied than expressed (see Donnison 1954; James 1998) but the rise in short-term case-work that followed the implementation of the Act increasingly forced the staff of the new Children's Departments into face-to-face work with families and encouraged an interest in preventative and family support work that was to find expression in the 1963 Children and Young Persons Act.

The 1963 Act, while primarily concerned with delinquency and the juvenile court system, began by granting local authorities specific powers to engage in preventive work (s. 1):

> It shall be the duty of every local authority to make available such advice, guidance and assistance as may promote the welfare of children by diminishing the need to receive children into care or keep them in care...

At the end of a decade which saw increasing economic pressure brought to bear on the universalism of the Welfare State, it was to be the 1969 Children and Young Person's Act that would represent the final flowering of a family-orientated, preventative treatment ideology that had begun in the Children's Departments of the 1950s. However, the 1969 Act was never fully implemented as the political tide turned in favour of a more conservative approach to welfare provision (see Hendrick 1994; Butler and Drakeford 2003). To a degree, this was reflected in the Children Act 1975, which reflected some of the concerns that had arisen following the first major child care scandal of the post-war period, the death of Maria Colwell. Amongst other provisions, the Act made it easier for local authorities to assume parental rights and more difficult for parents to remove their children from the care of the local authority (see Holman 1975, 1988; Jordan 1981; Thoburn 1999). The 1970s also saw the beginnings of a decisive shift away from prevention and towards the detection of child abuse (see Parton 1985, 1997).

By the 1980s both professionals and policy makers were becoming increasingly concerned, largely through the emergence of a body of research that called into question the quality of the care provided by local authorities, that an imbalance (Department of Health and Social Security 1985) had developed between the professional resources devoted to the 'blue light' child protection services and services aimed more at prevention and family support (see Department of Health 1995; Tunstill and Aldgate 2000, pp.1–6). The Children Act 1989 sought to address this imbalance by re-invigorating and recasting the role of local authorities in the provision of personal social services to children and families. According to Aldgate and Tunstill (1995, p.6), the 1989 Act 'represents a fusing of the concepts of prevention and family support' (see also Packman and Jordan 1991). Early Guidance stressed that the Act would enable families to 'look to social services for support and assistance. If they do this they should receive a positive response which reduces any fears they may have of stigma or loss of parental responsibility' (Department of Health 1991c, para. 2.14). As such, the Act implies not only a degree of flexibility in how support services might be delivered but also a different relationship between the providers of services and their users. This Unit will describe the statutory basis for social work practice to support children and families and explore the concept of partnership practice as it relates to the provision of support services. It begins with an account of the terms used in the Act to identify who might be eligible to receive such services.

Study Text 4.1: Children in Need

Part III of the Children Act 1989 establishes the local authority's duty to provide an appropriate 'range and level of services' for certain children with the aim of 'safeguarding and promoting' their welfare and, so far as is consistent with that aim, to do so by promoting 'the upbringing of such children by their families' (s. 17 (1)). The children concerned are those that the Act describes as 'children in need'.

The definition of a child 'in need' is to be found at s. 17 (10). A child is in need if:

(a)   he is unlikely to achieve or maintain, or to have the opportunity of achieving or maintaining a reasonable standard of health or development without the provisions for him of services by a local authority under this Part;

(b)   his health or development is likely to be significantly impaired or further impaired, without the provision for him of such services; or

(c)   he is disabled.

'Development' means physical, intellectual, emotional, social or behavioural development and 'health' means physical or mental health (s. 17 (11)). A child is 'disabled' if he or she is 'blind, deaf or dumb or suffers from mental disorder of any kind or is substantially and permanently handicapped by illness, injury or congenital deformity'. This definition of disabled is the same as that contained in the National Assistance Act 1948 and so a person with disabilities qualifies for services both before and after the age of 18. Services may also be available under other legislation, including the Chronically Sick and Disabled Persons Act 1970. The Children Act 1989 makes allowances for services to be provided for a child's family or any member of the child's family as well as to the child itself, if these are provided 'with a view to safeguarding or promoting the child's welfare' (s. 17 (3)). 'Family' is defined widely to include 'any person with parental responsibility for the child and any person with whom he has been living' (s. 17 (10)). This definition of need is deliberately wide in order to reinforce the Act's commitment to provide services across a broad range. Local authorities cannot exclude any category nor can the definition of 'need' be restricted only to those children at risk of significant harm.

Direct services for children in need will not only be provided by local authorities, however. The local authority is required to 'facilitate the provision by others' of support services (s. 17 (5)). So, even if you are employed in the voluntary or independent sector, your work may derive from the provisions of Part III of the Act. The local authority is required to 'take reasonable steps to identify the extent to which there are children in need within their area' (Sch. 2, para. 1(1)) and to publish information about the services that they provide, or which are provided by voluntary or other organizations, in such a way as those who might benefit from them are informed (Sch. 2, para. 1(2)). The duty to publish information is reinforced by the Human Rights Act 1998 (HRA). Article 10 ('freedom of expression') has been interpreted as to include the right to receive information. If adequate information about services were not available, a person who might benefit from the service would be able to challenge the local authority under the HRA. The local authority is also required to open and maintain a register of children with disabilities in their area (Sch. 2, para.2(1)). There is no duty on the individual to register. As well as in relation to children in need, the Act also confers some other duties upon local authorities to provide support services. The authority is required, through the provision of services under Part III of the Act, 'to prevent children within their area suffering ill-treatment or neglect' (Sch. 2, para. 4). It is also required to take 'reasonable steps' to reduce the need for care proceedings and criminal proceedings against children, to encourage children within their area not to commit offences and to avoid the need to place children in secure accommodation (Sch. 2, para. 7). (See Study Text 4.2 for a description of the range of services that may be provided to children in need.)

In order to determine whether a particular child is a child 'in need', the Act acknowledges that some form of assessment will be required (Sch. 2, para. 3). Such an assessment may be carried out as part of a wider assessment of special needs. We have already introduced you (in Study Texts 1.2 and 3.2) to the *Framework for the Assessment of Children in Need and their Families* (Department of Health and others 2000), which is now the preferred means of carrying out such assessments. The three dimensions (the child's developmental needs, parenting capacity, family and environmental factors) are often presented as three sides of a triangle with the child and the statutory duty upon local authorities to 'safeguard and promote' his or her welfare at the centre – see Figure 4.1.

The three domains

Family and environmental factors

Figure 4.1 The assessment framework

We will look in more detail in Unit 6 how the *Framework* is to be used in practice and consider further its immediate origins. For now, it is important to see with Rose (2001, p.40), that the *Framework*:

> represents a way of trying to capture the complexity of a child's world and beginning to construct a coherent approach to collecting and analysing information about each child. As such, it provides a conceptual map which will help professionals in their work with children and families.

We hope that we have already indicated to you what a useful 'conceptual map' the *Framework* is but, as we have also suggested at several points in this book already, we should not expect it to do more than *help* us in our work. The *Framework*, like the Children Act itself, provides the context in which social workers must exercise their professional skill and judgement. Neither the *Framework* nor the Act can be substituted for such skill or judgement. Social work cannot be done by numbers. The following exercise will make this point more clearly.

 Exercise 4.1: In Need?

For each of these mini case studies, using as much of the *Framework* as the case material will allow, decide whether the child concerned is a child in need as defined by the Children Act 1989 and write down as precisely as you can how the child satisfies the criteria established in Part III of the Act.

1. Sharon is 15 and pregnant. She intends to look after her baby herself, with the help of her mother. Sharon currently shares a bedroom with her sister, aged 11. Her two brothers and her parents occupy the other bedrooms in her semi-detached house. Her mother seems reconciled to the facts of Sharon's situation but her father is angry and upset and refusing to speak to Sharon. Tension between family members is rising and there are frequent arguments between various members of the family.

2. John, aged four, lives with his mum and older brother, Ian, in a council maisonette on a very large estate on the outskirts of a

major city. Mum survives on social security benefits but she is in debt (for about £500, used to buy a cooker) to a moneylender. John has few clothes and no winter coat. Food is not very nutritious but he never goes hungry. There are only a few toys in the home and the local playground has been vandalized.

3.   Mark, aged 14, has been involved with others in petty theft in and around his home area. He has not yet come to police attention officially but his family are concerned that this will only be a matter of time. Mark's parents are teachers and live in one of the better parts of town. Neither Mark nor his family are happy with the slowly deteriorating state of family relationships that is occurring as a consequence of rows over Mark's behaviour. Relationships have always been good up to now. When Mark's father heard that his son had been truanting from school he telephoned the social worker saying that he had had enough and that something had to be done.

4.   Robbie is aged 12. He is a keen supporter of the local football club and likes to dress in imitation of his heroes. Recently the club changed their first-team kit and Robbie now wants to buy a replica shirt and a suitable (and expensive) pair of trainers. He says that he has been excluded by his friends at school because he is dressed so badly and that he will soon have no friends left if he cannot keep up with them.

5.   Sanjit is the lone parent of Ayse, aged three, who has severe learning difficulties and some mobility difficulties. Ayse can do very little for herself and requires almost constant attention. Sanjit is finding the physical demands on her exhausting. Ayse's father was killed in a traffic accident and she and her mother have no other friends or family in the area. Sanjit works in the local launderette part-time where she can take Ayse but she often feels lonely and at the end of her tether.

6.   Mr Smith is having an affair with the wife of a family friend. He has been out of work for several years, despite numerous offers of work. Mrs Smith knows all about Mr Smith's affair and makes no secret of her contempt for her husband. Despite the fact that the family are in severe financial difficulties, both Mr and Mrs Smith have extravagant tastes and substantial credit card debts. The Smith's son, Jamie, is aged eight. He is a very timid boy who has

recently started to wet the bed at night. His bed is already ruined and Mrs Smith has asked you to help.

Points to Consider

1. What factors did you take into account when determining whether the development of the child concerned was at issue?

2. What factors did you take into account when determining whether the health of the child concerned was at issue?

3. How did you decide what was a 'reasonable standard' of health or development?

4. What factors did you take into account in deciding what 'significantly impaired' might mean in each case?

5. In your decision-making, did you accord more importance to the particular characteristics of the children concerned or to the circumstances in which they found themselves?

6. Was the degree of responsibility or culpability of the parents an issue in deciding whether each child was a child in need?

A RANGE OF NEEDS AND SERVICES

Each of the mini case studies used in Exercise 4.1 is based on a real example from our own practice but, until recently, we would have been hard pressed to know how 'typical' of the whole population of children in need these were. Some ten years after the implementation of the Children Act 1989, Aldgate and Statham (2001, p.25) noted that 'there are not yet reliable statistical data on children in need'. This has since been rectified with the publication of *Children in Need in England: First Results of a Survey of Activity and Expenditure as Reported by Local Authority Social Services' Children and Family Teams for a Survey Week in February 2000* (Department of

Health/Office for National Statistics 2000). Figure 4.2 contains some of the statistical highlights from this, the first robust survey of children in need, and some additional material from the 2000 *Children Act Report* (Department of Health 2001a).

- There were just over 380,000 children in need known to local authorities as requiring some form of social services provision (DH/ONS 2000, para. 8)
- Seventeen per cent of these (64,000) were children looked after (away from home) (DH/ONS 2000, para. 8)
- Local authority and regional variations are very marked with the rate of children in need varying from 10 per 1000 of the population aged 0–17 to over 70 (DH 2001a, para. 3.10) in different local authority areas
- Regionally, Inner London has an incidence of 43 children in need per 1000 of the population aged 0–17 compared to the West Midlands with an average incidence of 13. These variations are reduced considerably, however, if one takes into account levels of social deprivation (DH 2001a, para. 3.11)
- Almost a quarter of a million children had work undertaken on their behalf (or received some payment from the local authority) during the census week (DH/ONS 2000, para. 10)
- Ninety-two per cent of looked after children received services during the census week, compared to 54 per cent of other children in need (DH/ONS 2000, para. 12)
- Over 30,000 children looked after (56%) and almost 50,000 other children in need (28%) received a service for reasons of 'abuse and neglect' (DH/ONS 2000, Chart 2)
- Approximately 12 per cent of children in need are disabled and they received 14 per cent of gross expenditure on children in need (DH/ONS 2000, para. 30)
- About 30 per cent of children in need who are not looked after away from home are aged under five (DH/ONS 2000, para. 26)

- Some 16 per cent of children in need are of Black or minority ethnic origin. This constitutes an 'over-representation' of between 1.5 and 2.5 times the national average for the population aged under 18 as a whole (DH/ONS 2000, para. 28)
- Social services departments spend over £40,000,000 on children in need per week, equivalent to an annual expenditure of £2,130,000,000 per year (DH/ONS 2000, para. 18)
- The average cost per week for a looked after child is £435. Other children in need cost, on average, £85 per week (DH/ONS 2000, para. 20)
- Most work with children in need can be categorized as 'ongoing'; on average, 5.3 hours of work is undertaken per looked after child per week, compared to 3.3 hours for other children in need (DH/ONS 2000, Table 6)

Figure 4.2 The population of children in need
Sources: DH/ONS (Department of Health/Office of National Statistics) (2000); DH (Department of Health) (2001a) (Crown copyright).

One might acknowledge that definitional problems had, for some time, made research 'methodologically intimidating to researchers and politically intimidating to funders' (Tunstill 1996, p.154) (see also Tunstill and Aldgate 2000, pp.13–17) but one might still wonder why providing a census of this particular population should have eluded the UK's various means and mechanisms of 'social accounting' (an important part of which is the centralized collection of 'official statistics') for so long. It may be a reflection of the priority this group of children has had for policy makers and practitioners. In order to be officially counted, a given population has to count for something.

The sheer scale of the population of children in need may well have made an impression upon you but a clearer feel for the lived experience of these children is to be found in Aldgate and Statham's review (Aldgate and Statham 2001) of 24 research studies commissioned by the Department of Health to examine the workings of the Children Act 1989. They conclude that (2001, p.32):

- Many families of children in need are struggling to bring up their children in conditions of material and emotional adversity.

- Poor health and poverty are dominant themes in the studies for the majority of families.

- Domestic violence and drugs and alcohol misuse are present in families with more severe problems.

- There are differences in the level and scope of problems – families whose children are subject to care proceedings have more entrenched and long-standing multiple problems.

- Families of children in need can be grouped in three ways: those who need help with specific issues, acutely distressed families and families with multiple and long-standing problems.

- Families move from one category to another as problems improve or deteriorate.

Clearly, the daily struggle against what Beveridge once described as the five giants of want, disease, squalor, ignorance and idleness, continues for many children still. Yet, what is equally clear is that much of the daily experience of the children who are our concern is lived out of the public gaze. There are few newspaper headlines reporting the reduced life chances and frustrated potential of the children in need we have described (unless, that is, they are subject to abuse). We probably don't very often drive down the streets, past the houses where these children live, unless our job requires us to do so. It is comparatively easy to avoid close scrutiny of the quiet catastrophes that daily takes place in neighbourhoods very close to our own. You may wish to reflect further on why it is that these children do not raise the interest of journalists or the indignation of the general public more than they appear to do. As social workers, the Children Act 1989 provides you with some of the means to address the consequences of our society's general neglect of some of its most vulnerable citizens.

Study Text 4.2 sets out how the Act requires or permits certain forms of support service and provides a brief commentary on their relative effectiveness.

Study Text 4.2: Services for Children in Need

The Children Act 1989 (the Act) requires local authorities to make available the following services for children in need:

- advice, guidance and counselling
- occupational, social, cultural or recreational activities
- day care or supervised activity
- home help
- travel assistance
- assistance to enable the child to have a holiday
- maintenance of the family home
- financial assistance
- accommodation.

The local authority must provide or facilitate the provision by others of *advice, guidance* and *counselling* as well as *occupational, social, cultural or recreational activities* for all children in need living with their families (Sch. 2, para. 8). Such services may also be provided for other children not in need. Often such services will be available via family centres, which the local authority is required to provide under the Act (Sch. 2, para. 9). The nature and level of services offered by family centres vary enormously. Gibbons, Thorpe and Wilkinson (1990) have distinguished three main types of centre: the client-focused centre, where users are mainly referred by statutory organizations; neighbourhood centres, which have a more open-door policy and more flexible staff roles; and community development orientated centres, which are managed by local people and concentrate on providing self-help groups rather than facilities for case-work. The most common form is the neighbourhood family centre, which aims to combine some individual support with running advice groups for parents and day care facilities for children. Guidance (Department of Health 1991c, para. 3.20) differentiates between centres in a similar way and identifies therapeutic centres, where skilled workers carry out intensive work with families in extreme difficulty; community-orientated centres, which families might use as a meeting place and to take part in activities; and self-help centres, where services might be offered in a very informal, unstructured way.

Day care, which includes day nurseries, playgroups, toy libraries, out-of-school clubs and holiday play schemes, must be provided for all children in need aged five or under (if not in school) and may be provided for other children too (s. 18). The local authority has no power or duty under the Act to make provision for home help, travel assistance or holidays other than for children in need (Sch. 2, para. 8). Where a child in need is living away from home (but is not being looked after by a local authority), the local authority must take steps, if necessary, to promote the child's welfare, to enable the child to live with its family and/or to promote contact between the child and its family (Sch. 2, para. 10).

In exceptional circumstances, not defined by the Act, the local authority may offer assistance in cash. Any service offered, excluding advice, guidance, or counselling, may be subject to a charge to the service user (s. 29 (1)).

The local authority must provide accommodation for a child in need who requires accommodation if:

- there is no-one with parental responsibility for the child (s. 20 (1)(a))
- the child is lost or abandoned (s. 20 (1)(b))
- the person caring for the child is prevented from providing the child with suitable accommodation, for whatever reason and whether permanently or not (s. 20 (1)(c))
- the child is over 16 and the local authority considers that the child's welfare is likely to be seriously prejudiced if accommodation is not provided (s. 20 (3)).

Accommodation provided in this way is dealt with at greater length in Unit 5 but it should be noted at this stage that when a child is accommodated under the provisions of Part III of the Act, the pre-existing distribution of parental responsibility is unaltered. The local authority does not acquire any parental responsibility for the child, although it does acquire certain duties and obligations to safeguard and promote the child's welfare (s. 22 and Study Texts 3.2, 5.3 and 8.2).

WHAT WORKS?

Determining the effectiveness of the services provided by social workers (and others) is notoriously difficult. Contemporary interest in 'evidence-based practice' (see Butler and Pugh 2003) means, however, that questions concerning efficacy are more frequently and more urgently asked. Indeed, in October 2001, the Department of Health established The Social Care Institute of Excellence (SCIE) to further its aim of producing 'better knowledge for better practice'. SCIE has three main functions:

- reviewing knowledge about social care
- developing practice guides based on that knowledge
- promoting the use of practice guides in policy and practice.

Its website (see web resources at the end of this Unit) provides free access to a wide range of electronic resources which you may find useful.

As regards services for children in need, a review by Armstrong and Hill (2001) of the available research on the most common types of family support services concluded that 'each type can help improve family functioning' (p.356) (see also Aldgate and Statham 2001, pp.113–39). Armstrong and Hill went on to note:

- While many initiatives seem to have a positive impact on the social support, skills and confidence of mothers, it is not always clear how far this brings about improvements in parenting and benefits to children.
- There is little evidence about the effects of family support services on fathers and their parenting capacity.
- Intensive health visiting and high quality day care have many immediate and longer-term direct benefits for children.
- Programmes with a clear structure and frequent contact with users seem to have greater effects.
- The most vulnerable families are the least likely to engage with family support programmes and the most likely to drop out.
- Parenting education with behavioural and interactive elements is successful.
- The ideal is 'well co-ordinated multiple intervention'. (2001, p.357)

The last point made by Armstrong and Hill reflects what we know from the available research on the consequences for children of their experiences of being in need. Reviewing the literature on childhood risk factors leading to social exclusion, a risk that attends many children in need, Bynner (2001, p.292) notes that 'no single risk factor…is likely to lead to social exclusion. It is in combination that their potency for impeding children's cognitive and behavioural development becomes apparent'. However, it is important to note that such early childhood experiences are by no means determining. They are (to some degree) preventable and remediable. As Bynner notes in his conclusion (p.295):

> In most cases the continuing risk appears to derive less from any irreversible effect in early life than from continuing disadvantaged circumstances reinforcing and recycling the social relations identified with the risk.

Bynner goes on to comment on those interventive strategies that have been attempted, particularly at community level, both in the US and in the UK, before he makes the following statement (p.295):

> it is never too late to intervene.

Sometimes, however, our desire to help and our capacity to intervene may not easily coincide. We turn now to examine some of the obstacles to effective practice.

 MAKING CHOICES

It is important to recognize that 'need' is not an absolute or unitary concept; there are different kinds and degrees of need and a variety of ways of meeting it. The choice of appropriate response is rarely unconstrained, however. Often the social work task, in the context of insufficient resources to meet demand, is that of balancing the competing claims made by different groups or individuals, each of which has a legitimate case to make. It should be remembered also that just as certain kinds and degrees of need have higher or lower claims on an agency's resources, so it is also the case that certain forms of support service are more acceptable to some groups than others.

Consider for a moment how the parents of children with disabilities might feel at having their child included on a register maintained by the social services department. Some may welcome the formalizing of social services support but others may be offended by being associated for the first time with people who require social work intervention. They may regard a social worker's visits as stigmatizing and far less acceptable than having a health visitor call. Others may regard the supply of services by a voluntary agency as the equivalent of receiving charity. The following exercise will further illustrate the point.

 Exercise 4.2: Providing a Service

Return to the mini case studies used in Exercise 4.1.

1. Rank order the case studies from the highest level of need to the lowest.

2. List those services or combinations of services that you feel may be appropriate to those children whom you have identified as being in need. You may refer to the services already mentioned in the Unit and any others you may be aware of from your own experience.

3. Consider how acceptable such services might be to the person who would receive them and to their carers.

4. Now be realistic and, from your experience and knowledge of the current services in your locality, note how likely it would be that services could be delivered in the way that you have indicated.

Points to Consider

1. What factors did you take into account in determining levels of need?

2. Do you think that the concept of the child 'in need' is a helpful one in determining how to prioritize service responses?

3. Other than the level of need, what else is likely to influence the nature and level of service responses?

4. In your experience, which kinds of services are least likely to be stigmatizing?

5. Imagine that you are the parent of a child with a disability. You have heard that the local authority is opening a register for children with disabilities. What information would you be happy for social workers to collect?

6. What do you understand to be the primary purpose of providing support services to families?

A NEW ALLIANCE?

It should be clear that the supply of support services is a contingent process; not all families who have difficulties will be defined as 'in need', not all families who are eligible for services will receive them and not all of those who are eligible and who could receive them will choose to do so. Any reluctance to engage with social work support services, especially those supplied by the local authority, may be coloured by a sense of their Poor Law heritage (see also Aldgate and Statham 2001, p.72). However, there is ample research evidence to suggest that a great deal of child care practice has, in the recent past, been characterized by a persistent mutual mistrust on the part of the recipients and the providers of such services that is of much more immediate origin.

At least four important reports issued by central government since 1985 have argued consistently for a better working relationship between the families of children in difficulties and social workers. The consistent message of all of these reports is one of developing new alliances between the users and providers of services (between social workers and their 'clients') and between differing service providers.

The first report, *Social Work Decisions in Child Care – Recent Research Findings and their Implications* (Department of Health and Social Security 1985), noted in its foreword that: 'Sensitive and knowledgeable work by professional social work practitioners is required to secure a practical partnership with parents which will operate in the best interests of the children'. The report went on to argue for the need to 'consult, inform and work with parents' (p.20) and to urge (p.22) 'shifts in attitude[s] and priorities, increased understanding, more sensitive perception of client's feelings by social workers'.

The second report, *Patterns and Outcomes in Child Placement – Messages from Current Research and their Implications* (Department of Health 1991d), located the barriers to 'practical partnership' in tradition and bureaucracy, in the lack of skill, sensitivity and time available to social workers, the nature of parents' own problems and in problems over the balance of power and noted that (p.44): 'None of these characteristics offers an easy basis for reciprocal trust between parents and social workers and the latter will need to take initiatives and work hard to build a genuine partnership'.

A third report, *Child Protection – Messages from Research* (Department of Health 1995, p.86), in a section called 'Paternalism or Partnership?' found 'a clear link between better outcomes for children and greater involvement of parents' and added that:

> All family members stressed the importance of being cared about as people. They could understand that the professional had a job to do and that procedures were necessary, but they strongly objected to workers in whatever profession who did not appear to listen, did not show warmth or concern or who only did things by the book. (p.87)

The fourth set of 'messages from research' (Aldgate and Statham 2001) reinforces the importance of partnership and recognizes that it has proved 'a major challenge for social workers, a challenge to which, on the whole, they have responded' (p.142). Nonetheless, alongside some examples of excellent practice, there were also examples of: 'parents who felt marginalised and degraded, especially those who were involved in care proceedings and those whose children were looked after' (p.142). In the studies reviewed by Aldgate and Statham, failure to work effectively with parents often arose from the social worker's inability to exercise his or her authority appropriately. They note (p.142):

> The positive use of authority, combined with clear aims and objectives of intervention, could improve practice in the areas where there is a need to safeguard and promote children's welfare simultaneously in order to prevent risk of impairment, without the use of court action.

Understanding the nature of the power structure implicit in every relationship is important to understanding how to engage in effective partnerships. The following study text will sensitize you to this and to some of the broader currents of thought that influence contemporary ideas of partnership practice in child care, in preparation for the final exercise in this Unit, which provides an opportunity to consider partnership in the context of the provision of support services.

Study Text 4.3: Partnership Practice

PARTNERSHIP, POWER AND ANTI-OPPRESSIVE PRACTICE

At the heart of any discussion about the nature of partnership practice lies the question of power. In its everyday sense, the idea of a partnership implies a set of power relations that tend towards equality and mutuality. *The Shorter Oxford English Dictionary* defines a 'partner' as:

> one who is associated with another or others in some business, the expenses, profits or losses of which he proportionally shares – a husband or wife – a companion in a dance – a player associated on the same side with another.

If we add to this definition (which tells us more about where partnerships take place than anything about the idea itself) some of the assumptions we make about these settings, we can infer that a partnership:

- extends over time
- is for better or worse, richer or poorer
- involves shared aims
- involves a degree of mutual adjustment, like the partners in a dance.

However, there is a power inherent in the role and status of social workers, particularly, but not exclusively, when operating in a statutory context that tends towards the opposite of what is implied in the dictionary definition: away from mutuality and reciprocity towards an imbalance of power in favour of the social worker.

The power possessed by the social worker derives from a number of sources, not least legal mandate, and societal expectation (Davies 1994). It derives also from the possession of specialist knowledge and skills (Johnson 1972). There is a sense in which this is inevitable and, certainly, the assumption is deeply embedded in the social work literature and in contemporary practice. When the particular constellations of negative values that have hitherto characterized social work thinking (its euro-centricity and its gender biases, for example) are considered, many would agree that in relation to understanding oppressive practice of whatever sort, the issue of power, its sources and its uses, is central.

Phillipson has noted that understanding the uses and abuses of power 'is crucial to social work because social work needs to work with a frame-work for understanding those elements that are embedded in oppression and its repercussions' (1992, p.14). Individual practitioners may often feel that they have very little power. It is true, as Phillipson suggests, that there are structural dimensions to sexism, racism and other forms of oppression that are less amenable to the actions of any individual. At a more mundane level, even if you work in a large bureaucracy, strategic decisions over the allocation of scarce resources, for example, may appear to be taken at some remove from you. But, just as there are structural dimensions to oppression, so too are there personal ones. We have indicated already how 'gatekeeping' (facilitating access to existing services) often revolves around particular professional judgements in specific cases. The point at issue is not how much power social workers have or where else in society power is located. The point at issue is how the power that is possessed by social workers is used, either exclusively to impose definitions or assessments of problems or inclusively to enable or empower others. This is central to any understanding of the principle of partnership practice and the provision of support services to children and families. In so far as partnership is based on a commitment to genuine mutuality, reciprocity, negotiation and the prospect of a real alliance, it is a form of practice that can give substance to a commitment to anti-oppressive practice.

THE POWER OF PARTNERSHIP

It will not always be the case that power can be shared equally between social worker and service user. Sometimes this would not even be desirable. Partnership practice is not a form of utopianism but can make power differentials explicit and productive rather than covert or denied. However, as with all partial solutions, partnership practice also has the potential to be its own contradiction and to legitimate the existing structure of power relations. Coit (1978), writing about partnership in the context of community development, illustrates how partnership can be conservative:

- 'partnership' at a local level tends to mask structural inequalities and class antagonisms
- 'partnership' encourages compromise and conciliation in order to obtain minimum concessions
- 'partnership' is operated by professionals
- 'partnership' weakens local leadership.

Indeed, common sense would suggest that 'partnership' could easily be corrupted since it is essentially about power. Few ever give up power willingly. It may be more helpful to conceive of degrees of partnership – some more cosmetic than others – to see partnership operating along a continuum determined by the nature of the power relations.

Arnstein (1972) has described a general progression that begins at one end of the spectrum with 'manipulation', where it is only the worker who knows the rules, can diagnose the problem, pronounce upon the 'cure' and determine whether it has been achieved. One degree better than this is 'informing', where the service user is paid the courtesy of being told what will happen to them next. Then comes 'consultation', when the voice of the other is heard but is by no means necessarily heeded. Then 'placation', where Coit's 'minimum concessions' are won. Then on to 'partnership' itself, which still falls short of what Arnstein calls 'delegated power', where, for example, a budget might be delegated and then, finally, given over to 'citizen control' and the New Jerusalem. (For alternative continua of partnership, see Cox and Parish 1989 and Butler 1996b).

THE VALUE OF PARTNERSHIP

Partnership practice ultimately should be judged by its achievements: how it helps children and families deal with the problems with which they are confronted. Aldgate and Statham (2001, p.142) note how confusing it becomes for parents when partnership is seen as 'an end in itself rather than as a process to facilitate the attainment of good outcomes for children'. For the population at large, partnership is valued for what it helps one achieve, its instrumental value. For the users of social work services it is not to be valued only for how it makes one feel, its expressive value. If it has *real* value, partnership practice must have sharing as its determining character-istic; shared purpose, a sharing of knowledge, expertise, information and skills and a sharing of resources, power and decision-making. Partnership is more than a means to an end in that it implies a significant change in the philosophy and practice of many social workers. Atherton and Dowling (1989) offer a statement of values which lie at the heart of partnership practice that many would find challenging:

- Partners trust each other. So they can be open and honest in how they behave to each other. They try to understand rather than to judge.

- Partners respect each other. There is complimentarity rather than equality where the special skills and knowledge of the worker are made accessible to the client in the way that has been negotiated with the client.

- Partners are working towards the same broad objectives.

- Partners share power. Nobody has a monopoly on it and nobody takes over. That power may never be equal but it should be possible for the balance of power to shift by negotiation and agreement.

- Empowerment of the client can be assisted by ensuring that the views of each partner carry weight and are respected and by sharing information.

- Partners share in decision-making.

- Partners can call each other to account and have rights. Partnership practice does take the issue of accountability seriously and provides for any partner to call for explanations and challenge what work is going on.

 Exercise 4.3: Partners?

This exercise is based on the first of the mini case scenarios used in Exercise 4.1 and the worst kind of social work response that can be imagined. Read the additional material set out below and complete the tasks that follow.

Sharon's mother contacted the health visitor in order to see what kind of support might be available. She had hoped that the family might be able to obtain some practical help around the house when the baby was born and that the doctor might be able to write in support of an application to the housing authority so that the family could eventually move to a four-bedroomed house.

Later that day a social worker called to see Sharon. It soon became clear from the line of inquiry being pursued by the social worker that the matter was being viewed as a 'child protection' issue, although it was not clear whether the child concerned was Sharon or her baby. Sharon had told the social worker who the father of the child was and had been informed that this may prove to be a matter for the police as Sharon was 'under age'. The social worker told Sharon that her school had already been contacted. Sharon had not told anyone outside her family up to this point as she was not entirely sure what she wanted to do concerning her future plans. Sharon became very upset. The social worker told her that regular visits would be required from that point on, as Sharon did not seem to be emotionally capable of looking after herself, let alone her child. Sharon's mother asked the social worker to leave and was informed that it would be in the family's interest to allow such visits as 'there was always the possibility of going to court'.

TASKS

1. 'Quickthink' all of the potential support services that could have been made available to Sharon and her family.

2. Consider how Sharon and her family are likely to view any help that the social worker, health visitor or other professional is now able to offer them.

3. Consider how the response made will influence the likelihood of Sharon or her family asking for help in the future.

4. Describe an appropriate response by the health visitor and the social work agency.

 Points to Consider

1. In what sense and to whom are the professionals in this case accountable for their response? To whom should they be accountable?

2. How might Sharon and her family's objectives differ from those of the professionals involved? What might be the points of conflict?

3. Why might the social worker not trust Sharon and her family to know what help they want?

4. Who should be making the decisions in this case? Who will?

5. Is it realistic to think of partnership practice in the context of a potential child protection issue?

6. What are the limits of partnership practice?

CONCLUSION

In considering how families might best be supported through the difficulties that they encounter, we have suggested that the value and usefulness of that support and its appropriateness and acceptability are in some measure dependent on the terms on which it is offered. We have suggested that partnership approaches have a potential for establishing the kind of relationship best suited to helping families deal with their problems. Partnership practice depends on a willingness on the part of the social worker or other professional to think about their role in relation to families in difficulty quite differently to how they have done in the past. In turn, this requires a thorough appreciation of what personal qualities and professional style social workers bring to the helping relationship. It has been known for a long time that the characteristics of social workers that service users most value are:

> honesty, naturalness and reliability along with an ability to listen. [Service users] appreciated being kept informed, having their feelings understood, having the stress of parenthood accepted and getting practical help as well as moral support. (Department of Health and Social Security 1985, p.20)

> Social workers are experienced as helpful if they really listen and take pains to understand the difficulties from the family's point of view. They are also valued if they are practical as well as sympathetic and supportive and do more than just listen. Honesty and directness are important qualities that parents are well able to appreciate – even if some messages are hard and unpalatable... (Department of Health 1991d, p.47)

> Honesty and reliability were particularly valued. Clearly presented information about what was happening and the options available were both very important. (Department of Health 1995, p.46)

Parents value recognition of the circumstances that inhibit parental responsibility. Respect for different parenting styles is important... The power differential between parents and workers should be openly acknowledged. Parents respond well to being treated with dignity. (Aldgate and Statham 2001, p.73)

This is not a counsel of perfection. It is what is needed to do the job, assuming that the job is one of helping families resolve their difficulties.

NOTES AND SELF-ASSESSMENT

1. Why provide support services to children and families?

2. To whom do you regard yourself accountable in the exercise of your professional duties?

3. Do you trust the users of social work services?

4. In your working relationships with families, do you prefer to lead or to follow?

5. How well do you take guidance?

6. Is your practice characterized by 'honesty, naturalness and reliability along with an ability to listen'?

RECOMMENDED READING

Aldgate, J. and Statham, D. (2001) *The Children Act Now: Messages from Research.* London: The Stationery Office.

Horwarth, J. (ed.) (2001) *The Child's World: Assessing Children in Need.* London: Jessica Kingsley Publishers.

TRAINER'S NOTES

Exercise 4.1: In Need?

This exercise can be undertaken with or without reference to the *Framework*. Participants could also refer back to the material generated in Exercise 1.2 or 3.3 for broader conceptions of needs and rights. Groups may tend to focus rather more on the scarcity of resources than on the right to privacy and freedom from interference by the State when it comes to looking at an appropriate social work response. Participants should be encouraged to explore what limits there should be on the State's role in supporting children and families.

Exercise 4.2: Providing a Service

Task 1 can be undertaken as a kind of 'balloon debate'. A scenario could be imagined in which resources are particularly scarce and only one case will receive any services at all. Each case study is represented by one or more members of the group, who have to argue the merits of their case and persuade other group members that their case should be the one to receive services (in a balloon debate proper, the participants have to imagine that they are in a hot air balloon that is slowly descending as it loses air. In order to stay aloft, participants have to jettison, in turn, one member of the balloon's company until only one person remains.).

Task 3 can be undertaken as a 'dreams and nightmares' exercise. Half of the group is asked to imagine the worst possible way in which a particular service (from the list generated at Task 2) could be delivered. For example, day care could be provided in a vandalized building with untrained staff with convictions for child abuse, etc. The second half of the group has to imagine the perfect way in which such services could be delivered. Day care could be provided for free in a well-equipped building by caring staff who are all well qualified, etc. Then views are contrasted and a sense of what is practical and desirable established, as well as a possible action plan as to how the particular service could be developed.

Exercise 4.3: Partners?

This exercise works well as a role-play or as another 'dreams and night-mares' exercise. Participants should be encouraged to see the 'nightmare' response as capable of 'making sense', assuming a particular view of the role and tasks of social work. Participants should be prompted to see the internal logic of the response made in this case, which has a certain plausi-bility, and to recognize those characteristics in their own practice that would tend towards such an authoritarian, 'expert' response.

 WEB RESOURCES

http://www.scie.org.uk Social Care Institute for Excellence (SCIE) is an independent organization created in response to the government drive to improve quality in social care services. It provides free access to its own publications as well as to several very useful searchable databases.

In 1998, the Department of Health produced an on-line directory of training materials, courses and key texts to support the implementation of the *Framework for the Assessment of Children in Need*. It can be found at **http://www.doh.gov.uk /quality3.htm**.

There are a number of websites that exist to support parents in the tasks of parenting (see **http://www.parentcentre.gov.uk**, described in Unit 3). Three of the most helpful are:

http://www.gingerbread.org.uk Gingerbread enables lone parents to meet others who are bringing up children alone. Their website offers information on benefit/welfare and parenting problems.

http://www.nfpi.org.uk The National Family and Parenting Institute (NFPI) is an independent charity set up to enhance the value and quality of family life. NFPI works to support parents in bringing up their children, to promote the well-being of families and to make society more family friendly. The 'our parents' section provides access to a wide range of advice, from financial support and employment law to child health and living with teenagers.

http://www.parentlineplus.org.uk/ Parentline Plus is a UK-based charity set up to provide support for anyone who parents a child, including grandparents and foster parents. It also runs a helpline for parents.

UNIT 5

Looking After

OBJECTIVES

In this Unit you will:

- Learn about attachment and separation.
- Explore current issues in the care of children looked after by the local authority.
- Consider the provisions of the Children Act 1989 in relation to looked after children.
- Reflect on what is best practice in relation to looking after children.

 ## LOOKED AFTER CHILDREN

We noted in Study Text 4.2 that the provision of accommodation was included in the range of services made available to children in need by the Children Act 1989. We shall go on to learn (Unit 10) how a child may be received into the formal care of the local authority by virtue of an order made in court. Both groups of children, those provided with accommodation on a voluntary basis under Part III of the Act and those placed in the care of the local authority at the direction of the court, are described by the Act as 'looked after children' (s. 22(1)) and it is 'looking after' in this specific sense of the term that is the focus of this Unit.

Any episode of being looked after away from home begins with an experience of separation. This may be a painful process that makes enormous demands on the emotional and personal resources of everyone involved. Whilst this is no more than a statement of the obvious, it has, on occasions, been forgotten in practice, as the following extract from the Clyde report of the inquiry into child abuse on Orkney in the early 1990s makes clear:

> Mrs. B had got up as usual between 6.15 a.m. and 6.30 a.m. in order to wake WB[1] at about 6.50 a.m. in time to catch the school bus. On this morning she had gone out to the caravan[2], woken WB and gone back to the kitchen. Then she heard the noise of cars outside the house... The police approached and knocked on the front door. When Mrs. B appeared they then explained their presence. Mrs. B responded by shouting at them and the social workers were called over... WB had woken up before the police and social workers arrived. She emerged from the caravan in a dressing gown obviously distressed and stood in tears held by her mother in the confined space formed by the side of the caravan and the front wall of the house. Mrs. B grabbed her and hugged her, shouting observations to the social workers to the effect that they were evil, that they were not taking the children and why could they not let her prepare the children... The social workers attempted to calm her and encourage her to return to the house. While they were so engaged she led WB to the porch and WB slipped into the house, went upstairs and locked herself in the bathroom. Two police officers and a social worker followed her upstairs... (Clyde Report 1992, paras. 6.10/11)

While we make no comment on the causes of the social workers' concerns for the 'B' children or on the subsequent conduct of the case, the anguish and desolation of 'WB', made all the more awful by the detached manner in which her experience of separation is described, is almost unbearable. It is important that we begin any consideration of looked after children with an appreciation of the enormity of what separation, including much less

1   A girl, aged 13.

2   The caravan, where WB slept with her sister, was kept in front of the family home.

traumatic ones than that of WB and her mother, can mean to a child and its parents. The following study text provides a brief account of attachment theory as a prelude to an exercise that is intended to sensitize you to the emotional and broader psychological impact of separation.

Study Text 5.1: Attachment, Separation and the Looked After Child

ATTACHMENT

Attachment theory, 'a theory of personality development in the context of close relationships' (Howe 2001, p.194), derives from the work of John Bowlby (Bowlby 1970, 1973, 1980) and later commentators, in particular, Mary Ainsworth (Ainsworth and others 1978) and Vera Fahlberg. Fahlberg (1988) defines attachment as 'an affectionate bond between two individuals that endures through space and time and serves to join them emotionally' (p.13). She goes on to note that (p.13):

> A strong and healthy bond to a parent allows a child to develop both trust in others and self-reliance. The bond that a child develops to a person who cares for him or her in their early years is the foundation of their future psychological, physical and cognitive development and for their future relationships with others.

In other words, attachments form the basis of our later psychological integrity and our capacity to engage in rewarding and reciprocal social and emotional relationships. As Howe explains (2001, p.200):

> It is within close relationships that young children learn about the self and others, feelings and behaviour, emotions and social interaction. Interacting with other people helps children to understand themselves. And by understanding themselves they can begin to make sense of other people and social relationships.

Bonding is the process by which attachments are made. It starts before birth when a parent forms mental images of the new infant and begins to develop expectations and hopes for its future. From the moment of birth onwards, bonding proceeds as a consequence of a mutually reinforcing cycle of events that is part of many routine parent/child interactions. These interactions involve touch, sound and visual stimuli appropriate to the child's stage of physical and cognitive development. A typical successful interaction might occur, for example, when an infant is hungry or uncomfortable. S/he shows this by moving or crying. While in this state, the infant is unable to perceive anything else of the world. The carer notices and accurately meets the need or satisfies the child. The child feels better, is quietened and content. The parent is gratified by the response. The infant is able to perceive the world around him- or herself again and subsequently becomes aware of further needs and so the cycle continues, as in Figure 5.1. It is not only the child who might initiate these positive interactions, so too might the carer(s). For example, in the case of an infant, the carer might 'coo' or talk to the child, which may elicit a smile, which encourages the carer to 'talk' more, and so on.

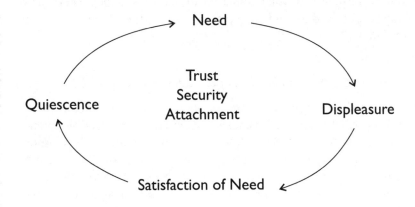

Figure 5.1 Arousal–relaxation cycle

There are many reasons why the bonding cycle may not be initiated or might be disrupted. It may be that the carer is not attached to the child for reasons relating to the nature of the pregnancy or the circumstances in which the child was conceived. Alternatively, it may be that the baby may have been born prematurely or with a medical condition that prevents the parent from entering into the child's routine care on a regular or sufficient basis for the virtuous circle described in Figure 5.1 to develop.

Secure attachment (Type B)

Securely attached children are less likely to cry or show signs of anxiety in the company of their primary carer, although they may cling to them in the presence of a stranger. If separated (for a short period) from their carer, such children will show distress and will respond positively upon their return. Carers' behaviour towards the child will usually be observed as positive and encouraging. Securely attached children develop positive feelings about themselves and experience their caregiver as available.

Anxious avoidant insecure attachment (Type A)

Children who experience their carers as consistently rejecting of them come to regard themselves as of little worth. Such children will show very little distress at the absence of their carers and may completely ignore them upon their return. They may show little difference in their general responses to their primary carer and a stranger. Their carers may be observed as cold, angry or 'distant' in their interactions with the child.

Anxious resistant or ambivalent insecure attachment (Type C)

Where a child's significant carer responds to the child inconsistently and unpredictably, the child comes to regard him- or herself as dependent and poorly valued. Such children tend to cry more, are less responsive to or even rejecting of physical contact. These children will be anxious ahead of any separation from their carer, very distressed during such an absence and ambivalent about renewing contact upon their return.

Disorganized disorientated insecure attachment (Type D)

Such patterns of attachment are often found in association with children who have suffered significant harm. They will have experienced their carers as frightening or threatening and themselves as helpless and of little worth. Such children may show a wide range of contradictory patterns of behaviour in their interactions with their carers.

Figure 5.2 Patterns of attachment

Mary Ainsworth and others (1978) and later commentators developed a typology (see Figure 5.2) of different styles or patterns of attachment that varied according to:

- the sensitivity of the carer to the needs of the baby
- the degree of acceptance (or rejection) on the part of the carer of the demands made on him or her by the baby
- the degree of 'co-operativeness' that develops between the carer and the child
- the degree to which a carer is available to (or ignores) the needs of the baby.

It should be noted that the personality of the child too might influence the development of attachments (see, for example, Buss and Plomin 1984). An understanding of the various forms of infant attachment styles may be helpful in making an assessment of parenting capacity when working with a child in need. It should be recognized also that patterns of attachment formed in early life are likely substantially to affect patterns of social and intimate relationships throughout the life course. It may be important to recognize, therefore, that a carer's current style of care-giving may echo strongly their experience as infants. This may be a particular consideration if you are trying to engage family members in providing additional support where parenting capacity is an issue.

Fahlberg (1985) notes the several deleterious effects of lack of normal attachment. These include:

- poor development of conscience
- poor impulse control and lack of foresight
- low self-esteem
- poor interpersonal skills and relationships
- lack of emotional awareness and sensitivity
- reduced cognitive ability
- some general developmental problems such as poor verbal skills and difficulty in aural comprehension.

One should note, however, that attachment theory has been criticized (see Gambe and others 1992, p.29ff) for its euro-centricity in that the theory moves from a 'universal concept of attachment to a context bound view' that emphasizes the importance of a primary caretaker and the child's developing sense of autonomy. This does not take into account different cultural patterns of child rearing which may involve multiple caretaking and a more positive evaluation of interdependency over individualized autonomy. Practitioners will need to be wary of drawing negative inferences from differing patterns of attachment within a particular family or cultural context.

SEPARATION

The separation of a child and its carer can occur for many reasons and it is important to understand normal as well as less adaptive reactions to separation (see Figure 5.2). Separation behaviour will vary, depending on the nature of the child's attachment to the primary carers; the nature of the primary carers' bonding to the child; the child's past experiences of separation; the child's perceptions of the reasons for the separation (especially whether the child views him- or herself as responsible for the separation); the circumstances of the move itself; the environment to which the child is moved and the environment from which the child was moved. Reactions will also vary according to the 'age and stage' of the child.

Each of these factors is, to varying degrees, susceptible to sensitive social work intervention, whatever the age or circumstances of the child. For example, providing space and time for the 'parting message' from a child's caregiver to be fully articulated and understood by the child; enabling the child to develop a 'coherent' sense of his or her own history and enabling some continuity of relationships with those from whom a child is separated (see Fahlberg 1994) will always be important considerations. We will return to the question of maintaining links with parents below.

SEPARATION AND THE LOOKED AFTER CHILD

It will often be the case that looked after children will have had less opportunity in the past to form strong attachments, particularly if their childhood is characterized by family breakdown or successive moves within the care system. However, given that the function of attachment behaviour is ultimately self-protective, both physically and psychologically, it may be the case that the prospect of enforced separation may come to represent sufficient threat to force a child into reliance on what limited attachments

they already have. Hence a child may well cling to an abusive parent and
exhibit hostility to the worker, who, in such circumstances, may represent
the greater threat as far as the child is concerned. Where normal prior
attachments do exist, workers must be careful not to misinterpret reactions
to separation. It is not uncommon for children to react aggressively during
separation and apparently to lose interest in their former carers or the
prospect of a return home as part of the normal self-protective response.

Goldman (1994) has identified four psychological tasks with which a
child or young person may be faced when adjusting to loss or separation:

- *understanding*: this involves regaining cognitive control of the
  crisis that a separation or more permanent loss can bring about

- *grieving*: this is a complex and often lengthy process (see Jewett
  1984) that does not apply only in the case of bereavement and
  which may involve a child moving through a number of phases
  in which s/he will demonstrate feelings that others will find
  very uncomfortable and distressing. These might include anger,
  denial and disbelief, depression and despair before the child is
  able to 'integrate' the experience of the loss

- *commemorating*: finding ways to remember the person from
  whom they are separated

- *going on*: looking to and investing emotionally in the future.

In your involvement with a child or young person experiencing a temporary separation or the more permanent loss of a significant carer, you will
need to recognize and respect the child's progress through the always difficult process of managing these tasks. The importance of the separation
experience to the subsequent process and outcomes of intervention cannot
be under-estimated. In a review of the research literature on admissions to
residential care, Bullock, Little and Milham (1993, p.16) concluded that
the 'secondary problems' associated with 'separation and strained relationships':

> can so preoccupy the child and his or her carers that the primary
> problems necessitating the child's removal from home are neglected
> … Indeed, the problems separated children experience as they try to
> preserve the continuity of their personal and family relationships may
> overwhelm any benefit that might reasonably be expected to accrue.

Exercise 5.1: Separation

Re-read the account of the removal of the 'B' children from their parents quoted in the introductory course text for this Unit.

1.　Using your imagination and your own personal experience of separation, write a 250-word account of the experience from WB's point of view (we would stress that you are not being asked to try to recreate what happened during the actual removal of the 'B' children or to imagine what *she* might have felt. You are being asked to imagine how *you* might have responded in similar circumstances). In particular, think about and describe:

- how you might have felt at the moment you awoke

- what you might have thought was happening

- what you might have wanted to do as soon as you were awake

- to whom you might have wanted to talk

- with whom you might have wanted to be

- what you might have felt as you heard the sound of other people's distress

- where you might think you were being taken

- what you might think would happen to you next

- when you might think you would see your bedroom or house again

- when you might think you would see your family again.

2.　Make a list of all of the steps that could have been taken that might have eased the experience that you have just described.

Points to Consider

1. In circumstances such as those described in Exercise 5.1, in what ways might the experience of separation be different for the parent of a child and for the child itself?

2. How might the experience for parent and child be different if the separation is at the request of one of them rather than at the insistence of someone else?

3. What might be the long-term effect of a traumatic separation on the child's and/or the parent's relationship with the worker(s) or agency implicated in the separation?

4. What might be the emotional cost to the workers involved in the separation of a child and its parent(s)?

5. What strategies, both productive and unproductive, might workers, parents and children adopt to protect themselves from the confusion and pain of a traumatic separation?

6. Is it possible to take all of the pain and confusion out of any enforced separation?

PARENTING AND THE LOOKED AFTER CHILD

Once the vitally important and often very difficult decision has been taken to separate a child from its carers, either by agreement or by order of a court, a significant proportion of the tasks and duties associated with parenting that child will fall to the local authority. We have seen already (Unit 3) how complex and demanding the task of parenting can be, even within the relatively narrow confines of the family. Parenting becomes even more challenging when it falls to the elected members, managers, social workers, teachers, health professionals and all the other individuals and departments that make up a local authority. Parenting of this sort is sometimes referred to as 'corporate parenting'. The local authority is directed in its task of corporate parenting by the Children Act 1989 and by formal Regulations and less formal Guidance issued by central and national government departments.[3] The following study text sets out the statutory framework that guides the local authority in its task of looking after those children for whom it has assumed some responsibility for parenting.

STUDY TEXT 5.2: THE CHILDREN ACT 1989 AND THE LOOKED AFTER CHILD

DEFINITIONS

Children are 'looked after' when they are either 'in care' by virtue of a formal order made by a court or 'being provided with accommodation' through a voluntary arrangement under the Act (s. 22 (1)).

---

3   No Act of Parliament can ever be expected to cover every conceivable situation in which its provisions might apply. Quite often, much of the detail of how an Act is to be implemented is contained in the Regulations which follow it. These Regulations are usually anticipated by a section of the Act itself. The Regulations carry the force of law and accordingly need to pass through a parliamentary process. Regulations, therefore, are sometimes referred to as Statutory Instruments (SI) as it is in this form that they are scrutinized by Parliament. (See 'Web resources' in Unit 1 for details of how to access SIs on-line.) Regulations are to be distinguished from Guidance. Guidance on how a particular Act is to be understood and implemented is often issued by the government department in which the Act originated or by a number of government departments that are to be involved in its implementation. Guidance does not carry the force of law but it should be regarded as authoritative and may well be referred to in court proceedings or in other forms of review.

GENERAL DUTIES

The local authority has a duty to all the children that it looks after. This is set out at s. 22 (3):

(a)   to safeguard and promote his welfare; and

(b)   to make such use of services available for children cared for by their own parents as appears to the authority reasonable in his case.

In addition, the local authority is under a general duty towards all the children that it looks after, or is proposing to look after, to consult widely before making any decisions concerning that child. The local authority must, so far as is reasonably practicable, ascertain the wishes and feelings of:

(i)   the child

(ii)   the parents

(iii)   any person who has parental responsibility for the child

(iv)   any other person whose wishes and feelings the authority considers to be relevant (s. 22 (4)).

It must give due consideration to these wishes and feelings (s. 22 (5) (b)). It must also give due consideration 'to the child's religious persuasion, racial origin and cultural and linguistic background' (s. 22 (5) (c)). However, these duties may be overridden when it is necessary to protect members of the public from serious injury (s. 22 (6)).

SPECIFIC DUTIES

1.   It is the duty of the local authority looking after a child to provide accommodation and maintain that child (s. 23 (1)).

2.   The local authority must make arrangements enabling the child to live with a parent or other person connected with the child 'unless that would not be reasonably practicable or consistent with his welfare' (s. 23 (6)).

3.   The local authority must, so far as is reasonably practicable and consistent with the child's welfare, secure that the accommodation is near the child's home and that where siblings

are being accommodated, they are accommodated together (s. 23 (7)).

4. The local authority must appoint an independent visitor for the child where communication between the child and parents has been infrequent or where the child has not been visited for 12 months, if it would be in the child's best interest (Sch. 2, para. 17 (1)).

5. The local authority providing accommodation for a disabled child must secure so far as is reasonably practicable that the accommodation is not unsuitable to the child's particular needs (s. 23 (8)).

6. The local authority is required, unless it is not reasonably practicable or consistent with the child's welfare, to endeavour to promote contact between the child and his/her parents, relatives, friends, and others connected with the child (Sch. 2, para. 15 (1)).

7. The local authority must allow the child in care reasonable contact with his/her parents, guardian and any other person with whom the child was living under a residence order, or an order under the inherent jurisdiction of the High Court, immediately before the care order was made (s. 34 (1)).

8. The local authority is required by regulations to conduct regular reviews of the circumstances of and plans for children it is looking after (s. 26).

9. The local authority must establish a procedure for considering representations (including complaints) made to it both by children it is looking after and other children in need, their parents, local authority foster parents and other persons whom the local authority considers have a sufficient interest in the children's welfare (s. 26 (3)). There must be an independent person involved in the procedure (s. 26 (4)). Under Article 6 of the European Convention on Human Rights, an individual is entitled to a fair hearing within a reasonable time by an independent and impartial tribunal established by law in the determination of his/her civil rights and obligations. The Court of Appeal has ruled that the presence of one independent person on a social services complaints panel is sufficient to meet the requirement of 'independence' when coupled with judicial review as a further appeal route (R v (Beeson) v Dorset County Council CA

18 December 2002). A new s. 26A has been inserted into the Children Act 1989 concerning advocacy services. Every authority must make arrangements to provide assistance, including representation, to people who wish to make representations under the complaints procedure established by the Act. Authorities are required to publicize these arrangements (Adoption and Children Act 2002).

Unit 8 (Figure 8.1) will go on to describe the specific arrangements in place for children leaving care introduced by the Children (Leaving Care) Act 2000.

INCLUSIVE PARENTING

The government has set out its expectations of the local authority as corporate parent (see Figure 5.3). It should be clear that the corporate parent is expected to do all that a 'good parent' should but it must do so drawing on a range of agencies and services and, most important, it must exercise its parenting functions alongside those of the child's parents and carers. We have already described how the Children Act 1989 defines and allocates parental responsibility (Study Text 3.3) and explored some of the challenges of working in partnership with parents (Study Text 4.3) in the context of working with children in need. Both the government's expectations of the corporate parent (Figure 5.3) and Study Text 5.2 (above) make it clear that working with parents is central to the task of looking after children living away from home, who are, after all, included in the category of children in need.

The government expects social services and education authorities to:

- provide care, a home and access to health and education and other public services to which all children are entitled according to their needs

- provide a mixture of care and firmness to support the child's development, and to be the tolerant, dependable and available partner in the adult/child relationship even in the face of disagreements

- protect and educate the child against the perils and risks of life by encouraging constructive and appropriate friendships, and discouraging destructive and harmful relationships

- celebrate and share their children's achievements, supporting them when they are down

- recognize and respect their children's growth to independence, being tolerant and supportive if they make mistakes

- provide consistent support and be available to provide advice and practical help when needed

- advocate their children's cause and troubleshoot on their behalf when necessary

- be ambitious for their children and encourage and support their efforts to get on and reach their potential, whether through education, training or employment

- provide occasional financial support, remember birthdays and Christmas or annual celebrations within the individual child's religion and culture

- encourage and enable appropriate contact with family members – parents, grandparents, aunts, uncles and brothers and sisters

- help their children to feel part of the local community through contact with neighbours and local groups

- be proactive, not passive, when there are known or suspected serious difficulties.

Figure 5.3 The corporate parent
Source: Extract from a letter to local authority councillors from the Secretary of State for Health, September 1998. Reproduced from Department for Education and Employment (2000b), p.88 (Crown copyright).

We know relatively little of how children themselves make sense of the relationships that they maintain with their parents and any substitute carers with whom they might be placed. One study (Heptinstall, Bhopal and Brannen 2001, p.14) reported that 'no matter how inadequate or unavailable their parents may be, they still form an important part of children's own representations of family life'. Siblings too were important to fostered children in that they 'represented continuity in the face of considerable disruption and change'. This study concluded (p.15):

> Children may have unrealistic and idealised views of their families, but these images remain important... Children in general do not necessarily talk about their family relationships nor their feelings of family change, much less explain them. As well as taking account of the context and manner in which children reveal information, it is important to pay attention to what is *not* said and to consider the meaning of these silences.

Another study (Aldgate and Bradley 1999), looking at children's experiences of *short-term* placements with carers, lists amongst its conclusions (p.201ff) that:

- The majority of children had some difficulties settling with the carers. Most were homesick and in some cases, this did not diminish with familiarity.

- How children managed their homesickness was an important finding. Many chose to cope with their feelings in solitude rather than talk to parents or carers.

- In spite of some similarities in lifestyle between carers and families, children found some differences. Most diminished with time and none of the differences was unsettling enough to affect the arrangements drastically.

- The majority of children liked their carers and increasingly enjoyed the time they spent there.

There is ample research evidence (see Department of Health 1991d) to suggest that longer-term dissolution or disruption of family links is enormously disadvantageous to the looked after child. The preservation of family links, including sibling links, is vital to ensure 'continuity, roots and identity' (Department of Health 1991d, p.22), given the instability of much of the care system and in order to avoid lengthy and unnecessary extensions to the period for which a child remains in care. However, translating strategic intent into practical reality is rarely straightforward. This is especially so when the policies (if not the politics) are personal, which is the case in the context of foster care. The following exercise is intended to sensitize you to some of the difficulties of deciding which aspects of parenting are to be taken on by whom and how relationships between all parties need to be actively considered and maintained when a child is placed in a substitute family care setting.

Exercise 5.2: Rebecca's Story

Re-read that part of Unit 3 dealing with 'good enough parenting' and the following account of Rebecca's placement with foster carers and answer the questions that follow.

> The Griffith family is registered as a short-term foster carer for babies and very young children. The Griffiths have two children of their own: Bethan aged ten and Michael aged six. One day a social worker telephones and asks if the family could possibly stretch to taking a seven-year-old girl, Rebecca, who has been removed from home. Her 13-year-old sister has made allegations against her father of serious sexual abuse. The Griffiths agree to accept Rebecca on a temporary basis. They know that it means making up a bed in Bethan's small bedroom but the family are confident that she will not object.

> Rebecca arrives. She lived in one of the large council estates in town where there were riots a year or two ago. Rebecca is dirty, ill clad, and has nits. She is carrying a small bag of unwashed clothes. She is brought in by her mother and the social worker. Mum looks unwell and harassed. She does not speak during her short stay at the house. Rebecca seems unperturbed by her departure. Rebecca's mother is moving into a hostel later that day on the far side of town. There is no obvious means of contacting her there and no arrangements are made for Rebecca's mother to visit her at the Griffiths'.

During the next few days and weeks, the Griffiths find clothes for Rebecca that Bethan has grown out of. It becomes difficult to recognize this smart, clean and smiling Rebecca as the child who first arrived on the Griffiths' doorstep. She settles well into a new school and is beginning to form a strong relationship with Bethan. There has been no contact between Rebecca and her mother.

One major concern, however, is her father, who keeps ringing up. He appears to talk to Rebecca as if she is an adult. He cries and says that he is missing her. Rebecca is very distressed after these calls. The social worker is trying to arrange supervised contact with the father, who can be very violent. In the event, contact takes place in the residential unit where Rebecca's sister lives. (Up until now, Rebecca has been prevented from having any contact with her sister as a police investigation has begun into the allegations of abuse made against their father.) The first contact session does not go well and the father accuses everyone, the Griffiths included, of stealing his daughter from him. Rebecca refuses to attend any more contact sessions. Her father is still ringing daily. Rebecca asks to see her mother.

Rebecca continues to live with the Griffiths as care proceedings are begun. A social worker is visiting to talk to Rebecca about the sexual abuse. The Griffiths tell him that Rebecca is telling Bethan and Michael what happened to her and Bethan has already asked whether her daddy would ever do such a thing. The Griffiths are not involved in the counselling sessions with the social worker although they comfort Rebecca when she has dreams afterwards. The final hearing is due shortly and a case conference is to be held within a few days.

TASKS

1. How are the various roles and tasks of parenting Rebecca being allocated between the Griffiths, the local authority and Rebecca's parents? How should they be allocated?

2. Describe what you think the appropriate relationship should be between:

   (a) Rebecca and each member of the Griffith family

    (b)   each member of the Griffith family and members of Rebecca's birth family

    (c)   the social worker and Rebecca, her birth family and the Griffiths.

3.   What are the advantages/disadvantages of maintaining Rebecca's family links in this situation?

Points to Consider

1.   Has Rebecca been placed *in* or *with* the Griffith family?

2.   How might the Griffiths' parenting of their birth children be affected by Rebecca's arrival?

3.   How much of a voice in decision-making would/should a foster carer have in situations like this?

4.   What are the differences in the kind of parenting provided by a foster carer and the kind of parenting usually provided by a child's birth family?

5.   What responsibility does the social worker have for the effects of this placement on each member of the Griffith family?

6.   What motivates people to become foster carers? Would you consider becoming one? Why/not?

SPECIAL PESSIMISM

While it is the case that fostering has become the dominant form of substitute care, we wish now to turn to a consideration of residential care as we complete our exploration of the current professional, policy and practice issues that bear on the care of children looked after away from home. We wish to place the emphasis on residential care at this point for a number of reasons. First, popular and professional interest in residential care has been more intense during recent years than for many years previously. This is substantially because of the evidence of abuse that has emerged in the various reports of child care 'scandals' during this period (see Butler and Drakeford 2003). In reviewing several of these, the National Commission of Inquiry into the Prevention of Child Abuse (1996) concluded that (p.19):

> The catalogue of abuse in residential institutions is appalling. It includes physical assault and sexual abuse, emotional abuse; unaccept- able deprivation of rights and privileges; inhumane treatment; poor health care and education.

One needs to be cautious in extrapolating from the reports of 'scandals' and public inquiries, which constitute a very particular filter through which residential care is viewed. Such reports, even in aggregate, serve 'to reinforce the idea that the problems of institutional care are sporadic, acute and somehow peculiar to the institutional world' (Butler 2001, p.179). Nonetheless, one would also need to acknowledge that such reports have provided much of the motive force for recent policy and practice develop- ments in residential care, some of which we discuss below (Study Text 5.3).

Second, the fact is that much more research has been undertaken into residential care than into most other forms of care provided for looked after children and our knowledge base is accordingly a little more sound in this area than in others. This is not to say that the available research is par- ticularly current or that it is comprehensive. There are some notable gaps, particularly in relation to the effects of the Children Act 1989 on practice and outcomes (see Department of Health 1998a; Aldgate and Statham 2001).

The third reason is a more personal one. It is our experience that field social workers and other professionals tend to undervalue, or even discount, residential care as a learning resource while in training and, more important, they tend to disregard residential care as a viable resource in practice. Few become engaged in the continuing debate about the role, function and future of residential care. This is a wide-ranging and impor- tant debate encompassing attitudes and values as well as substantial changes in the population of looked after children and in the range and type of provision available. In our practice, we see little to persuade us that the conclusion reached by the Department of Health and Social Security in 1985 (p.46) does not apply still:

> Virtually all social workers appear to view admission to care very negatively. They see it as a last resort and as a sign of failure to prevent the break up of families. They are also worried about what the care experience will do to children and parents. Residential care is looked on with special pessimism.

Study Text 5.3: The Policy Framework for Looked After Children

By the early 1990s, the policy and practice response to the very long drawn-out and seemingly perpetual crisis in residential care had been, according to one important review (Utting 1991), 'formidable in volume and complexity'. Far from being a 'tool for practitioners', official guidance and regulations may have become more 'a subject for their research' (Berridge and Brodie 1998, p.172). Indeed Utting, in his later review of 'the safeguards for children living away from home' (Utting, Department of Health, Welsh Office 1997), with perhaps unintentional irony, noted that (p.17; our emphasis):

> Regulations and guidance and other forms of advice provide a full and detailed *web* of safeguards.

The process of unifying and, to a degree, simplifying, the policy framework to deliver better quality services for children living away from home began with the publication in November 1998 of the Government White Paper *Modernising Social Services* (Department of Health 1998b). Drawing on the findings of a series of critical Joint Reviews,[4] the White Paper

---

4   Joint Reviews of social services departments are carried out by the Social Services Inspectorate and the Audit Commission, combining a regard for professional standards and value for money.

spelled out the Government's commitment to the 'third way for social care' which would move the focus 'away from who provides the care, and [place] it firmly on the quality of services experienced by, and outcomes achieved for, individuals and their carers and families' (Department of Health 1998b, para. 1.7).

This White Paper was followed by the publication in 1999 of *The Government's Objectives for Children's Social Services*. These objectives, taken with other policy initiatives directed at achieving 'best value', now form part of the *Personal Social Services Performance Assessment Framework* (Department of Health 2003a). In essence, this consists of a series of standards and performance indicators against which the performance and (ultimately) the funding of local authority social services are measured and judged (see Humphrey 2002, 2003). The priorities for local authorities are periodically reviewed and Figure 5.4 sets out selected objectives for children's services relating particularly to children looked after, as they stood in March 2003. More recent revisions to the objectives and indicators can be found via the Department of Health website referred to at the end of this Unit.

You might care to note that the national targets associated with C1.1, C4.1 and C5.1 were as follows:

- The national target associated with C1.1 was that every council should have less than 16 per cent of looked after children having three or more placements by 2001.

- The national target associated with C4.1 was that 50 per cent of children leaving care should have one or more GCSEs/GNVQs by 2001 and 75 per cent by 2003.

- The national target associated with C5.1 was that the level of employment, training or education amongst young people aged 19 in 2001/02 who were looked after in their 17th year is at least 60 per cent of the level amongst all young people of the same age in their area.

You may wish to find out how far your local authority managed to achieve these or more recent targets.

In addition to the setting of objectives, indicators and targets for social services, the New Labour Government introduced new inspection arrangements via The Care Standards Act 2000 (CSA) and associated Regulations. The CSA established the National Care Standards Commission

C1.0   To ensure that children are securely attached to carers
       capable of providing safe and effective care for the duration
       of childhood.

   C1.1   *To reduce the number of changes of placement for children
           looked after.*

   C1.3   *To maximise the contribution adoption can make to
           providing permanent families for children in appropriate
           places.*

   C1.4   *To minimise the period children remain looked after before
           they are adopted.*

   C1.5   *To minimise the period children remain looked after before
           they are placed in long-term foster care.*

C4.0   To ensure that children looked after gain maximum life
       chance benefits from educational opportunities, health care
       and social care.

   C4.1   *To bring the overall performance of children looked after,
           for a year or more, in National Curriculum tests closer into
           line with local children generally.*

   C4.2   *To ensure that children looked after enjoy a standard of
           health and development as good as children of the same age
           living in the same area.*

   C4.3   *To reduce the offending rate of children looked after.*

   C4.4   *To ensure that children looked after from black and ethnic
           minority groups gain maximum life chance benefits from
           educational opportunities, health care and social care.*

C5.0   To ensure that young people leaving care, as they enter
       adulthood, are not isolated and participate socially and
       economically as citizens.

   C5.1   *For young people who were looked after at the age of 16 to
           maximise the number engaged in education, training, or
           employment at the age of 19.*

   C5.2   *To maximise the number of young people leaving care after
           their sixteenth birthday who are still in touch with Social
           Services, or a known and approved contact, on their 19th
           birthday.*

> C5.3 *To maximise the number of young people leaving care on or after their 16th birthday who have suitable accommodation at the age of 19.*
>
> C8.0 To actively involve users and carers in planning services and in tailoring individual packages of care; and to ensure effective mechanisms are in place to handle complaints.
>
> C9.0 To ensure through regulatory powers and duties that children in regulated services are protected from harm and poor care standards.
>
> C10.0 To ensure that social care workers are appropriately skilled, trained and qualified, and to promote the uptake of training at all levels.
>
> C11.0 To maximise the benefit to service users from the resources available, and to demonstrate the effectiveness and value for money of the care and support provided, and to allow for choice and different responses for different needs and circumstances.

Figure 5.4 Objectives for children's services (selected)
Source: Taken from Department of Health (2003a), p.1ff (Crown copyright).

(NCSC), an independent, non-departmental public body to take over the inspection and regulation of social (and some health) care services that were previously regulated by local authorities. Amongst the categories of services regulated by the NCSC are children's homes. In addition to monitoring the application of the appropriate Regulations (for our purposes, the Children's Homes Regulations (SI 2001 3967)), the NCSC applies national minimum standards (NMS) in deciding whether a particular service or establishment is to be entered on its register, a condition of being able to provide a service and in subsequent, periodic inspections. The NMS and the Regulations to which they refer apply to services provided by the local authority and those provided in the private, independent and voluntary sectors. Figure 5.5 sets out the main headings under which standards are set and, for the purposes of illustration, reproduces Standards 12 and 14.

Planning for Care (Standards 1–7)

- statement of the home's purpose
- placement plans
- reviews
- contact
- moving in and leaving the home
- preparation for leaving care
- support to individual children.

Quality of Care (Standards 8–15)

- consultation
- privacy and confidentiality
- provision and preparation of meals
- personal appearance, clothing, requisites and pocket money
- good health and well-being:

    Standard 12: The physical, emotional and health needs of each child are identified and appropriate action is taken to secure the medical, dental and other health services needed to meet them. Children are provided with guidance, advice and support on health and personal care issues appropriate to the needs and wishes of each child.

- treatment and administration of medicines within the home
- education:

    Standard 14: There is an educational policy that shows how the home intends to promote and support the educational attainment of children throughout the time they live there. This includes supporting the child by facilitating their prompt arrival at school with the necessary school equipment.

- leisure and activities.

Complaints and Protection (Standards 16–20)

- complaints and representation
- child protection procedures and training

- countering bullying
- absence of child without authority
- notification of significant events.

Care and Control (Standards 21–22)

- relationship with children
- behaviour management.

Environment (Standards 23–26)

- location, design and size of the home
- accommodation
- bathroom and washing facilities
- health safety and security.

Staffing (Standards 27–31)

- vetting of staff and visitors
- staff support
- adequacy of staffing.

Management and Administration (Standards 32–35)

- monitoring by the person carrying on the home
- monitoring of the operation of the home
- business management
- children's individual case files.

Specific Settings (Standard 36)

- secure accommodation and refuges.

Figure 5.5 National minimum standards for children's homes
Source: Extracted from Department of Health (2002a) (Crown copyright).

There are other NMS set for adoption services, residential family centres, fostering services, boarding schools and residential special schools. These can all be found at the NCSC website given at the end of this Unit. The *NMS for Children's Homes* does address many of the sources of concern that child abuse inquiries, government reports and academic research have identified over the last twenty years although, given that the Standards only came into effect on 1 April 2002, it is not possible to say at this point what impact they will have on the experience of being looked after.

Modernising Social Services (Department of Health 1998b) also contained a commitment to fund the reforms in welfare services that it sought. As far as children's services were concerned, one of the main vehicles for driving change was to be the 'Quality Protects' programme (known as 'Children First' in Wales). Originally conceived of as a three-year initiative and launched in September 1998, it has since been extended. 'Quality Protects' provides access to (substantial) targeted funding via the achievement of a management action plan (MAP) that should form part of the local authority's Children's Services Plan and which is subject to scrutiny by the SSI. The MAPs are focused on the *Government's Objectives* (Department of Health 1999) and also form part of the *Performance Assessment Framework* (Department of Health 2003a).

The Department of Health's review of those MAPs submitted after the first three-year phase of 'Quality Protects' (Department of Health 2001b) reveals a very mixed record of progress in achieving the objectives. In relation to Objective C4.0 (see Figure 5.4), 'education indicators are moving in the right direction, but slowly, and more slowly than predicted … The evidence on health, once again, shows slow progress (Department of Health 2001b, p.8 paras. 25 and 26). On the other hand, in relation to Objective C5.0: 'all show significant movement in the right direction' (Department of Health 2001b, p.9 para. 30). We will return to a consideration of the education and health of looked after children below.

To reinforce the programme's commitment to improving outcomes for children looked after, 'Quality Protects' has also seen the establishment of project teams to take forward ideas on forms of 'best practice'. Project teams have been set up to look at such issues as the involvement of councillors in improving services; children's participation, assessment and recording; child protection; leaving care; disabled children; placement choice; Black and ethnic minority children and reducing offending. Details of the work of all of these project teams can be found via the website given at the end of this unit.

Finally in this study text, we wish to turn to a brief exploration of specific policy initiatives in relation to the education and health of looked after children. This will not only help to illustrate some of the progress that has been made either directly or indirectly through 'Quality Protects' and the other regulatory and inspectorial mechanisms now in place, but it will also demonstrate that some of the reasons for the diminished life chances available to those in the public care over recent years are to be found in the attitudes and practices of social workers just like you and me, as much as they are to be found in the 'failure of the care system' or in exceptional instances of bad practice.

THE EDUCATION OF LOOKED AFTER CHILDREN

In his review of the research on the education of looked after children, Goddard (2000, p.79) notes that there is strong evidence to suggest that 'one of the major handicaps which [looked after children] face is a relatively low level of educational achievement'. Some of this can be explained by relatively high rates of school exclusion amongst looked after children and by frequent moves within the care system, disrupting children's experience of school. Behind such factors as these, though, lies the contrast between the priority attached to the education of looked after children by those professionals working with them and the priority given to their children's education by most parents. Many parents would regard the school catchment area as a decisive consideration in deciding where to live, for example. In contrast, research (Stein 1994) suggests that most social workers have very little idea of the educational needs or achievements for those children for whom they are responsible. There is strong evidence that residential care staff have demonstrated even less concern for the education of looked after children (Jackson 1989; Berridge and others 1996; Berridge and Brodie 1998). Work by Firth and Horrocks (1996, pp.87–8) sums up the differences between the expectations we might have for our own children and those we might have for those for whom we have a professional responsibility:

Natural parents talk about further, higher education and career development and the family support necessary for this while care system
professionals talk about jobs, claiming benefit and independent
living.

In May 2000, the DfES[5] published its Guidance on the *Education of Young
People in Care* (Department for Education and Employment 2000b). It
contains a useful summary of the research evidence of looked after children's 'unacceptable levels of underachievement' (p.1. para. 1.4) and elab-
orates on some of the reasons which lie behind them. The Guidance notes,
in plain terms (p.16):

> *Quality Protects* demands that local authorities have higher expecta-
> tions in their role as corporate parents. This must translate into consis-
> tently high expectations on the part of all those with day-to-day
> contact with young people in public care. These high expectations
> need to translate into action: ensuring regular attendance, securing a
> school place without delay, homework and study support, and behav-
> iour support where appropriate. It is about the mutual high expecta-
> tions of all parties involved in corporate parenting, so that the shared
> objective of raising the attainments of children is achieved.

The Guidance urges local authorities to provide all children with a
Personal Education Plan within 20 days of becoming looked after or of
changing school (p.28ff); it recommends the appointment of Designated
Teachers in schools to act as advocates and as points of reference for looked
after children (p.31ff); it sets timescales for managing admissions, exclusions and transitions (p.56ff) and it directs local authorities to establish
protocols for sharing information and improving communication (p.23ff).

The evidence we have cited already in relation to Objective C4.0
(Figure 5.4) would suggest that the Guidance is not being as urgently
applied as its authors might have wished. This is certainly the view of the
Children Act Report (Department of Health 2001a). On the basis of the data

5   The Department for Education and Skills (DfES) was formerly known
     as the Department for Education and Employment. Hence, some
     publications are attributed to the DfEE and some to the DfES
     although, essentially, they originate from the same source.

available via local authorities' statistical returns to the Department of Health, the report notes (p.54) that in 1999–2000 only 30 per cent of young people left care with any GCSE or GNVQ qualification. It should be noted that the data is not as 'robust' as one might have wished, partly because in some areas 'the right links between social services, schools and education departments were not in place' (p.55). The report makes clear that: 'This is a deficiency which councils must take urgent action to rectify…'. You may wish to find out how far progress has been made in implementing the Guidance where you work.

THE HEALTH OF LOOKED AFTER CHILDREN

One can trace problems with the health of children who enter care, many with a background of deprivation, to the very origins of public provision for children and the endemic eye diseases of children living in the metropolitan workhouses in the early nineteenth century (Pinchbeck and Hewitt 1973). A study by Brandon and others (1999) reported that looked after children, in common with their peers living with their families, express serious concerns about their state of health in the present day too.

Despite the relative paucity of statistically sound data on the health of looked after children, the Department of Health, in its Guidance on *Promoting the Health of Looked After Children* (Department of Health 2002b), felt able to declare (p.6):

> A series of Government reports have highlighted the health neglect, unhealthy life-style and the mental health needs that characterise children and young people living in care. Looked after children are the epitome of the inverse care law – their health may not only be jeopardised by abusive and neglectful parenting but care itself may fail to repair and protect health. Indeed, it may even exacerbate damage and abuse.

The Short Report (1984) had expressed similar doubts some twenty years previously. We have suggested elsewhere (Butler and Payne 1997) that the requirements of the Children Act 1989 to provide for medical assessments of looked after children have been more honoured in the breach than in the observance. In our research, we found that only a quarter of the medical assessments for children looked after were actually carried out and that the content of these was seriously deficient in many cases. Part of the explanation for this was felt to be the low priority given to 'looked after medicals' over many years, not only by the Social Services Department but also by the Community Child Health Service.

Amongst the key changes introduced by the Guidance (and the associated Regulations, namely the Children Act (Miscellaneous Amendment) (England) Regulations 2002) are the following:

- a health assessment is to be undertaken as soon as practicable after a child starts to be looked after, once available health information has been collated

- the audit of a child's health at the health assessment is expanded and now includes physical and mental health, and health promotion

- the first health assessment will be undertaken by a suitably qualified medical practitioner

- a written report of the health assessment and a health plan is to be prepared for each child

- the frequency of subsequent health reviews for children aged between two and five is increase to at least once every six months. For children over five, the review should take place at least once a year

- such health reviews may now be undertaken by whoever is considered most appropriate (e.g. a nurse or midwife).

The health of looked after children was not set as a priority target for local authorities as part of the Department of Health's performance review process in the first five years following the publication of the *Government's Objectives* (Department of Health 1999). Local authorities were set specific targets in relation to the prevention of drug misuse and the reduction of teenage pregnancy, however. Again, you may wish to find out what is being achieved in your area.

PERSONAL OBJECTIVES

There can be no doubt that there has been an intense policy interest in the quality of services for children looked after away from home since the late 1990s. As yet, progress towards meeting the aims of the policy framework that has been put in place has been, at best, uneven. One might argue that this is because insufficient time has been allowed for the various policy initiatives to take effect. This is undoubtedly the case in some respects. However, the deficiencies of the 'care system' have been well known for many years and little of what has been put in place can be described as radically new, although it is the case that policy has never been so explicitly stated nor carried the authority of central government to the same degree. We would simply remind you of the danger of relying on systems and procedures without taking into account those who have to operate them. A personal commitment to make the policy work 'on the ground' will be important too.

We will look shortly (Exercise 5.3) in a little more detail at what we mean by this. For now, we want to pass on something that we sometimes say to our students: 'What is wrong with social work practice currently, is our fault. What will be wrong with it in ten years' time will be yours.' What will you do to help achieve the *Objectives* set for looked after children?

Exercise 5.3: David's Story

There are few 'smoking guns' in social work. What we mean by this is that very often the failure to look after children adequately does not lie in the 'gross failures' of the statutory or regulatory framework, stark deficiencies in our professional knowledge base nor even in the inadequacies of the network of provision available to children. Very often they reside in the 'small carelessnesses' to which each of us is prone. Consider the following account of one young person's experience of being looked after and answer the questions that follow:

Day One – Friday Night

A telephone call from the Emergency Duty Team is received at Paddlebrook Residential Unit at 1.00 a.m. It is a request for a placement for a 15-year-old youth. He had been missing from home for a few days and upon his return, his mother had been afraid to let him in. Father is out of town at the moment. A neighbour called social services after David was seen 'wandering the streets'. His mother refuses to have him home until father gets back and agrees to the social worker providing accommodation for David.

David asks the social worker to take him around to his uncle's, who lives across town, as he will look after him. The social worker refuses to do so as he says he does not have time and has made other arrangements. At 2.00 a.m. the 'out of hours' social worker brings David in. The social worker says he was busy, hence the delay, and then leaves almost immediately. He leaves behind details of the young person's name and his address.

The 'sleeping in' residential social worker deals with the admission, much to his annoyance, as he has to be on shift again in the morning. He makes his feelings very clear to the waking night staff. With David in the room, he takes the opportunity to complain about how the emergency social worker had dealt with the whole business. A member of the night staff gives David a quick physical examination. David is told that he is just looking for bruises and any signs of infection. No toothbrush, soap or towel can be found for David, who is looking quite grubby and dishevelled. A bed has to be made up and there is a problem of finding a full set of bedclothes. Eventually David is sent up to bed without supper or a drink, his clothes are taken from him, his pockets emptied and his clothes taken down to the laundry.

Day Two – Saturday Morning

David stays in bed waiting to be told he can get up. He can't find his clothes. A log entry is made that David wouldn't get up. David is given a tracksuit belonging to some past resident and comes downstairs. He has missed breakfast. A social worker who had called to collect another young person, and who specializes in home finding, is told all about last night's admission. This discussion takes place in the office with all but one member of staff present. This member of staff comes in to the office at one point and complains about being left with the kids all morning. David sits and watches TV. At lunchtime, David refuses to eat the food that is offered to him. He approaches a member of staff whom he addresses as 'Sir', much to everyone's amusement, and says he doesn't like it. He is told to 'like it or lump it'. A confrontation then ensues in which David loses his temper and swears at staff. A log entry is made for the afternoon staff to be especially vigilant as David is clearly potentially violent.

At 6.00 p.m. David 'absconds'. At about 6.30 p.m., David's father turns up at the residential unit. He says that he has only just found out where David was put last night. He asks to see his son. He is told that this can only happen with the social worker's permission and the area office will be open on Monday. He is sent on his way. At approximately 7.30 p.m. David returns to the unit in a calm frame of mind. He says he has been to see his uncle who would look after him until his father gets home. He offers to cook his own tea but permission is refused.

At 9.30 p.m., David leaves the unit again without permission. He is reported to the police at 10 p.m., as per the authority's guidelines. He is returned to the unit at 11.15 p.m. by the police. He has been glue sniffing with two other residents from the unit and is to be interviewed in the morning about the theft of glue from the local garage. He is argumentative and difficult and is manhandled into his room.

Day Three – Sunday Morning

David gets up and immediately informs the duty senior that a member of staff hit him last night. He is told to stop making such allegations or people will turn against him.

TASKS

1. Using your knowledge of children's needs and rights, the requirements of the Children Act 1989 and your understanding

of the principles of good practice in relation to looked after children, identify the points in this case when social workers acted inappropriately.

2.   Suggest an alternative course of action at each of these points.

3.   Try and explain why the professionals in this case acted in the way that they did.

Points to Consider

1.   What could David's parents have reasonably expected from the professionals in this case? What could the professionals reasonably have expected of David's parents?

2.   What might David now expect of both the professionals involved and his parents?

3.   What does this case tell you about the difficulties faced by the 'corporate parent'?

4.   What does David's story tell you about the kind of 'secondary problems' that can overshadow the original reasons for being looked after?

5.   What steps would you take now to recover the ground lost?

6.   What will you do to prevent yourself being governed by the same kind of bureaucratic and organizational imperatives that produced such poor practice in this case?

CONCLUSION

When you see (or more likely hear) a small child's reaction to finding itself temporarily 'lost' in a supermarket or busy thoroughfare you can begin to appreciate the primal nature of the emotional response to separation.

There are times when separation is necessary in the interests of the child's broader welfare or through force of circumstance, and not all separations will be so traumatic. Some will come as a relief and all are mediated to some degree by age and experience. Nonetheless, the measure of the task facing those who will look after such children is reflected in the lost child's tears and protests. Making good the loss while building hope for the future is what looking after children really means.

NOTES AND SELF-ASSESSMENT

1. Do you know where the photographs of you taken as a baby are kept?

2. Can you remember the bedroom you had as a teenager?

3. Have you been to a family wedding?

4. Do you know where each member of your immediate family lives?

5. What difference would it make to you if the answers you gave to questions 1 to 4 were actually the complete opposite of those that you did give?

6. Who have you lost?

RECOMMENDED READING

Daniel, B., Wassell, S. and Gilligan, R. (1999) *Child Development for Child Care and Protection Workers.* London: Jessica Kingsley Publishers.

Butler, I. and Drakeford, M. (2003) *Social Policy, Social Welfare and Scandal: How British Public Policy is Made.* London: Palgrave/Macmillan.

 **TRAINER'S NOTES**

Exercise 5.1: Separation

This can be a difficult exercise for groups and trainers will need to be mindful of how painful memories can easily be triggered by this topic. Participants should be given an absolute right not to share their accounts with the larger group. The removal of 'WB' can be role-played but this requires a great deal of the person(s) playing 'WB' herself. Quiet consideration of the issues raised is, in our view, a better way for participants to explore the issues raised by this exercise.

Exercise 5.2: Rebecca's Story

The case material can easily be adapted to provide the scripts to role-play the imminent case conference. Questions about role, task, status and power emerge quite naturally in most simulated (and many real) case conferences. An interesting variation can be introduced if the case conference (or a simulated family conference) is asked to make arrangements for the termination of Rebecca's placement. The issues around separation as well as role and task are even more complex at this point. Alternatively, the exercise material can be used to explore attachment and loss behaviours.

Exercise 5.3: David's Story

Participants could be asked to use the material generated by the exercise as the basis of a procedure manual or good practice guide for field and residential workers. Alternatively, participants could be asked to write an information leaflet either for children and young people looked after or for their parents. A larger group, suitably divided, could be asked to do both. It is instructive to note the points of similarity and difference that inevitably emerge.

WEB RESOURCES

http://www.doh.gov.uk/qualityprotects The 'Quality Protects' 'home page'. Access to project teams, publications, e-bulletins, best practice guides etc. This is an important and useful site for all qualifying and qualified social workers.

You might also want to explore the website of Research in Practice (RIP) (**http://www.rip.org.uk**). This partnership of academic institutions and over 70 local authorities, voluntary child care organizations and health trusts provides (to its member agencies) a range of information resources and briefings. The site provides public access to the *Quality Protects Briefings* produced jointly by RIP, the Department of Health and Making Research Count. The briefings, which cover such topics as *Understanding and Challenging Youth Offending; Leaving Care; Meeting the Needs of Disabled Children; Placement Stability; Young People's Participation* and *Child and Adolescent Mental Health*, have been produced in printed form for distribution to relevant child care professionals in England and Wales. The on-line versions contain a more detailed account of the sources used in preparing the briefings, which are intended to provide practitioners with accessible digests of research related to the various topics covered.

http://www.carestandards.org.uk This is the home page of the National Care Standards Commission (NCSC). It provides a description of the role and function of the NCSC and provides access to downloadable copies of published NMS. It also provides access to the reports of inspections undertaken by the NCSC.

Voices from Care was founded in 1990 to bring looked after young people together from across Wales in order to improve the conditions of looked after children and young people and to provide them with a voice in the development of policy and practice. Their website, of relevance to children and young people living throughout the UK (**http://www.vfcc.org.uk**), is an exciting mixture of helpful information (e.g. on children's rights when living away from home) and e-fun! A more established website is that of First Key (**http://www.first-key. utvinternet.com/movingon.html**) which provides useful advice and information of particular relevance to care leavers.

BAAF Adoption and Fostering (**http://www.baaf.org.uk**) is an independent organization and registered charity that aims to promote the 'highest standards of child centred policies and services for children separated from their families of origin'. The website provides access to newsletters and briefings on a great many topics associated with fostering and adoption. It is particularly useful if you are interested in the implementation of the Adoption and Children Act 2002. Some areas are restricted to members, but it is possible to become an individual member. BAAF publishes the journal *Adoption and Fostering*.

Child Abuse

OBJECTIVES

In this Unit you will:

- Explore child abuse from an emotional, intellectual and practice-based perspective.
- Learn how child abuse is defined and classified.
- Consider appropriate responses to abuse.

 CHILD ABUSE AND YOU

No qualifying or newly qualified social worker should be responsible for cases involving child abuse. The development of knowledge and skills in this area should form part of a social worker's post-qualifying experience and training. But, even though you are at an early stage in your professional development, it is important to begin preparing yourself for work in this area as soon as possible, for you may find yourself confronted with child abuse much earlier in your career than you anticipate. You may already have a statutory duty to respond to allegations of abuse as part of your job or during training. Your preparation must precede your professional obligations and it is never too early to start. This Unit is intended to develop your awareness and understanding of what is meant by 'child abuse'. Many of the themes introduced in this Unit are developed in Unit 9, which explores key elements of child protection practice.

We have suggested several times already that *you, your* attitudes, *your* values and the knowledge that *you* bring to a situation, are important influences on both the processes and the outcomes of social work with children and families. We begin this Unit by exploring what agenda you bring to work in the area of child abuse.

Any number of radio, television or newspaper headlines reporting an incident of child abuse or the conclusions of the latest inquiry into a child death would serve to demonstrate the significant emotional content of work in this area. Child abuse can raise powerful feelings in everyone, including the social worker. It is important to recognize the emotional impact child abuse has on you. Ignoring your emotional responses may interfere with the work you are trying to do. Once acknowledged, however, you can use your own emotional responses to practical effect. Exercise 6.1 will demonstrate what we mean.

 ## Exercise 6.1: A Personal Account

The account below was written specifically for the purposes of this exercise by someone who had been abused as a child. Although it is very graphic in some ways, you will have to supply most of the details of what took place yourself.

Read the text, take a few minutes to think about it and then carry out the tasks below.

> There are two things that I remember more clearly than anything: the fact that he could be so nice sometimes and not being able to stop thinking about it. Even days afterwards I'd think about what had happened while I was doing something else, like at school. After the physical pain had gone I still used to feel it, that it had happened – not always him doing it but the feeling afterwards and the certain knowledge that it would happen again. But then, it wasn't him, in my mind, it was two other people.

I still felt bad because I knew, somehow, that it shouldn't happen and I'd try things in my head, stupid things to try and make sure it wouldn't happen again. He was always so apologetic. I'd work out how to stay on the right side of him but, of course, I couldn't. I certainly didn't want anyone else to know, not then. You know, when you have not done your reading or your work for a class and you hope it's not you that gets asked but you know, you just know, that you will be, it's like that. You think people know already, you see, but you wish that they didn't.

If someone tells you that they love you and they're sorry then you want to believe them and you hope that it's all over. Maybe I should have done more to stop it. I think perhaps that I should but I didn't. I didn't know what he felt about me then and I don't think I do now. There is no excuse for what he did to me.

How I didn't talk about it, I don't know. What would have happened if it hadn't stopped, I don't know. You can't imagine what it did to my head when I was older. I was so angry and felt such a fool. I nearly died the first time this kid asked me out.

TASKS

1. Make a list of words to describe how you feel about what you have read.

2. Write down how you feel about the child concerned.

3. Write down how you feel about the adult involved.

4. Write down how you feel the child and the adult may have felt at the time of the abuse and now.

 Points to Consider

1. Were you surprised by any of the feelings that the piece raised in you?

2. Which of the feelings that you had towards the child might be helpful to you from this point?

3. Which of the feelings that you had towards the child might be unhelpful to you from this point? For example, do you see how a feeling of anger may motivate you to work hard for this child? Do you see how anger might also cloud your judgement and make it more likely that you will make mistakes? Do you see how fear might prompt a 'fight or flight' response?

4. What might be the consequences for you of denying those feelings that you have described?

5. What might be the consequences of showing or hiding your feelings from the child and/or the adult involved?

6. What reasons might there be for someone not wishing to acknowledge his or her emotional response to child abuse?

 ## INTELLECTUAL RESPONSES TO CHILD ABUSE

While our initial response to an incident or account of child abuse might be at an emotional level, social workers cannot confine themselves to a response at this level only. You are required to explore intellectually what is meant by the term. You might view such a suggestion as unnecessary. Surely, everyone knows what abuse is? At the extremes, we might concede that there is likely to be a fairly ready consensus as to what constitutes abuse. The deliberate starving to death of a child is clearly abusive, we might assume, but in what sense is the 'quiet catastrophe' that we referred to in Unit 1, that results in 40,000 children in the developing world dying every day from malnutrition and preventable diseases, abusive? Is it abusive that 100 million primary school-aged children have no school to go to (UNICEF 2000)? Risking children's health in dangerous working conditions is clearly abusive, but have you thought about where your morning coffee, your trainers or your household furnishings come from in those terms? We do not expect you, as social workers, to take on such geo-political issues. Our point is that what we describe as abusive, even at the extremes, is selective. At the more immediate level of the kind of abuse that confronts social workers in the UK, we believe there remains an essential ambiguity. Exercise 6.2 will demonstrate what we mean.

Exercise 6.2: Is it/Isn't it Abusive?

Read the following mini case studies and answer the question: 'Is or isn't it abusive?'

1. Wayne is six years old. He has some behavioural problems and is generally boisterous and disobedient. He threw a stone, narrowly missing his baby brother, and broke a downstairs window. His father made him pick up the glass. Wayne cut his hands but his father made him clear the whole room nonetheless 'as a lesson to him'.

2. John is 13. His father has a large collection of pornographic videos that he allows John and several of his schoolfriends to watch together. John's father has said that he is only making sure that the boys understand the facts of life properly and that there is nothing to be ashamed of in being so 'open' about sex.

3. Julie is 14 and has run away from a children's home. She is staying with a much older man who has provided her with a home, food and clothing, but she is expected to pay for her keep by sleeping with him and working as a prostitute. Julie says that she likes the life and the money and does not want to return to care.

4. Sandra has moderate learning difficulties. She has twin boys aged 11 months. She keeps several dogs and the house is very dirty and disorganized. Sandra goes out every Thursday night and leaves the twins with the 12-year-old boy from next door. Both twins are dirty and have severe urine burns and a nappy rash. Both are underweight. Sandra says that she cannot afford to buy more nappies than she does and, as she does not have a washing machine, she cannot keep up with the twins.

5. Tom is 16. He is not very 'sporty' and prefers to spend more time with his books and computer than he does with young people his own age. He is very shy in the company of girls. Some of his classmates have begun calling him names. They say that he is 'gay'. Tom has begun to pretend to be ill in order to avoid going to school. He says that the name-calling is 'getting to him' and fears that, sooner rather than later, 'someone will sort him out' at school.

6. Rosie is 16. Her parents are members of a strict religious sect. Rosie is made to dress very plainly and is not allowed to wear cosmetics, listen to music or watch TV. She is not allowed out alone other than to walk to school. Her parents searched her school bag and found a 'love letter' from a classmate. Rosie was locked in her bedroom and kept away from school for over a month.

7. Megan is 13. She lives with her mother and stepfather and her two half-brothers. The boys receive almost all of their parents' attention. Megan is not included in family outings and is made to do a disproportionate amount of helping out with the household chores. She is often not allowed to eat with the rest of the family. She is constantly told that she is 'useless' and will never make anything of her life.

8. Alun and Mary live in a particularly run down and deprived area. Their prospects of work, beyond a government scheme, are practically nil. Both are very depressed at the prospect of a life on the dole and say that the only pleasure they get from life is from sex with each other and occasional solvent abuse. Both sets of parents allow them to sleep together. Both are 14. Alun's father is worried about the solvents but feels he has nothing better to offer his son.

Points to Consider

1. When making your decisions, how far did the nature and degree of any harm done and the degree of responsibility of the adults involved influence you?

2. Were you influenced by the immediate or by the longer-term consequences of the possible abuse?

3. Were you influenced by how much control the adult had over the circumstances in which the possible abuse took place?

4. To what extent did the 'maturity' of the young people involved affect your decision?

5. Would the determination of abuse be different if you were to ask the children concerned? Or the adults?

6. Are you aware of anything in your own experience of childhood that might prevent you from recognizing abuse?

DEFINING CHILD ABUSE

Some definitions of child abuse are provided later in this Unit. Defining abuse is not the same as explaining it, of course, and we address some of the issues that arise when trying to define abuse in Study Text 6.1.

Study Text 6.1: Defining Child Abuse

In a report written by the Directors of Social Work in Scotland, concerning child abuse and child protection, the following honest and sobering observation is made: 'Practitioners…are within a field of evolving knowledge and changing public attitudes and expectations. Often they find themselves at the forefront of discovery without the support of established theory' (1992, p.5).

This statement provides a number of clues as to why it is so very difficult to make unequivocal statements about child abuse, its nature and causes, and appropriate responses. It is not that child abuse is a new phenomenon; rather it is that our knowledge and understanding of it are constantly evolving. Moreover, the statement hints at the fact that child abuse is a negotiated process – that is to say that both the term and the idea mean different things to different people at different times. An NSPCC-sponsored report found that there is not much agreement in the literature either: 'there is a lack of social consensus on what is abuse, apart from homicide or the very grossest injuries' (Cleaver, Watton and Cawson 1998, p.5). Consequently, there remains at the very heart of our understanding of child abuse a fundamental and unavoidable uncertainty. This study text explores that uncertainty so that you can build it into your own understanding of child abuse and so that you develop an appropriate critical approach to your wider reading in this area.

We have already explored in Unit 1 how childhood is socially constructed and re-constructed, mostly by adults and often for reasons that have little to do with the rights, needs or interests of children. It is increasingly recognized that the same is true of child abuse (and child protection). There are few absolutes as, culturally and temporally, childhood is continuously defined and redefined. Similarly, child abuse and child protection services cannot be understood without reference to the way in which we account for, and respond to, children generally.

It is perfectly possible, for example, to trace an explanatory, therapeutic and analytical history of child abuse and child protection, just as it is possible to trace the social history of children. Arbitrarily, one might begin with the nineteenth-century concern with what has been called a 'narrative of the body' (Hendrick 1994) where the visible poverty, palpable squalor, physical illness and the depredations of harsh working conditions were to be remedied with cleanliness, godliness and the cottage home; through to the development of a 'narrative of the mind' where the psychic traumas of childhood are internal, individual and, latterly, sexual. History is not a linear process, however, and ideas from one period may last well into successive ages; and sometimes, of course, old lessons have to be re-learned. Nonetheless, it is simply not possible to extract the concept of abuse from the context in which it occurs and the climate of ideas in which it is defined (see also Butler 2000; Corby 2000a).

Contemporary constructions of childhood rest on assumptions, as we have suggested in Unit 1, that childhood is not simply quantitatively and qualitatively different from adulthood (which is simply to state the obvious) but that children are also, *by their very nature*, inferior. This imputed inferiority refers not only to children's intellectual, emotional and cognitive capacities but also to their status as social beings and actors in their own biographies. It is not simply a matter of relative competence. It is in the cultural presumption of the inferior social status of childhood that we locate their consequent powerlessness and it is this relative powerlessness that is implicated in any explanation of the phenomenon of abuse itself. Unsurprisingly, such a construction of childhood has had profound effects on the process and structures of child protective services in the UK. If children are generally, and almost by definition, viewed as incompetent and inferior, yet fully understood by adults, it is no surprise that some children are abused nor is it a surprise that child protection measures may prove incapable of adequately protecting some children.

Growing awareness of this has led to the development, in recent years, of 'ecological' accounts that locate abuse in the various power relationships in society and which argue for responses to child abuse that are more broadly preventative and which emphasize children's rights. Such approaches can be criticized on the grounds that they may absolve individual abusers of responsibility and that there is a fine line between respecting children's rights and leaving them to fend for themselves.

Clearly, any explanation, categorization or definition of child abuse carries the impression of the precise moment in which it is made and conveys as much about those making the distinctions as it does about the phenomenon itself. Consider how child abuse might be defined (and explained) depending on where one stood in relation to the events in question. Here we are not referring to any particular incident of abuse but to the idea of child abuse itself.

We might identify several 'stakeholders' in any account of child abuse. First, the community at large has a legitimate interest in that the public 'wants children protected from a variety of depredations: it wants parents' rights and family life to be safeguarded against unwarranted interference by the State…and it expects all of this to be done quietly, smoothly, efficiently and effectively' (Parker and others 1991, p.20). Second, practitioners, based on their training and experience, will have particular views on what constitutes abuse. This may owe more to their sense of what can be done to manage a particular set of circumstances than any particular theoretical orientation, of course. Research has shown that a team's response to allegations of abuse can be influenced by 'status' of the referrals. 'High' status referrals, such as those from police and teachers, enter the child protection system earlier (Cleaver and others 1998). Third, resource gatekeepers, such as elected members and management committees, may also have an interest in defining abuse in terms of their own strategic interests and responsibilities. If resources are limited, eligibility thresholds can shift. Fourth, the families of vulnerable children are clearly actual and potential contributors to how abuse is defined. Then there is the child him- or herself.

Hitherto, the child's account of abuse has had very little impact on how the phenomenon is understood and acted upon by adults (Butler 1996b). Bullying, for example, would almost certainly rate much more highly on children's hierarchy of abuse than it does on adults'. Bullying may actually result in the death of more children than any other form of 'abuse'.

We have hinted already that certain forms of harm or injury to certain categories of children would not constitute abuse for many adults (e.g. racism in this country or starvation amongst children living in the developing world; bullying and corporal punishment in the UK or child labour and economic exploitation elsewhere; certain categories of asylum seekers in the UK or refugees in 'foreign' wars). Depending on your point of view and relationship to the events in question, your definitions of, and explanations for, abuse may be different from ours. What matters, however, is that in your reading around these issues (which will extend well beyond the confines of this particular book), you examine critically, carefully and comprehensively any definition, explanation or account that you encounter. Certainly not all, maybe not any, definitions of abuse are universally reliable, valid or exhaustive.

A fundamental uncertainty around what constitutes abuse is at the heart of intellectual or academic debate in this area. It finds a significant echo in direct work too. Living with the uncertainty, rather than ignoring it or taking refuge in simple (and simplistic) explanations or definitions, is one of the most difficult steps in developing as an effective professional capable of working in this field. At the heart of good child protection social work lies the exercise of good judgement. The next exercise reinforces the point.

 ### Exercise 6.3: Defining Abuse

Below you will find six thumbnail 'definitions' of abuse (more detailed definitions are introduced in Study Text 9.1). Read them carefully and jot down, for each one, an example of what is being described. Then go back and read the mini case descriptions provided for Exercise 6.2 before completing the tasks set out below.

1. *Physical abuse*: where a parent (or somebody else caring for a child) physically hurts, injures or kills a child.

2. *Sexual abuse*: when adults seek sexual gratification by using children.

3. *Neglect*: where parents (or whoever else is caring for the child) fail to meet the basic essential needs of children (e.g. adequate food, clothes, warmth and health care).

4. *Emotional abuse*: where children are harmed by constant lack of love and affection, or threats.

5. *Deprivation*: where children's needs fail to be met or their potential and life-chances are damaged by social forces and/or institutions.

6. *Exploitation*: where individuals and social institutions (including institutions of the State) satisfy their own needs or purposes by inappropriately using children.

TASKS

1. Allocate each of the mini case descriptions to one or more categories of abuse.

2. Describe clearly your reasons for doing so.

3. Describe how adequate each definition is for each case.

4. Amend each of the thumbnail definitions to reflect your appreciation of the cases and your broader understanding of abuse.

And/or

5. Rank order the cases – first from the point of view of the child concerned and then from the (imagined) point of view of the editor of the local tabloid newspaper.

 Points to Consider

1. Was it difficult to place particular cases in single categories?

2. What does this tell you about the phenomenon and the concept of abuse?

3. Whose definition of abuse counts for the most and why?

4. Whose definition of abuse counts the least and why?

5. How adequate is your own definition of abuse?

6. What are you going to do to improve it?

 RESPONDING TO ABUSE

As someone who wants to work with children and families, part of your motivation, we assume, is that you want to do something to stop or reduce child abuse. We have seen how difficult it can be to determine what abuse means. Not surprisingly, it is equally difficult to work out in practice what protecting a child involves exactly. Sometimes, for example, the removal of a child from his or her home may be protective. Sometimes such a separation will prove harmful (see Unit 5). At this stage in your professional development, you may not be in a position to make such judgements. That does not mean, however, that you have no obligation to respond to situations in which child abuse may have taken place. The final part of this Unit deals with responding to child abuse, when you are least prepared for it and least expecting it.

Not everyone confronted with a potential incidence of abuse will respond. Unless the abuse is very obvious (and it rarely is) it may be possible to persuade yourself that you don't have 'enough evidence' on which to act. You may persuade yourself that the child is 'making it up' or 'attention seeking'. You may not want to find yourself caught up in an investigation or a court appearance at a later date. The incident may reawaken bad memories of your own. All of these reasons for not responding are understandable but ultimately insufficient, especially if you consider the consequences of inaction if your suspicions are well founded.

If the abuse is not stopped it is impossible for children to receive the help they may need to redress the damage they have experienced. If abuse takes place and the abuser is not prevented from re-abusing it may be that other children may also be in danger. These are powerful reasons why we should all take our responsibilities very seriously if we suspect that abuse is happening.

So what should you do? Exercise 6.4 examines how you might react if a child was to disclose abuse to you.

Exercise 6.4: Jane's Story

Read the following case scenario and answer the questions. Complete each individual section before attempting the next.

Jo, a student social worker, is taking her daughter to Brownies and the Leader asks to have a word with her. She starts by apologizing and says that she knows that Jo is something to do with social services. 'Can I talk to you in confidence?' she asks, 'It's about Jane [another Brownie]. I'm very worried about the bruises she has on her face and arms.'

1. What would your response be to a request for confidentiality in a situation such as this?

Jo has a look and is appalled at what she sees. Jo asks Jane how she got the bruises.

2. Was this the right thing to do in the circumstances? If not, what else could Jo have done?

Jane starts to cry and says that she fell over. She begs Jo not to say anything to anyone else. She seems really upset. Jo is beginning to feel a bit embarrassed about all the fuss and wishes that she had not become involved in the first place. Jane is clearly relieved when Jo tells her not to worry; Jo is not going to say anything.

3. Is this how you might have reacted?

4. What are the possible consequences of Jo's decision not to tell a child protection worker?

Later that night, Jo realizes that the incident with Jane is bothering her. It gives her a restless night. The next day Jo mentions it to a colleague in the office where she is on placement who says that Jo ought to discuss it with someone from the child care team. Jo delays doing this all day and finally, at 4.45 p.m., she goes and talks to the child care team leader.

5. What are the consequences of this delay:

    (a) if Jane's injuries were sustained from an assault?

    (b) if Jane really had simply fallen down the stairs?

The team leader listens to Jo's description of the bruises and is very interested in the fact that Jane was distressed and begged Jo not to tell anyone else. The team leader decides that there is sufficient reason to investigate further.

6. What are the possible consequences now if:

    (a) Jane has been abused?

    (b) Jane has not been abused?

7.   Could Jo have done anything else which might have assisted the investigation which will now take place?

Points to Consider

1.   List some possible reasons for someone in Jo's position not wishing to 'get involved'. Might any of these apply to you?

2.   What might Jane be expecting from someone to whom she does tell her story?

3.   What particular needs of the child should your response be directed towards meeting?

4.   What particular rights of the child must your response respect?

5.   Where might *you* turn for advice if you were to find yourself in a similar position to Jo?

6.   What might inhibit you from seeking advice in such circumstances?

Study Text 6.2: Responding to Abuse

Unit 9 deals in more detail with the process of investigation and the co-ordination of responses following an allegation or suspicion of abuse. The purpose of this study text is to help to prepare you for exposure to abuse when investigation is not explicitly part of your professional role. It begins with some direct advice on what you need to bear in mind should you find yourself in a similar position to Jo. This is presented in the form of a series of 'bullet points' in the hope that you will be able to easily absorb and recall what is required of you. We then consider the question of confidentiality in situations where abuse is suspected.

AN INITIAL RESPONSE

As a student or as a volunteer or sessional worker, or even as a qualified social worker, you can do a great deal to prepare yourself for the unexpected discovery of possible child abuse by making sure that you are familiar with your agency's child protection procedures. All health and social care agencies *will* have detailed procedures and protocols in place that should be explained to you as part of your induction to working in that agency. Almost every other kind of organization working with children, from church groups to sports clubs, *should* have such policies and procedures in place. It is your responsibility to know what is expected of you should you have cause for concern whenever you accept any position of trust or responsibility in relation to children. There is no possible defence for not finding out what your responsibilities are under your agency's child protection procedures. 'No one told me' is not an excuse.

In your professional role, or even in a situation such as the one in which Jo found herself, there are certain principles that you should observe should you find yourself dealing with a child or young person where you have suspicions that he or she may have been abused:

- *Listen*: If someone, particularly the child directly concerned, begins to tell you about a possible abusive incident or series of events, listen. Do not 'cross-examine' the child or begin some form of quasi-investigation. Be particularly careful not to jeopardize any possible criminal investigation by, for example, asking leading questions or 'putting words into the child's mouth'.

- *Be supportive*: It is important that the child feels supported and that you do not transmit any of the anxieties that you may have to the child. You will need to balance any emotional response that you may have with an appropriate intellectual response. Try to relate to and communicate with the child in a way that is appropriate to his or her age and understanding.

- *Don't judge*: It is vital that you do not patronize the child or otherwise seek to diminish what you are being told. Keep the information that you are being given separate from your interpretation of it. It may prove necessary to repeat what the child says to the child protection workers later and it may be helpful to make notes of what you have been told, as soon as practicable after you have spoken to the child.

- *Don't make promises that you can't keep*: Particularly, do not promise a child unconditional confidentiality. (We return to the question of confidentiality below.) Be honest and offer reassurance wherever possible. It is far preferable to say to anyone, child or adult, who asks you not to tell: 'I don't know what you are going to tell me. I may have to talk to someone else if I think you or someone else is in danger but, if I can keep what you tell me in confidence, I will.'

- *Don't dither*: Check out your concerns with a more experienced worker and report them to a senior worker in your agency, ideally your line manager. Delay, in Jane's case for example, could have led to the bruises, that is the 'proof', fading and the opportunity for her to be further harmed. Or, if she hadn't been assaulted, delay may have made it more difficult for her parents to convince the social worker that the faded bruises were the result of a fall.

CONFIDENTIALITY

One of the more vexed questions that can arise in situations such as that suggested by the previous exercise is that of confidentiality. Sharing information is a vital consideration in child protection work. You should be aware that it is often only when information from a variety of sources is pooled that the circumstances of a particular child can be properly understood and the risks to that child fully evaluated (see Department of Health 1999, paras. 7.27 and 7.29). As a social worker, your agency will have a particular part to play in the local child protection arrangements (these are described in Unit 9) and arrangements for the sharing of information will usually be formalized and explicit once the process of investigation has begun. Guidance issued to social workers, the police, doctors, nurses and other child protection professionals (Department of Health and others 2003) deals with the issue at some length. It is important, however, that you reflect on your understanding of confidentiality at the point *before* the formal systems begin to operate.

Your starting point should be that you have a professional obligation to preserve the confidences entrusted to you as a social worker. The *Code of*

Practice for Social Care Workers, issued by the General Social Care Council, the regulatory body for social work established by the Care Standards Act 2000, makes specific reference to your duty to respect and maintain 'the dignity and privacy of service users' (para. 1.4); to respect 'confidential information and clearly [to explain] agency policies about confidentiality to service users and others' (para. 2.3) and 'not to abuse the trust of service users and carers or the access you have to personal information about them' (para. 5.3). (See the web resources at the end of this Unit.)

This professional imperative is supported by the common law duty of confidence that you owe to the children and families with which you will be working. The common law[1] duty of confidence arises when someone shares information with another person where it is reasonable to expect that the information shared will remain confidential. This duty may be owed to a child or young person just as much as to an adult, subject to their capacity to understand and make their own decisions. This means that, as a general rule, you should treat all personal information that you gather in relation to a child or family in the course of your work as confidential. Article 8 of the European Convention on Human Rights (ECHR) (as per the Human Rights Act or HRA 1998) gives additional weight to an individual's right to privacy and disclosure of confidential information *could* give rise to a legal claim. However, in neither the common law nor in relation to the ECHR is the duty of confidence an absolute one.

As far as the common law is concerned, the disclosure of information may be justified if:

- the information itself is not confidential in nature
- the person to whom the duty of confidence is owed gives consent to its disclosure
- the public interest justifies disclosure
- the court orders disclosure
- there is a statutory duty to disclose information.

1 Common law is that law established by the tradition' as opposed to statute law that is Parliament.

Generally, it is better to proceed to the disclosure of confidential information with the consent of the person concerned unless obtaining consent would be prejudicial to their welfare (or that of others – see below). The consent can be express (either verbally or in writing) or implied. Consent may be implied if you have reasonable grounds to believe that the person to whom the duty of confidence is owed would expect that information would be disclosed. A person making an allegation of abuse to a social worker could reasonably be expected to understand that the social worker would need to disclose that information to colleagues and possibly other professionals, for example.

In the absence of consent, the law recognizes that the disclosure of information may be justified in the broader public interest. The public interest may be expressed in terms of the possibility of serious harm to others or in terms of the fair administration of justice (see Brayne, Martin and Carr 2001, p.35ff for a discussion of relevant case law). In the first instance, the principle is that the protection of the public from violence takes precedence over the general public interest in preserving a duty of confidence. In the second instance, disclosure might be justified in order to allow an individual the benefit of a fair hearing before the law.

In either event, the key factor in the disclosure of confidential information is proportionality (the 'need to know' basis). Guidance states (Department of Health and others 2003, Appendix 3 para. 11):

> The amount of confidential information disclosed, and the number of people to whom it is disclosed, should be no more than is strictly necessary to meet the public interest in protecting the health and wellbeing of a child. The more sensitive the information is, the greater the child-focussed need must be to justify disclosure and the greater the need to ensure that only those professionals who have to be informed receive the information…

This general rule applies just as much within a particular agency as it does to the passage of information between agencies.

Where matters go before a court, then the public interest in the equitable and fair administration of justice takes precedence over the duty of confidence. (We will explore in Study Text 10.2 how information is put before court and how it can be shared with others who are involved with the proceedings in question.) In addition, there are certain statutory duties to disclose information deriving from specific Acts of Parliament (e.g. the Prevention of Terrorism Acts; the Police and Criminal Evidence Act 1984 and the Misuse of Drugs Act 1971). Both of these considerations are beyond the scope of this Unit, however, but see Brayne and others 2001, p.37ff for a fuller discussion.

In relation to the HRA, Article 8.2 of the ECHR states:

> There shall be no interference by a public body with the exercise of this right [to respect for private and family life] except such as is in accordance with the law and is necessary in a democratic society...for the prevention of disorder or crime, protection of health or morals or for the protection of rights and freedom of others.

It would seem that if the disclosure of confidential information can be justified under the common law duty of confidence and does not contravene specific statutory duties, it should meet the requirements of the HRA.

As a social worker, you may feel anxious about passing on information given to you 'in confidence', particularly if this is given to you by a child. However, as we have indicated, the duty to preserve confidentiality is not an absolute one. There are times when it must be overridden in order to serve better the interests of children and young people. The law allows for this. You can avoid the most obvious crises of conscience by being honest, from the outset, over the degree of confidentiality that you can offer and, subject to the child's welfare being properly safeguarded, seeking consent to disclose information where this proves necessary. In our view, certainly as a student social worker and afterwards, you would be entirely justified in talking over any concerns you might have about the safety of a child with a more senior and more experienced colleague.

You might now like to compare the answers you gave in Exercise 6.3 with those given in the trainer's notes for this Unit.

 CONCLUSION

We have suggested in this Unit that a central element in working in this field is an acknowledgement of the essential uncertainty and ambiguity that surrounds child abuse. There are no simple check-lists that you can apply to determine whether abuse is taking place or not; there are no simple steps you can take to make the abuse go away or magically 'get better'. You will go on to learn how to understand, evaluate and reduce the risks for the child and the worker in child protection situations as your career develops, but you may find yourself involved long before you think you are fully ready. At this point in your professional development we would want you to think carefully about what you see or are told about child abuse and critically to evaluate and reflect on your wider reading.

But, most important of all, we want you to be ready to act when your suspicions are aroused. There can be no justification for simply turning away.

 NOTES AND SELF-ASSESSMENT

1. Are there certain forms of behaviour that you would always categorize as abusive?

2. How does your understanding of abuse relate to your particular construction of childhood?

3. What are the major influences on your understanding of abuse?

4. Do all instances of child abuse require action?

5. What might stop you from responding to any abuse of which you become aware?

6. Do you know how to take the appropriate next step in responding to abuse in your particular post or practice placement?

RECOMMENDED READING

Corby, B. (2000b) *Towards a Knowledge Base*. Second edition. Buckingham: Open University Press.

Macdonald, G. (2001) *Effective Intervention for Child Abuse and Neglect: An Evidence Based Approach to Planning and Evaluating Intervention*. Chichester: John Wiley.

TRAINER'S NOTES

Exercise 6.1: A Personal Account

Encourage group members to share feelings, possibly by 'quickthinking' them on to a flip chart. You may wish to consider the range of feelings expressed and their intensity. Are there feelings that are commonly felt? Are some much more personal than others? (Group members should be reminded that they do not have to explain or 'justify' their responses.) One important aspect to consider is whether some of the feelings expressed would be helpful in working with a family where abuse was suspected. If so, to whom would they be helpful? In the exercise, for example, we note how anger can be both a negative and positive influence – negative in the sense of rendering a worker unable to hear the needs of the person who has been abused, positive in the sense of providing the energy to 'do' something in the face of other overbearing emotions. What other feelings amongst those you have elicited from the group might have similar double-edged effects?

Exercise 6.2: Is it/Isn't it Abusive?

A larger group could be broken down into pairs and the decisions compared and debated between sub-groups. A much more effective (but much more difficult to manage) way to proceed is to work in a large group and to take each case in turn and to proceed only when unanimous agreement has been reached. This has the advantage of making participants explore in fine detail their reasons for whatever view they hold and it makes visible the kind of disagreements that really do exist about the nature of various forms of abuse.

Exercise 6.3: Defining Abuse

This exercise can be used in a group in the same way as the preceding exercise. For Task 4, sub-groups or pairs can work together to produce definitions that can be debated and 'adopted' by the whole group. Task 5 is best done by two 'opposing' groups, who complete their rankings and then, in role, argue the merits of their case.

Exercise 6.4: Jane's Story

The case material can:

- be given to each student as it is and the whole group works individually on the answers

or

- be read out by the trainer, posing the questions in sequence and having group discussion

or

- be prepared as a booklet for use in small groups. The booklets would have a scenario and question on each page so that issues could be discussed before the next instalment was revealed on the following page.

The following are some suggestions for discussion 'prompts':

1. What would your response be to a request for confidentiality in a situation such as this?

    ○   You can't guarantee confidentiality.

    ○   It's difficult to say no.

2. Was this the right thing to do in the circumstances? If not, what else could Jo have done?

    ○   Depends on how it is done. Might be OK if Jo is subtle but perhaps a bit overpowering for Jane who, after all, doesn't know Jo.

    ○   Perhaps better to talk only with the Leader and enable her to do the talking to Jane and pass on information to Jo.

3. Is this how you might have reacted? After all, the bruises could have been caused by a fall.

    ○   Has Jo the right to tell Jane that she will respect her confidence and not tell anyone else?

    ○   What do you think Jane might be feeling now?

    ○   How swayed are you by Jane's distress?

4. What are the possible consequences of a decision not to tell a child protection worker?

    ○   Jane might be more severely bruised tomorrow.

    ○   Jane might be too terrified to tell anyone in the future.

5. What are the consequences of this delay:

    (a) If Jane's injuries were sustained from an assault:

    ○   Bruises will fade and 'proof' of harm will be more difficult to come by.

    ○   There will be more opportunities for Jane to be further harmed.

    (b) If Jane had really simply fallen down the stairs:

    ○   Nothing for Jane but if the social services department decide, when they are informed, that there is a case to investigate the fact that there are faded bruises might make it more difficult for Jane's carers to convince the social worker that it was simply a case of a fall.

6.   What are the possible consequences now if:

(a)   Jane has been abused:

- ○   Jane may be protected from further abuse.
- ○   The perpetrator may be stopped from harming Jane or any other children in the household.
- ○   Jane will be given the opportunity to talk about what has happened to her, to let out some of her distress. This may be the start of action to repair any damage, mental or physical.
- ○   The family will experience disruption and investigation by outsiders.

(b)   Jane has not been abused:

- ○   The family, of which Jane is a part, will experience disruption and stress.
- ○   Jane herself may feel guilty for setting the investigation in progress.
- ○   If Jane feels that she is not believed then the protection may seem more like persecution.

7.   Could Jo have done anything else which might have assisted the enquiry?

- ○   Enabled the Brownie Leader to collect together clear information about what she had seen.
- ○   Written down what she had seen: time, extent, reasons given, Jane's comments, etc.
- ○   Told the Brownie Leader whom to contact and offered to go with her.
- ○   Been more honest with Jane and explained that she is very concerned about her bruises and the fact that she seems very frightened.

WEB RESOURCES

http://www.nspcc.org.uk The National Society for the Prevention of Cruelty to Children, the NSPCC, campaigns to raise awareness of child abuse in Britain as well as providing direct services to children and families. Its website contains information and advice both for the general public and for professionals and academics working in the area of child protection. In particular, you should find the library section extremely useful. You should certainly visit the 'reading list' section that provides extensive (downloadable) reading lists of key texts and, for registered users, an on-line enquiry service. You can reach this service by navigating to the 'NSPCC inform' page (**http://www.nspcc.org.uk/inform/CH_Home.asp**).

http://www.childline.org.uk This is the website for Childline, the free 24-hour helpline for children and young people in the UK. It has a user-friendly 'help and advice' page, dealing with a wide range of topics, such as bullying and racism, as well as child abuse.

http://www.kidscape.org.uk This is the website for the charity Kidscape, which describes itself as working 'to provide individuals and organisations with practical skills and resources necessary to keep children safe from harm'. Kidscape provides a helpline to support parents whose children are being bullied as well as a series of advice and information leaflets and posters, some of which can be downloaded.

The General Social Care Council (GSCC) was established in October 2001 under the Care Standards Act 2000, as the guardian of standards for the social care workforce in England. The GSCC's function is to increase the protection of service users, their carers and the general public by regulating the social care workforce and by ensuring that work standards within the social care sector are of the highest quality. In September 2002, the GSCC issued the first ever codes of practice for social care workers and employers. The codes set out the standards of practice and conduct social care workers and their employers should meet. In April 2003, the GSCC launched the Social Care Register and began the process of registering all social care workers in England. To be able to register, workers must have an appropriate qualification, commit to uphold the *Code of Practice for Social Care Workers* and be physically fit to do their jobs. The Code of Conduct can be downloaded from the GSCC's website: **http://www.gscc.org.uk**.

PART II

Developing Specialist
Knowledge and Skills

UNIT 7

Assessing

OBJECTIVES

In this Unit you will:

- Learn some practical techniques for gathering and ordering information.

- Consider means to effectively engage children and families in the process of assessment.

- Begin work on an extended case study and consider the application of what you have learned to practice.

 IN THE BEGINNING

'In any social work situation, you should always start at the beginning.' That sounds like the kind of common-sense advice that you might expect to find in a book like this. The trouble is that the 'beginning' can be a very difficult place to find! Even if you are the first point of contact for people using the services of your particular agency, the situation that prompted the referral will obviously have a history that extends beyond your introduction into events. All of the individuals, families or groups involved will also have histories, both discrete and interconnected. It might be more appropriate, although not very helpful, to seek 'the beginning' in the 'life, universe and everything' kind of question that we usually leave to philosophers or theologians. The truth is that your involvement in any child and family situation never occurs 'at the beginning'. You are always going to be joining in a sequence of events that is already in progress and which will continue long after your involvement has ended.

We make this very obvious point for two reasons: first, because some social workers and other professionals can forget that this is the case and assume that nothing of importance or interest could conceivably have pre-dated their arrival on the scene; and second, because, ignorant of the past and uncluttered by too many facts, it is all too easy to go on to make judgements about the situation of the child or family and how it is to be tackled. These assumptions have much more to do with what the worker brings to the situation than with what the family brings and are usually unproductive, if not actually harmful.

The key to avoiding them lies in a commitment to the process of assessment. The reference to 'commitment' is deliberate. It is perfectly possible to proceed to action without assessing the circumstances or context in which that action takes place, with potentially disastrous results. We can all be too busy, too stressed, or too confident in our diagnostic skills. We refer to a 'process of assessment' deliberately too. Assessment isn't an event. It is not something you do once to someone else and exclusively for your own purposes. Assessment is a continuous and mutual process of making sense of what *has* happened and what *is* happening now.

Veronica Coulshed offers a useful definition of assessment which she describes as a 'perceptual/analytic process of selecting, categorising, organising and synthesising data' (1988, p.13) with the main purpose of assessment being to develop an 'informed impression leading to action' (Timms and Timms 1982, p.16). The process of assessment 'leads the worker and the client to a better understanding of the reasons or causes for the problem and the factors that may aid or hinder its resolution' (Cournoyer 1991, p.8).

It should be noted that, while assessment has been integral to social work practice for many years, it has not necessarily been as inclusive a process as Cournoyer would appear to suggest. Indeed, Seden (2001), in her account of the development of assessment in social work, notes that it was not until the 1970s that the ideological shift 'away from a diagnostic focus towards understanding the perspectives of the service user within a holistic and person centred framework' (p.9) took place.

The *Framework for the Assessment of Children in Need and their Families* (Department of Health and others 2000) that we have introduced at various points already (Study Texts 1.2, 3.2 and 4.1) gives particular emphasis to such an inclusive and focused approach to assessment:

> Nothing can be assumed; the facts must be sought, the meaning attached to them explored and weighed up with the family. (p.13)

> Understanding what is happening to a vulnerable child...must necessarily be a process of gathering information from a variety of sources and making sense of it with the family and, very often, with other agencies concerned with the child's welfare. (p.14)

The purpose of this Unit is to encourage you to develop your understanding of assessment as a dynamic, interactive and reciprocal process that will be of equal use and value to you, the child and the family concerned.

So, even if we can't really start at the beginning, where can we begin the assessment? If assessment is to be understood in broad terms as 'making sense of what has happened and what is happening now', the obvious place to start is with the information that you have in front of you. Often the most immediate and voluminous, if not necessarily the most accessible, source of information will be in the form of a case file. Such files come in all sorts of shapes, sizes, colours and degrees of organization. As a student or a newly qualified worker, perhaps the majority of your work will be encountered, in the first instance, via the case file.

As well as offering the foundation of a thorough assessment, a good working knowledge of the file has other benefits too. For example, acquaintance with the contents of the file should reduce the possibility that information previously provided to your agency will need to be collected again. Sometimes this information will have been gained at considerable cost to the service user. Your ignorance of key events already known to your agency will convey an unhelpful sense that what has been shared previously has been forgotten or discounted. You will have more time available for the task in hand if you do not have to trawl for information that your agency already possesses. Moreover, confidence in you and your ability to help will inevitably be diminished if you make a point of demonstrating that you have not had either the time or the inclination to prepare adequately. The following study text demonstrates some ways in which you might begin the process of assessment, by exploring how you can make most use of such a file.

 Study Text 7.1: Starting Points

One key dimension along which we ordinarily fix and structure our own experience is by reference to time. Many interventive techniques, particularly those derived from the psychoanalytic tradition of casework, rely on establishing a detailed and accurate chronology of events as a basis for interpreting and understanding current situations and motivations. Even if you do not intend to base your own practice in this tradition, establishing the order of events is a useful first step towards developing your understanding of the histories and processes in which you are becoming involved.

Most case files are, nominally at least, compiled in chronological order. However, while case notes may be sequential, they often cross-refer to other sections of the file – such as correspondence or reports, which may be ordered thematically or in relation to particular events. In reality, the 'timelines' can be very difficult to trace through even a relatively new file. You could begin to get a sense of past events simply by writing the year down on one side of a piece of paper and, using the file, writing down the significant events of that year alongside. Alternatively, you could use a card index record – this allows you a little more flexibility to add additional information as your assessment proceeds. You could also represent the information graphically, in the form of a flow chart (see Figure 7.1). With a little imagination, the flow chart could be turned into a river or a railway line that might help to elicit further information later in the assessment or to interpret the flow of events to a younger child as part of your direct work with them.

1971	1972	1973	1975	1978	1982
September 12th Born Northtown. Twins! Me 5lbs 4 oz. Jane 5lbs.	Whooping cough. In hospital for two weeks. Jane also poorly.	Family moved house. Brother Matthew born, June 24th.	Started school. Liked it. So did Jane. Started speech therapy, hated that.	March, fell off my bike. Broke my arm.	Started Grammar School. Jane went to girl's school. Mum and Dad split up.

1987	1989	1990	1991	1992	1994
Took GCSEs. Did well. Jane didn't. She was very disappointed.	Took A levels. Got into university. Jane didn't. She started nurse training but dropped out after a few months.	Dropped out of university. Joined the army.	Gulf war. Jane got married. Missed the wedding. Home on leave in September when I met Becky.	February! Married Becky. Posted to Germany. Jane had baby son. Quite a year!	Back in UK. Infertility treatment started. Jane now has three children!

1995	1996	Future
Confirmation that we can't ever have children of our own. Mum dies.	Make first contact with adoption agency. Social worker starts to visit.	We want to have a family of our own...

Figure 7.1 The flow chart

A second key dimension along which we fix and order our experience is by reference to patterns of relationships. The nature of relationships can also be a focus for specific interventions and is usually an important consideration in child and family work. One commonly used technique for representing relationships through time is the genogram. At its simplest, a genogram is little more than an annotated family tree. The annotations can include major family events, occupations, places of residence and even patterns of contact. The genogram uses conventional notation: a square represents a male; a circle represents a female; a triangle represents those circumstances where the sex is unknown (e.g. an unborn child or a distant relative) and a cross drawn through one of these figures represents a death. Lines show the strength of relationships between individuals: an enduring relationship by a firm line and a transitory relationship by a broken line. These lines can be crossed through by a single line in the event of separation or by a double line in the event of a divorce. When drawing a genogram, the children of a particular couple are usually entered according to age, starting with the oldest on the left. It can be useful to draw a dotted line around all of those living in the same household. Figure 7.2 illustrates the basic form of a genogram covering three generations.

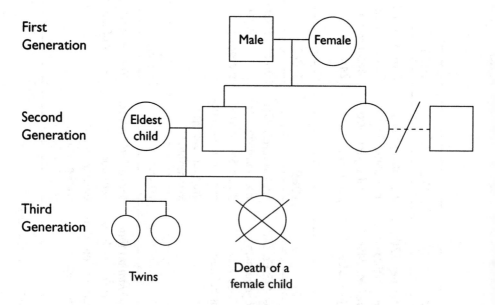

Figure 7.2 The genogram

At its best, the genogram can present complex family relationships in a very concise and accessible form. It can highlight themes and patterns that are echoed across the generations and it can serve to map key relationships and patterns of communication.

While the family is one important context in which to establish relationships, it does not provide a big enough picture (see Figure 3.3). Individuals and families have relationships with individuals and groups around them and their particular household. Such groups, or 'systems', can include neighbours, school, friends, health services, etc. One way of representing the various affiliations and the nature of a family or individual's relationships to the wider community, is the ecomap (see Figure 7.3). Ecomaps can be drawn for families or individuals. In either case, a circle in the middle of the page represents the key person(s). Around this, sometimes at distances intended to represent the 'closeness' of the relationship, other circles are drawn that represent important connections, to other members of the family, particular individuals or groups. As with the genogram, the lines used to join the various circles can also carry additional information: a solid line can represent a strong relationship; a dotted line, a weak one and a hatched line, a stressful one. Arrowheads can be added at either or both ends of the line to demonstrate the 'flow' of information, interest or resources between the parties.

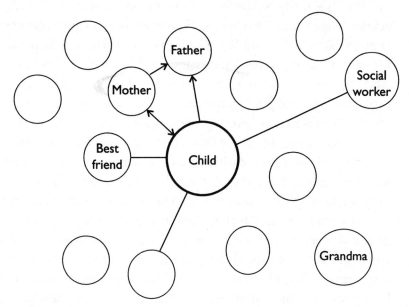

Figure 7.3 The ecomap

While we have presented each of these techniques as a useful means of sorting existing information, it should be clear also how they might be used in direct work, either to elicit further information on the basis of the gaps that show up in available data or to convey or interpret information that is not shared or understood by members of the family or individuals with whom you are working. Representing a child's journey through life as a railway line, for example, may allow opportunities for the child to reflect on who was waiting for him to arrive, who is travelling with him and where might his next and later destinations be. Conducting this exercise with a child and a set of marker pens is one of the better uses for flip chart paper that we have come across!

There are some obvious dangers in the process we have described so far, however. Files can be substantially inaccurate. They can be incomplete, outdated or record as factual what is merely conjecture. Frequently, simple mistakes, such as the failure to record a date of birth accurately, can be repeated over many years. Careful reading should help identify gross errors, but you should always confirm key information before acting upon it. This is an important route into the mutuality of assessment that we mentioned earlier. Sharing, comparing and reviewing the information that is the basis of your assessment is a vital part of the process of becoming engaged with the family with whom you are going to work.

The essentially subjective nature of any assessment needs to be acknowledged too, even where that assessment begins conventionally enough with the 'facts on file'. Cournoyer (1991) makes the point well in his account of the several stages involved in preparing to begin direct work. He describes what we have encouraged you to do so far as 'preparatory reviewing' and goes on to explore 'preparatory empathy' and 'preparatory self-exploration'. Preparatory empathy involves the worker imaginatively recreating the salient issues from the service user's point of view. This may heighten your sensitivity to the thoughts and feelings that others may have about the 'facts' of their life. Preparatory self-exploration is intended to identify the potential negative impact on the service user of the worker's characteristics, biases, emotional tender spots, 'unfinished business' and prejudices. It is also a very specific way of making explicit your commitment to anti-oppressive practice. Both preparatory empathy and preparatory self-exploration, however tentative, will demonstrate to you how much assessment is more of an interpretative art rather than an exact science and, as such, has always carried the indelible signature of its makers.

A CASE IN POINT

If you are fortunate, many of the files allocated to you will contain a summary prepared when the case was closed or in anticipation of its transfer. What follows is a representation of such a summary, with the addition of a report of the most recent events that have led to the particular family involved presenting themselves at the Southtown social services department. Assume that you are working in a child and family team in the social services department and that the case is being allocated to you. Read through the file and then attempt the exercise that follows.

Exercise 7.1: Getting to Know You

Note: for the purposes of this exercise, and for all of those exercises that use this case material, the sequence of events is important. In order to ensure that this book has a 'shelf-life' we have adopted a particular convention regarding dates. Days and months are given in the usual way. The current year, however, is always 100. For example, in this exercise you are asked to assume that you are reading the file in early January 100. Michael, one of the characters in the case material, was born in June 90. This makes him nine years old for the purposes of this exercise; i.e. it is nine years from 6/90 to 1/100, from the year he was born to 'now'.

Assume that you are reading this file in January 100.

TAYLOR FAMILY CASE FILE

Background Information

Alison (1/3/89) and Michael (5/6/90) live with their mother, Tracy (2/2/73). Tracy prefers to be known as Tracy Taylor, her family name, since her divorce in June 96 from Ron Jones, Alison and Michael's father. No formal court orders concerning the children were made during the divorce.

Ron now lives in Northtown, some 140 miles away. He remarried 18 months ago. He has a newborn son, Wayne. Ron is an electrician by trade and it is believed that he has begun to build up a successful business with his cousin in Northtown. Tracy has had another child since the divorce, John (1/12/97). His father, Alun Evans, lives with Tracy and the three children at her council-owned house in New Estate, Southtown. Alun and Tracy have been living together for three years. No record exists of previous contact with Alun. Previous social workers do not seem to have seen him at all, although there is a note saying that Mr Evans would not meet the social worker as he had 'had enough of them when he was a kid'.

Tracy and Ron met when she was still at school. She became pregnant before she left and married Ron, four years her senior, just days after her sixteenth birthday. Her family has been known to the social services department for many years. She is one of six children, the eldest four of which, including Tracy, were the subject of three-year matrimonial care orders following the breakdown of her own parents' marriage in the summer of 79. Tracy and her three older brothers and sisters were fostered briefly in 80 as there was concern for the poor standard of care the children received from Mrs Taylor and their poor school attendance. The files relating to this period of Tracy's life have been lost and no further details are available.

When Alison was born Tracy found it very difficult to cope and moved away from her recently allocated council house in Old Estate, Southtown back to her mother's house, a few streets away. Ron went to stay with his parents in Northtown during this time (June to December 89), although he did make very frequent visits to Tracy and Alison. Mrs Taylor (senior) still lives in Old Estate. Tracy's father died in August 90.

In November 89 there were several anonymous telephone calls stating that the child living at Mrs Taylor's (senior) house was being neglected and that the house was in a filthy state. Two duty social workers visited and found the physical condition of the house appalling – the kitchen unhygienic, scarcely any food in the house, evidence of a recent fire in one of the bedrooms, a blocked toilet, broken glass all over the garden and dirty nappies spilling out of the bin.

Alison was clearly not well and, with Tracy's agreement, was admitted to hospital for a week. Ron visited regularly and Tracy stayed with Alison in hospital. At a child abuse case conference called before Alison was discharged from hospital, it was decided, by consent, that Alison would be placed with foster carers while Ron and Tracy moved back into their former house in Old Estate. A support programme involving a family aide and regular visits from the social worker was initiated and the child was not placed on the 'at risk' register. Within a month Alison was home and, with the right kind of support and practical assistance, the family settled down and social work attention eased off gradually.

The social worker was still visiting when Michael was born. This time Tracy and Ron were better prepared and, although Tracy did not have an easy time during the later stages of pregnancy and during labour (Michael was a high forceps delivery), the early weeks at home seemed to go very well. However, in the late summer of 90, the health visitor reported that Tracy was becoming very depressed and was unable to look after the children properly. Ron was not always around as he was working with his cousin in Northtown and the health visitor was becoming concerned for the children. In her opinion, Alison was developmentally delayed and Michael was not thriving as he should. Additional support, including help from staff at the local family centre, was put in place.

The situation did seem to be holding together but Ron was clearly very distressed by all that was going on. He decided that Tracy and the children should go with him to Northtown where his family would look after them and he could see them every day. He agreed to allow a social worker from Northtown Social Services Department to call in to see that all was well.

From September 90 until October 92, the children lived with Tracy, Ron and his cousin's family. According to a report from Northtown Social Services, who only visited once, the children were being very well looked after and both thriving. Tracy was not happy in Northtown for long, however, and had begun to spend longer and more frequent periods at her mother's house in Southtown.

In October 92, the family moved back to Southtown, this time to New Estate, which is on the far side of town to Old Estate and Tracy's mother. Ron had reluctantly agreed, although he kept his job in Northtown. A social worker visited and was more than satisfied with the welfare of the children but did note the tension in Tracy and Ron's relationship. As no help was requested in this regard, the case was closed.

The file has a note attached of a conversation with a probation officer, dated June 96, indicating that a welfare report had been written for the divorce court but that no further involvement was envisaged.

A further note from a health visitor announces the arrival of John but does not express any concern. No referral is made and so the file is not re-opened.

Current Situation

Tracy came into the neighbourhood office on New Estate during the week saying that she was at the end of her tether and very anxious about the safety of her children.

It would seem that Alison and Michael have been spending occasional weekends and most holidays with Ron since the divorce. All has not been going well recently, however, and Alison, in particular, has been complaining to her mother that she doesn't enjoy going to visit Ron. She particularly dislikes the way her brother Michael is treated so differently. According to Tracy, this is becoming increasingly obvious as they are growing up. Last time the children went to stay, Michael spent most of his time with his father whereas Alison was expected to spend all her time with Ron's wife and Wayne. She found it hard, particularly as Ron's wife seemed to dote on the new baby and ignore her. Michael, on the other hand, says that he enjoys being with his father, uncles and 'new brother'.

The situation has caused a lot of arguments between Alison and Michael, which has spilled over into arguments between Tracy and Ron. Ron has said that he is unhappy with the way that the children were being brought up and that they would have a better upbringing with him and his new wife and family. He is talking about going to court to have the children live with him.

The situation at home is becoming unbearable and Tracy says that she doesn't know if she can keep going. She says it is affecting her relationship with Alun and she feels that John is getting a raw deal. Alun is not, apparently, very supportive and she feels he would probably want to see 'the back of' the two eldest. He has never liked Ron, according to Tracy, and is beginning to take it out on all of the children and on her. Tracy does not want to 'lose the children again'. She wants a social worker to come and help. Mrs Taylor (senior) is aggravating the situation, as she doesn't get on with Alun. The tension at home is rising and Tracy hinted to the duty social worker that 'something will break' if she doesn't get help.

TASKS

1. Establish the basis of this family's history in chronological order using the card index method described above.

2. Draw a flow chart for Tracy Taylor.

3. Prepare an ecomap for Alison. Include all the members of her family referred to in the case file.

4. Draw a genogram for the whole family.

QUESTIONS

1. How old was Alison when her parents divorced?

2. How old was Ron when Alison was born?

3. How old was Alison when she was first fostered?

4. How long did John live in Northtown?

5. How old was Alison when Michael was born?

6. How old was Michael when John was born?

7. How old was Tracy when her father died?

8. How long after the birth of Michael did Tracy's father die, and how long before she moved to Northtown?

9. How old was Tracy at the birth of each of her children?

10. How old is Tracy now?

11. How long was she married?

12. How old was Tracy when her parents divorced?

13. How old was she when she became pregnant?

14. How old are each of the children now?

15.   What relation is Wayne to Alison?

16.   Who are John's grandparents?

17.   Who are Alison's grandparents?

18.   How many maternal aunts/uncles does John have?

19.   What relation is Alun to Wayne?

20.   What relation is Alun to Alison?

Points to Consider

1.   What are the key pieces of information in the file that you might want to confirm with family members?

2.   Have you begun to form an idea of what gaps exist in your knowledge of this family? If so, list them.

3.   From the information that you have, write down what impression you have begun to form of Alun and Ron.

4.   Can you identify just how much of that impression is based on what you found in the 'file' and how much of it comes from preconceptions of your own?

5.   Describe Tracy's history of involvement with your department. What might her expectations be of you and what you might do?

6.   Write down what expectations you have of Tracy. Do your expectations focus on Tracy's potential weaknesses or on her strengths?

ART OR SCIENCE?

After completing the previous exercise, most students are surprised by how much they have managed to 'learn' about the Taylor family. This experience, despite our earlier cautions, might lead them to think that the process of assessment can be reduced to a set of technical exercises or even simply to filling in a few forms. Nothing could be further from the truth. Any assessment will require, as well as the intelligent, structured and purposeful acquisition of information, the synthesis and analysis of that information and the exercise of your professional judgement.

The value of such technical devices as the ecomap or the genogram or the wide variety of other 'assessment tools' that are available to social workers (not least those associated with the *Framework for the Assessment of Children in Need*) lies in the way in which they structure the process of gathering information and help to present it in such a way that it can be systematically reviewed and interpreted. You should note that there is rarely a consensus on what constitutes a reliable assessment 'instrument'. Indeed, there is sometimes considerable controversy over what constitutes a reliable and useful model of assessment. Prior to the introduction of the *Framework for the Assessment of Children in Need* (Department of Health and others 2000), for example, much attention was drawn to the work of Professor Roy Parker and his colleagues and the materials that they produced that were designed to structure and integrate systematically the assessment process with action planning on behalf of looked after children. The materials, popularly known as the 'LAC Materials', include a series of age-related 'Assessment and Action Records' that, from the mid-1990s, became widely accepted as the basis of assessment and planning in respect of looked after children.

Essentially, the 'Assessment and Action Records' involve the systematic review of key areas of a child's life and critical evaluation of progress made, not only by those involved professionally in delivering services to the child/family but also by the child him- or herself. In this way, one is able to assess 'how a local authority fulfils all rather than some of its parental responsibilities' (Parker and others 1991, p.35) while still being able to concentrate on outcomes for children. The authors examine many of the conceptual and theoretical issues that are associated with outcome measures before outlining the key 'dimensions for assessment' (p.77) that the framework includes. These are set out briefly in Figure 7.4. You will note the similarities with the *Framework for the Assessment of Children in Need.*

- *Health*: A parent is usually very sensitive to even small changes in a child's health, the physical nurture of a child being the 'basic parental task' (Parker and others 1991, p.84). For children looked after by the local authority, both this kind of intuitive knowledge as well as the more straightforward factual knowledge of the child's health record can easily be lost.

- *Education/Skills Training*: Parents will sacrifice much for the sake of a child's education and its general importance to most families is evidenced by how estate agents regard proximity to good schools as a major selling point. Children in the public care will often already have come with a disrupted educational background and there is evidence, according to Parker (Parker and others 1991), to suggest that the education of 'looked after' children does not receive adequate attention.

- *Emotional Development and Behaviour*: It is often emotional and behavioural problems that go beyond parents' or carers' capacity to cope that will precipitate a young person coming to be looked after by the local authority. Instability and discontinuity in care can themselves produce emotional and behavioural disturbance and so, while rarely straightforward, the persistence or reduction of such problems is a key indicator of a successful outcome for a child.

- *Social, Family and Peer Relationships*: In Unit 5 we explored some of the difficulties of maintaining links for 'looked after' children and we would agree that the creation or maintenance of a 'supportive, affectionate and reliable network of relationships' (Parker and others 1991, p.95) with brothers and sisters, the extended family, friends and neighbours is an enormously important outcome in child care.

- *Self-Care and Competence*: Children do need to look after themselves, in every sense. They need to acquire the basic life skills of decision-making, handling money and making and sustaining relationships, for example, and this is not something that can be crammed into a 12-week preparation for leaving care 'package'. It is a lifelong process that begins at birth.

- *Identity*: A knowledge of yourself, your history and your potential is vital to your sense of well-being. Often, 'looked after' children will have learned to take a very negative view of all three.

- *Social Presentation*: Social attractiveness does matter. Children are likely to be shunned on account of their 'unattractive appearance, unlikeable personal habits and inappropriate social behaviour' (Parker and others 1991, p.100), particularly by other children.

Figure 7.4 Assessing outcomes in child care

In 1998, an article by Knight and Caveney appeared in the *British Journal of Social Work* that questioned the normative view of parenting and family life that the authors believed to be at the heart of the 'Assessment and Action Records' and the lack, in Parker's approach to assessment, of any serious consideration of the adequacy of the resources available to deliver appropriate services to children and young people. They criticized the 'check-list' approach to assessment for the way in which it would strengthen the bureaucratic nature of being in public care and maintain the existing, unequal power relations between the adults and the children involved. Knight and Caveney (1998) concluded that any worthwhile improvement in the circumstances of looked after children would need to be founded upon a clear recognition of children's rights and a recognition of the power adults hold over children. This article led to a spirited response by Sonia Jackson (1998), who had worked with Professor Parker on the development of the 'Assessment and Action Records'. This, in turn, led to further discussion on the 'political' nature of the social work process (see Garrett 1999) as it affects looked after children and, for some, the debate continues. We do not seek to persuade you to any particular point of view in relation to the value of the 'Assessment and Action Records', but neither do we wish you to accept them uncritically. Both the 'Assessment and Action Records' and the *Framework for the Assessment of Children in Need* should be kept under critical review and applied creatively in practice to suit the needs of the situation and circumstances in which social work help is required.

While the structured and systematic gathering of information ('the science' of an assessment) is of vital importance, it is our view that the quality and usefulness of an assessment ultimately lies in the way in which information is analysed and reflected upon by all of those involved in the process (the 'art' of an assessment). In this way, assessments also have therapeutic value; they become part of the process of helping. As Adcock (2001, p.84) points out:

> An assessment provides an opportunity for families to engage in reflection with the aid of a helpful worker and to begin to develop explanations for concerns. Any insights may provide a way to find alternative coping strategies and possible solutions.

In this sense, assessment is every bit as much part of the solution as it is part of understanding the problem. This is much more likely to be the case where the assessment is carried out on the kind of inclusive basis that is implicit in Adcock's observations. We have noted already, at several points, how the balance towards inclusive approaches, not only to assessment, has decisively shifted within the practice of social work and we have introduced you also to some of the challenges and opportunities of working in partnership with parents (see Study Text 4.3). A further important dimension of partnership practice is the engagement of children. The following study text should sensitize you to the importance of developing your capacity to actively involve children in any assessment affecting them.

Study Text 7.2: Children's Participation

POLICY CONTEXT OF CHILDREN'S PARTICIPATION

We have seen in Unit 1 some of the cultural presumptions that get in the way of children's participation in critical decision-making processes affecting their lives. What progress has been made towards the democratization of family life and how far children have achieved any substantial political emancipation are topics too large for us to pursue here. What is clear, however, is that, for at least a generation, there has been a significant public policy interest in the question of children's participation. The Children Act 1989, for example, reflecting the United Nations Convention on the Rights of the Child, confers specific obligations on courts and local authorities to elicit the views of children and young people in certain circumstances (see Study Texts 1.3 and 5.3). Early Guidance to the Children Act made the point very clearly that (Department of Health 1990, p.12):

> Young people's wishes must be elicited and taken seriously. Even quite young children should be enabled to contribute to decisions about their lives in an age appropriate way. Learning to make a well informed choice is an important aspect of growing up…

More recently, the rationale for children's participation has been expressed using the rhetoric of 'modernized' public services, citizenship and social inclusion rather than the rhetoric of personal/psychological development. For example, the Children and Young People's Unit (see web resources at the end of this Unit) at the Department for Education and Skills has produced a set of 'core principles for the involvement of children and young people' (DfEE 2001, p.6). These principles are intended to help government achieve its aims of:

- *Better services.* It is accepted that the effectiveness of services depends on listening and responding to customers. Giving children and young people an active say in how policies and services are developed, provided, evalued [sic] and improved should ensure that policies and services more genuinely meet their needs.

- *Promoting citizenship and social inclusion.* Promoting early engagement in public and community life is crucial to sustaining and building a healthy society...

- *Personal and social education and development.* Good participation opportunities produce more confident and resilient young people...

It is interesting to note how expressions of public policy in respect of children's participation draw on both 'needs-talk' and 'rights-talk' (see Study Text 1.2) for its justification. However it is accounted for, many of the public policy documents that we have introduced to you so far are permeated by participation-speak; for example, Objective 8 of the *Government's Objectives for Children's Social Services* (Department of Health 1999); Standard 8 of the NMS for Children's Homes (Department of Health 2002a); there is also a 'Quality Protects' project team working on Children's Participation.

PARTICIPATION IN PRACTICE

Perhaps not surprisingly, at a practice level, progress toward children's participation in decision-making has been less consistent than the expressed intentions of policy makers might indicate. Some of the difficulties are inherent in the complex situations in which children's voices are only one of many to be heard. As Eileen Munro has very tellingly put it (2001, p.136), 'Essentially, adding another voice to the decision making process adds another potential dissident'. Her research on 'empowering looked after children', while providing further evidence of children's capacity and their willingness to participate sensibly in decision-making, recognizes the complex backdrop of sometimes competing interests (parents, care staff, social worker, 'management interests' etc.) against which children's participation has to be set. (Incidentally, Munro also warns against the dangers of 'standardization' in child care practice that militates against individualized decision-making and limits children's opportunities to learn the skills of effective participation.) Thomas and O'Kane's work (1999) on 'children's participation in reviews' makes many similar points and notes also how the dynamics of 'needs and rights' can create additional tensions for workers (1999, p.229):

> There can be a tension in work to involve vulnerable children in difficult or complex decisions, between an approach based on sensitive casework and the building of relationships of trust and one based on children knowing their rights and being encouraged to use them. In our view, there is no fundamental contradiction between the two. On the contrary, a combination of both approaches is needed if we are to empower children...

Aldgate and Statham too have concluded from their review of several studies that considered the question of children's participation (2001, p.86) that:

> There are inherent tensions and dilemmas in giving due consideration to children's views and acting upon them when, in the judgement of the adults, the children's wishes and feelings may not be compatible with their welfare. The matter of listening to children's views and taking them seriously has to be set within the context of safeguarding them.

We have taken a slightly different view elsewhere (Butler and Williamson 1994). Here we expressed the view that without children's participation, there can be no realistic prospect of safeguarding them. We contrasted the way children and adults in our study used the word 'safe'; children used it as a term of approval and respect – someone who was 'safe' was someone in whom a child had confidence, who would take him or her seriously and listen to what the child had to say. Adults tended to use the word 'safe' in the way that Aldgate and Statham appear to be using it – to mean 'protected', by adults. We noted then (p.144):

> The former [sense of the word] demands flexible, sensitive interventions... These will require adults to respect and keep the confidence and confidentiality of children and young people to a far greater extent than they are used to doing; it will require adults to countenance much more self determination by children and young people which may be experienced as taking even greater risks; it will require greater trust and faith than either party would currently seem to have in and for the other. The latter form of intervention calls for rigid procedures imposed from above in response to political and professional imperatives, where it is the adult who feels safe from the uncertainties of an uncertain world and the hostility of an unforgiving public and press. The latter may satisfy the 'social conscience' but only the former can enable children and young people to equip themselves with the resources to deal with the social realities they currently encounter or expect to encounter in the future.

The most enduring lesson that the various child care scandals of the last 30 years have taught us (see Butler and Drakeford 2003) is the most obvious one, namely that there can be no guarantee that either parents or professional carers will always act in ways that are compatible with children's interests. We believe that the best safeguard available to children lies with them and in their fundamental right to speak, be heard and to have their views respected. In taking this position, we do not seek to privilege children's accounts. We do not see why either parents' or children's or workers' interests should predominate. But we do want to argue strongly that children's accounts should be rendered on the same terms as adults; and weighed equally in the balance in finding the best means of ensuring a child's safety and promoting his or her welfare.

Where we would unreservedly agree with Aldgate and Statham is in their call for greater clarity in the minds of social workers about what they understand by children's participation, a more clearly differentiated response by workers to reflect children's own volition and a far greater respect for children's competence and capacity to act.

TOWARDS PARTICIPATION

There seems to be a ready consensus on what it is that children value in their social workers and what is likely to be the basis for a relationship in which the child will be an active and constructive participant (see Figure 7.5).

Children value social workers who:

- *Listen* – carefully and without trivializing or being dismissive of the issues raised

- are *available and accessible* – maintaining regular and predictable contact

- are *non-judgemental and non-directive* – accepting, explaining and suggesting options and choices

- have a sense of *humour* – it helps build a rapport

- are *straight talking* – with realism and reliability; no 'false promises'

- can be *trusted* – maintain *confidentiality* and consult with children before taking matters forward.

Figure 7.5 The complete social worker
Source: Department of Health and others (2000, p.46) (Crown copyright).

Such a relationship can be expressed very directly in practice. Shemmings and Shemmings (2001) provide some very practical advice on how to promote participation by children and other family members (p.125ff):

- be clear right from the start what your role is

- don't wait to be asked for information

- show families what you are recording about them

- invite them to meetings and prepare them properly

- use 'check-lists' as part of a 'guided conversation' (not bureaucratically)

- continue to acquire more knowledge about the impact of culture, gender, sexuality and poverty in the lives of families

- communicate in straightforward, jargon-free language
- share your thinking
- 'deal with others as you would be dealt by'
- be prepared (and equipped with suitable 'play materials') for children who wish to use different forms of communication
- be prepared to work with someone advocating on behalf of a child.

Engaging a child's participation, just like the wider assessment itself, is a process to be entered into and worked on by both parties. It cannot be assumed or be guaranteed and it needs to be able to develop at an appropriate pace. Bannister (2001) identifies four distinct phases. First, there is the need to build rapport. Then there is the matter of 'creating a safe space', which involves an active consideration of where work with the child will be carried out. In our practice, we are frequently disappointed by the number of social workers who believe that they have an automatic right of entry into a child's bedroom or who think that a High Street burger bar is a suitable place to discuss matters of extreme intimacy or importance to a child. Creating a 'safe space' is more than a matter of geography, however. It involves the patient building of an honest relationship with a child in which the boundaries are acknowledged and where the social worker demonstrates the qualities that we referred to in Figure 7.5.

The third phase Bannister describes (p.136) as 'reassuring, clarifying and moving on'. The final stage, 'therapeutic containment', involves the measured and reassuring 'closing down' of the process and facilitating the child's return to 'his or her usual ways of coping' (p.137). We are often saddened by the peremptory way in which some social workers, once they have taken what they want from an assessment (usually in the form of 'information' for a 'report'), simply break off contact. If this were only discourteous and disrespectful it would be bad enough, but it is worse than that; it presents to the child yet another adult who cannot be reliably trusted and who has not dealt honestly with them. We think this is unforgivable in a social worker.

CHILD CENTRED OR 'PIGGY IN THE MIDDLE'?

We suggested to you in Unit 1 that the way in which you personally understand (or 'construct') childhood will have a direct bearing on your practice with children and young people. You may be more or less inclined to see children in deficit terms or to focus on their strengths and capacities, for example. You will recall also that, as well as being expressed in a variety of important policy documents (see Study Text 7.2, above), the *Framework for the Assessment of Children in Need* unambiguously places the child at the centre of the process of assessment, both figuratively and conceptually (Department of Health and others 2000, p.10):

> Fundamental to establishing whether a child is in need and how those needs should be best met is that the approach must be child centred. This means that the child is kept in focus throughout the assessment and that account is always taken of the child's perspective.

Shortly, we will be asking you to think through an assessment of the Taylor family and the problems they are experiencing. In order that you attempt that exercise taking a child-centred approach, it might be helpful to consider what barriers there might be to keeping the children 'in focus throughout the assessment'. They may perhaps be more subtle than you think. We have written elsewhere (Butler 1996b) of how child care professionals can easily lose sight of the object of their attentions, even when it is right in front of them. For example, while attending a conference on substitute family care, we were once presented in a workshop with what we judged to be abusive forms of practice. The presenters clearly thought otherwise. In the name of a variety of perfectly well articulated and plausible therapeutic imperatives, children and young people were subjected to sustained and intensive emotional working over, on videotape. Children as young as three or four were left in great sobbing heaps in the middle of a large sofa or on a rug in a vast office as their therapist's off-screen voice intoned at them to 'really get in touch with their pain' or to 'face the reality of their situation'. The distress of the children did not register either with their therapist or with most of the participants at the workshop. Therapist knew best. There were few objections raised by the audience either to the exploitation of these children for the purposes of the conference or to the interventions being demonstrated. Such objectors as there were received very short shrift and were accused of being too emotionally involved with the case material – note 'case material', not children. The 'case material' would achieve the 'proper outcome' in due course. All means, to the zealot, it would seem, justify the ends.

Much more common, is the situation where a child is 'engaged' in an assessment in so far as he or she is required for forensic or evidential purposes or simply for administrative convenience to play a part in the process. The aims and outcomes of the process are quite separate from the needs and wishes of the child, but the child's involvement is required in order to facilitate the process. This often results in the child being not so much in the centre of activity but, rather, caught between those activities in which the adults are engaged, a kind of 'piggy in the middle'.

The following exercise is intended to help you explore what might get in the way of keeping the child at the centre of your work.

Exercise 7.2: Barriers to Maintaining a Child-Centred Approach to Assessment

Using the example of Alison Taylor, answer the following questions:

1. What is there about Alison and her situation that may prevent you from keeping her at the centre of your work?

2. What is there about the other members of her family that may prevent you from retaining a focus on Alison?

3. What is there about you and your attitudes, values and habits of thought that might prevent you from taking account of 'the child's perspective'?

Points to Consider

1. Do you think that (most?) children will expect to be considered as central to the process of assessment? Why might this be and what effect might this have on the process of assessment?

2. Do you think that (most?) children's parents and carers will expect the 'child's perspective' to be given very much weight?

3. Do you think that children are genuinely able to contribute to the adults' understanding of family disputes or problems?

4. What skills might be required to engage children in the process of assessment? Do you feel that you have such skills?

5. What limitations would be imposed on an assessment if the children's experiences, views and opinions were not paid sufficient attention? Do you see any risks to the child in such a situation?

6. What are the risks in adopting a child-centred approach? What might happen to the legitimate interests of other family members or to the proper concerns and statutory obligations on the worker?

BEGINNING THE ASSESSMENT

The Guidance to the *Framework for the Assessment of Children in Need*, reflecting the requirements of Objective 7 of *The Government's Objectives for Children's Social Services* (Department of Health 1999), distinguishes between two levels of assessment and sets appropriate timescales for both.

The expectation is that within one working day of a referral or of new information coming to light in relation to an existing case, the agency (usually the local authority social services department) will make a clear decision as to what it will do next. If the agency decides to gather more information, this constitutes an *initial assessment*. This is defined as 'a brief assessment of each child referred to social services with a request for services to be provided' (Department of Health and others 2000, p.31). Such an initial assessment should be completed within a maximum of seven working days and must address all of the dimensions of the *Framework for the Assessment of Children in Need*. The initial assessment will have regard to determining whether the child concerned is a child in need and what responses or services, if any, are required. The family must be informed of the conclusions of the assessment and, if a child is a child in need, of the plan for providing services.

If, after (or during the course of) the initial assessment, it becomes clear that the situation of the child is more complex and that a further, more detailed assessment is required, then a *core assessment* may be begun. A core assessment is defined as 'an in-depth assessment which addresses the central or most important aspects of the needs of a child and the capacity of his or her parents or caregivers to respond appropriately to those needs within the wider family and community context' (Department of Health and others 2000, p.32). A core assessment should be completed within 35 working days.

You should note that should a child protection concern arise at any point, subject to the additional procedures that apply in such circumstances concerning the convening of a strategy meeting and the consideration of any inter-agency action (these are explained in Study Text 9.3), the necessary assessment will take place (or continue, as the case may be) using the *Framework for the Assessment of Children in Need* although the pace and scope of the assessment may well change.

Bearing these timescales in mind and remembering what you have learned from Exercise 7.2, the following exercise is designed to encourage you to think through what is involved in undertaking an initial assessment, using the *Framework for the Assessment of Children in Need*.

Exercise 7.3: An Initial Assessment

A senior colleague of yours has reviewed the notes on the Taylor family made by the duty social worker and has determined that an initial assessment of the family should be made. This task has been allocated to you.

TASKS

1. Drawing on the Taylor Case File and the information you reviewed in Exercise 7.1, make notes under each of the headings ('dimensions of assessment') of the *Framework for the Assessment of Children in Need*, setting out what you 'know', what you will need to verify and what gaps there are to be filled in your knowledge of this family.

2. Using these notes, decide what topics, themes or issues you will want to explore with the Taylor family at your first meeting with them. (Of course, in a 'real situation', you would want to reserve some space to ensure that the family's priorities are also properly explored.)

3. For at least two of the topic areas you have prioritized, write down what questions you will need to ask, of whom, when and where, to inform your assessment. Make a list also of what other information-gathering techniques (other than asking questions) might be helpful in relation to the particular areas that you have chosen.

4. For one of the topic areas you have prioritized, give examples of the kinds of responses that might cause you concern.

Points to Consider

1. How well did you keep the children as the centre of your focus during this exercise?

2. Are you able to justify asking for all of the information that you intend to gather?

3. How would you explain to Tracy why you were asking for the information that you are seeking?

4. How would you explain to the children why you were asking for the information you are seeking?

5. How might you interpret a refusal to provide information?

6. How well able are you to articulate the standards against which you will be judging the information you gather?

 ## CONCLUSION

We have only hinted at the practicalities of undertaking an assessment and said even less of the agency context in which it will take place. Our intention has been to encourage and enable you to reflect upon the process of assessment and to recognize that it is a negotiated one. There are many different routes to 'make sense of what has happened and of what is happening now', some more formal and codified than others. Assessment is the foundation for planning and so for direct work, but it is an interpretative process throughout. Assessment is a complex and demanding task that should never be reduced to routine, certainly not to an exercise in form-filling. It needs thoughtful preparation and creativity in your approach to practice.

One of the real rewards of social work is encountering the real-life histories of the real live people you will work with. Each and every one of the complex biographies through which you pass should be treated with respect and your attempts to make sense of them for the purposes of your work should be approached with some humility.

NOTES AND SELF-ASSESSMENT

1.   How would you explain to a ten-year-old what you mean by 'assessment'?

2.   How comfortable are you articulating the theories that inform your work?

3.   Who should 'own' the assessment?

4.   How easy to assess are you?

5.   How would you feel about being assessed by a social worker? Write down why you feel as you do.

6.   What aspects of your own life or personal history would you find most difficult to introduce into an assessment being made of you?

RECOMMENDED READING

Seden, J., Sinclair, R., Robbins, D. and Pont, C. (2001) *Studies Informing the Framework for the Assessment of Children in Need and their Families.* London: The Stationery Office.

Butler, I. and Williamson, H. (1994) *Children Speak: Children, Trauma and Social Work.* London: Longman.

TRAINER'S NOTES

Exercise 7.1: Getting to Know You

Task 1 is best done individually as each member of the group will need a thorough knowledge of the 'file' for subsequent work. Tasks 2, 3, and 4 are best distributed amongst the group – the resulting material can then be shared with other group members and retained for use in later sessions. This works well if the material is prepared using flip chart paper. The 'twenty questions' can be used to test the group's knowledge of the case after a simple reading of the file (i.e. before attempting any of the tasks) and then again after the tasks have been completed. This is usually a powerful demonstration of how much information can be gleaned from only a few pages after a little less than an hour's work. We have deliberately not supplied any answers to the questions as we do not want anyone (including the trainer) to take a short cut to a working knowledge of the case.

Ignoring information gaps, forming impressions based on personal prejudices or over-emphasis on weaknesses and the priorities of the worker are common faults amongst newly qualified workers and group members should be encouraged to illustrate the discussion with material drawn from their own experience.

Exercise 7.2: Barriers to Maintaining a Child-Centred Approach to Assessment

Each of the three tasks can be split between three small groups as the basis for a whole group discussion later. Alternatively, each task can be allocated to three small groups as the basis for a role-play with the 'scripts' for a first meeting between the 'social worker', 'Alison' and 'Tracy' (or another family member) being developed by each small group. The role-play should be observed by the whole group and would form the starting point for the subsequent discussion. The role-play can be modified as it progresses by the introduction of certain rules that 'disadvantage' each of the players. We suggest, for example, not allowing 'Alison' to speak for two minutes; having 'Tracy' answer every question put to 'Alison' ('Alison' can then answer for herself); having the 'social worker' repeatedly interrupt 'Tracy' to ask 'Alison' what she thinks. We are sure you can think of variations of your own. The idea is to prevent those playing the parts of 'Alison' and 'Tracy' from acting too quickly like social workers!

Exercise 7.3: An Initial Assessment

This exercise is intended as a summarizing or reinforcing exercise. It can be used most effectively to integrate practice and classroom study if, instead of preparing an assessment using the Taylor case, a real case from group members' own experience or current practice is used. This can be combined with a skills rehearsal exercise around the presentation of formal assessments. Instructions can be given as follows:

> This exercise is intended to provide opportunities for you to share your practice experience with your colleagues and to benefit from the practice experience of others; to encourage you to reflect on the relevant skills that you possess or need to develop; to provide you with an opportunity to rehearse your skills in communicating your assessments to others.
>
> For the (next) session prepare a five-minute presentation (no more and no less) of a case or incident of which you have direct knowledge that has involved you in the process of assessment of a particular child or family situation.
>
> Structure your presentation as follows:
>
> 1.   Describe the particular situation and circumstances that gave rise to the assessment that you made and some indication of what conclusions you have or are beginning to form about the child/situation.
>
> 2.   *Either* identify the skills that you used in making the assessment *or* describe any particular technique(s) that you used that might be of interest to your colleagues.
>
> 3.   Identify what this piece of work has taught you about assessment that you would want to pass on to others.

WEB RESOURCES

http://www.cypu.gov.uk The Children and Young People's Unit (CYPU). The CYPU describes its function as follows:

> [The] Social Exclusion Unit…looked at how we could encourage young people to be more involved with some of the decisions (policies) affecting them. Government is keen to make sure that all these policies are easy to find out about and that all departments involved with young people talk to each other regularly. This ensures that each Government Department does the right thing, at the right time and is able to find out from young people themselves, how things are going.

The website contains information on what initiatives government departments are pursuing to achieve these aims as well as some useful links.

The full text of many of the key documents associated with the *Framework for Assessment* are available on-line. Most can be reached via the 'Quality Protects' website page for the project team working on Assessment and Recording (**http://www.doh.gov.uk/qualityprotects/work_pro/project_3.htm**). The full text of the *Framework* can be downloaded from the Department of Health website at **http://www.doh.gov.uk/scg/cin.htm**

In developing your knowledge base to assist you in the complex task of making assessments, as well as following up the references in this book (!), you will also need to keep abreast of the most recent research in the field. Much of this is first published in the professional and academic journals. Your library will take a number of these and you should go and explore its catalogue. Many journals now have a web presence and most offer on-line access, including the facility to download articles (to subscribers), as well as e-mail postings of forthcoming 'tables of contents'. You should at least visit the following:

The British Journal of Social Work **http://www.bjsw.oupjournals.org**

Child and Family Social Work **http://www.blackwellpublishing.com**

Children and Society **http://www3.interscience.wiley.com**

Journal of Child Health Care **http://www.sagepub.co.uk**

Journal of Early Childhood Research **http://www.sagepub.co.uk**

Child Abuse and Neglect **http://www.authors.elsevier.com**

Child Abuse Review **http://www3.interscience.wiley.comcgi-bin/jhome/5060**

UNIT 8

Planning

OBJECTIVES

In this unit you will:

- Consider the relationship between assessment and planning.
- Learn about the process of goal-setting.
- Learn about the statutory basis for planning in child care.
- Explore the use of written agreements in child care.

 WONDERLAND

Even if you don't know the story of *Alice in Wonderland*, you may have heard of the Cheshire Cat. Alice is lost in a wood and is anxious to find her way out. She sees the Cheshire Cat sitting in a tree and decides to ask his advice. She asks him which way she ought to go. He replies that it rather depends on where exactly she wants to get to. Alice says that she doesn't much mind where that is, at which point the Cat interrupts and tells her that it doesn't matter which path she takes then. Alice completes her question: '...so long as I get somewhere'. 'Oh you are sure to do that', replies the Cheshire Cat, 'if you only walk long enough.'

Alice's uncertainty about where she is now, her sense of urgency to get 'somewhere' and her apparent unconcern for just where that 'somewhere' turns out to be are familiar feelings for many social work practitioners.

What Alice needs is a plan! Not just a two-dimensional map of Wonderland, although with that she could at least work out which paths lead
where, and she would know a little better where she had been and what
might be waiting around the next corner. Her progress through Wonderland would, at least from that point on, be a more rational and predictable
one.

A simple map wouldn't help her decide her destination, however, and
it wouldn't necessarily tell her whom she would meet on the way or of any
new short cuts or hold-ups; for that she would need to use knowledge
drawn from her experience in the wood, and elsewhere, and be certain of
her purpose. She would need to make a series of decisions that would take
her further towards where she wanted to be – she would have to engage in
a process of rational and purposive decision-making to really make
progress through the wood. It is this process of rational, purposive
decision-making, or planning, that is the subject of this Unit.

To give a more practical illustration, consider the point at which the
previous Unit on assessment ended. Once you had decided your priorities
and approach, especially to seeing and talking to the children (see Exercise
7.3), you would then have to think about the actual process of carrying out
the assessment. There are a number of questions you would need to
consider at this point: Whom are you going to consult? Whom will you
want to speak to in person? In what order will you see people? Where will
you meet them? Who will you see together and who separately? What
would be a good time to see the children? After school? What if that conflicts with meal times? And so on.

You could simply answer each question as it arose and proceed on that
basis. You may even be able to complete an assessment in this way. People
do. There is considerable evidence (Department of Health and Social
Security 1985; Department of Health 1991d) to suggest that a great deal
of child care social work has taken place in the recent past in a planning
vacuum. In relation to looked after children, research would suggest that,
while local authorities are increasingly taking care planning seriously (see
Grimshaw and Sinclair 1997), 'effective care planning remains one of the
most significant challenges facing Social Services' (Aldgate and Statham
2001, p.123).

Alternatively, you could organize, prioritize, take positive decisions
about what you will do and *plan* the assessment. If assessment is about

'making sense of what has happened and what is happening now', planning is about making sense of what will happen next. Like assessment, though, planning is a continuous process in need of constant review and updating and one which overlaps with other phases in the social work process. But, accepting that planning cannot be easily divorced from other elements in the social work process, what can we say about beginning to plan and how that relates to assessment?

Planning begins with the identification of the planning required, with the question 'planning for what?' – the answer to which can only derive from the nature of the assessment that is underway. Usually, during the assessment stage, some preliminary decisions must be taken about the immediate future and about the expected direction of events later on. Indeed, in an emergency, decisions often have to be made and action taken before the situation can be even partially assessed. But, these kind of situational responses are not plans in the sense in which we intend; this would imply that planning is far too reactive a process. Planning is itself a form of causality, it is about *making* things happen rather than simply responding to events as they occur. So, while planning is inextricably bound up with the assessment phase (assessments need to planned too), it is not coterminous with it. While the assessment phase may well be ongoing and may well be revisited and revised during the course of the social work involvement, there is a very general sense in which it is concerned with what has happened or is happening now. Planning is about what happens next – understood in the instrumental sense of what is intended *should* happen next. Understood in this way, planning rests upon decision-making directed towards a desired end or goal.

Volume 4 of the Guidance and Regulations that accompanied the Children Act 1989 developed this point and has described planning as involving (Department of Health 1991e, para. 2.60):

- translating the assessed needs into goals and objectives

- listing and appraising the specific options available (or which may need to be created) for achieving these objectives

- deciding on the preferred option, setting out the reasons for the decision.

The core social work process of goal-setting is the subject of Study Text 8.1.

Care planning has not received quite the same degree of attention as has assessment in the various key documents that have come to shape social work with children and families since the publication of *The Government's Objectives for Children's Social Services* (Department of Health 1999). Objective 8 does address the question of planning but, essentially, in pursuit of the broader aim of securing participation:

> To actively involve users and carers in planning services and in tailoring individual packages of care…

Standard 2 of the *NMS for Children's Homes* (Department of Health 2002a) requires a 'placement plan' for each child, 'consistent with any plan for the care of the child prepared by the placing authority'. But the NMS adds, 'where other plans cover the above, the placement plan may simply refer to existing documents without any need for duplication' which, while perfectly reasonable at one level, may be thought to weaken the force of the standard. *The NMS for Fostering Services* (Department of Health 2002c) at several points (e.g. Standard 8, 'Matching'; Standard 10, 'Promoting Contact' and Standard 14, 'Preparing for Adulthood') are predicated on the existence of a care plan but planning itself is not the subject of a particular standard. (See Study Text 8.2, below, for further details of the 'placement plan'.)

As we shall see shortly (Study Text 8.2), however, the framework for planning introduced by the Children Act 1989 has itself been modified to accommodate practice and policy changes that have taken place since the publication of the earliest Guidance that accompanied the Act. Where this has been significantly extended is in relation to planning with young people leaving care as a result of the introduction of the Children (Leaving Care) Act 2000 (see below).

In policy terms, greater emphasis has been given to planning at the level of service provision to ensure a greater diversity of placement choice, the better to meet the needs of children looked after. We do not intend to pursue this important topic here but we would recommend that you visit the website for 'Choice Protects', the government's review of fostering and placement services, and to examine the work of the 'Quality Protects Placement Choice Project Team'. Both can be accessed via the web resources given at the end of this Unit.

At the heart of the planning process, as we have described it, is the question of goal-setting and it is to this that we now turn.

Study Text 8.1: Goal-Setting

What do we mean when we use the term 'goal'? Amongst the definitions offered by the *Shorter Oxford Dictionary*, two seem particularly apt for our purposes: 'Goal: the object of effort or ambition, or the destination of a (difficult) journey'.

In a social work context, Hepworth and Larsen (1982) note that goals serve the following valuable functions in the helping process:

- Goals provide direction and continuity to the helping process and prevent needless wandering.
- Goals facilitate the development and selection of appropriate strategies and interventions.
- Goals assist practitioners and clients in monitoring their progress.
- Goals serve as outcome criteria in evaluating the effectiveness of specific interventions and the helping process.

Moreover, it is suggested that the process of goal-setting with service users contributes substantially to the effectiveness of the helping process itself. Goal-setting is motivational. Knowing that there is at least the possibility of arriving somewhere beyond the circumstances that bring you together can often bring a renewed sense of optimism and confidence for both service user and worker.

What kind of appropriate 'destinations' might be defined as goals? Goals are not to be expressed in global terms. They cannot be generalized to the level of life, the universe and everything. To be useful, goals must remain specific to the current person/situational circumstances. Hence, statements such as 'to make X better', 'happier' or 'better able to cope' are not goals so much as pious intentions. Goals must reflect the nature of the issues that originated the social work contact in the first place; for example, 'to improve the quality of parenting', 'to increase participation in social groups', 'to improve verbal communication' or 'to relate more comfortably with the opposite sex'. In this way, goal statements, although somewhat abstract, are still rooted in the circumstances (person/situation dynamic) that bring the social worker and the service user together. Goals expressed at this level of generality should be distinguished from objectives or aims, which Anderson (1984) describes as 'statements of intended accomplishments that are specific, attainable, appropriate and measurable' (p.488). In other words, objectives are the steps we take along the path to reaching our goals.

A well-constructed objective statement will answer the five key questions of who, what, to what extent, when and where:

- *Who?* The objective statement is often made with reference to the service user. This does not necessarily imply that the identified service user is the only object of any objective statement. For example, if the social worker is engaged with a family, it is important to specify whether the objective is to be attained by all family members, specific family members or by others altogether, including representatives of outside agencies.

- *What?* The task here is to formulate statements that are specific to the desired outcome. For example, such a statement as 'To get Chris to attend school' is inadequate. Does that mean just once more or every day for the next two terms? Without this degree of specificity, how can one begin to evaluate progress? To blur this distinction between specific outcomes and more generalized statements of intent can be very tempting. To promise a court 'To get Chris to attend school' leaves plenty of room for negotiation if at any point you have to report back. It also lets you off the hook in other ways in that lack of specificity allows you to set, in effect, very low-level objectives. Getting Chris to attend school once in the next two years may satisfy your objective statement but it does little for Chris's educational development.

- *To what extent?* Answers to this question do not have to be set only in positivistic, numerical terms. Other formulations are possible: for example, 'to stop sniffing solvents on my own' describes a specific context rather than any quantitative element. Nevertheless, whether expressed in qualitative or quantitative terms or any combination of them, the message is one of specificity.

- *When?* This question addresses when the expected outcome is going to occur. The period will need to be realistic in order to achieve a balance between motivation and setting a course for inevitable and avoidable 'failure' judged by not meeting arbitrary deadlines.

- *Where?* Often, problematic behaviours occur in specific settings or at specified times during the day. Answering this question of the objective statement tells everyone where to look for the expected outcome.

It should be noted that despite the apparent deterministic approach reflected in the above, the goal-setting process is a mutual one. Just as with assessment, goal-setting is not something done to clients by social workers (a particular way of ensuring the mutuality of the goal-setting process is the subject of Study Text 8.3). However, in order for you to practise what is involved in the goal-setting phase of the planning process, we want to return to the Taylor family, to catch up on events and to begin the process of planning with them.

 Exercise 8.1: Goal-Setting

First, read the next instalment of the developing case of the Taylors and then attempt the tasks that follow.

It is now just over a week since Tracy Taylor called into the office. You have been able to make just a brief introductory visit to the family since receiving the referral. This means that, unfortunately, you have not been able to really get going with your assessment. Indeed, you have been overtaken by events once more, as the following case notes reveal:

TAYLOR FAMILY CASE FILE

The weekend following your last visit, Ron came down to collect Alison and Michael. Alison refused to go. There was a very heated discussion on the doorstep, which ended in a fight between Alun and Ron. Ron eventually left without the children, who had witnessed the fight and who were very distressed. On the Sunday, Alun and Tracy also came to blows over the situation and Tracy left with the three children and went to stay with her mother. You have visited Mrs Taylor's (senior) house and spoken to Tracy and the children.

Tracy is adamant that she will not go home to Alun and does not want to try and remove him from the family home at this point. The tenancy is in his name. Unfortunately, she is aware also that she cannot stay where she is indefinitely as the children are already getting on their grandmother's nerves and the tension is beginning to mount. Tracy feels that she could manage John but cannot cope with Alison and Michael, who have not stopped quarrelling since they arrived at Tracy's mother's house. Michael blames Alison for what has happened and is being very loud and aggressive. Alison is being very sullen and keeps bursting into tears.

You have already phoned Ron but he has made it clear that he cannot have Alison and Michael stay with him, except at weekends. Wayne has been poorly over recent weeks and his wife has been very upset at what happened over the weekend. His family have advised him to consult a solicitor to resume the formal care of the children but he is clearly reluctant to do so. He is prepared to talk about the children and does want to see that they are well looked after. At the moment, he cannot offer accommodation.

Tracy is asking that the older children 'get looked after by a foster family' for a while until things settle down. You have contacted the placement unit and they have told you that they do have two 'short-term beds' with the Williams family. The Williams, who run a small-holding, live about six miles out of Southtown. The only other option is to place the children in a residential unit, Brummell Drive. This is a small unit, due for closure shortly, that is more used to dealing with older children.

You have not had very much time to get to know the children. Michael appears to be very fond of his father and protective of both Alison and John. His relationship with his mother is being tested but you feel that there is a strong bond. He is probably appearing braver than he feels at the moment. You know that he is doing very well at school and is very keen on football and computer games.

Alison, although older than Michael, seems emotionally much less mature. She is very 'clingy' with mother and seems to think that dad is trying to break them up. She seems resentful of John. Both children speak very harshly of Alun, whom they are clearly in no hurry to see again.

John is very quiet for his age and seems to you to be developmentally delayed. He has very little language and is still in nappies. You have been meaning to have a word with the health visitor but have not been able to yet. You were beginning to be worried about him before this last episode occurred and recent events have not lessened your concern.

Mrs Taylor (senior) is blaming the whole world for what is happening and switches from being very aggressive towards you, Tracy and the children to being utterly indifferent. She leaves you in no doubt whatsoever that the children cannot stay with her. Tracy and her mother insist on foster care for the children. Tracy will not allow them to go to any of her brothers and sisters as 'most of them have got social workers already'. Mrs Taylor (senior) tells you bluntly 'I know what is right for my grandchildren and I know that you have to listen to what I say. I want them fostered for a week or two till we can get things sorted out.' In the circumstances, you are inclined to agree.

TASKS

1. Drawing on your answers to Exercise 7.3, but adding relevant information contained in these case notes, begin to plan for the immediate future of these children. You should assume that the children will need to be looked after by the local authority for at least a short period.

2. Identify clearly what it is you are planning for and prepare statements of the goals you intend your plans to achieve.

3. Identify the specific objectives that you intend to achieve on the way to the overall goals that you have determined.

    Points to Consider

1. Have you included goal statements in respect of where the children will live and who will parent them?

2. How well do you think your goals will meet the needs of the children?

3. How well do you think your goals will meet the wishes and feelings of the children?

4. How well do you think your goals will protect the rights of the children?

5. How well have you reflected the needs, wishes and feelings of all the adults involved in the goals you have chosen?

6. Are your statements of objectives 'specific, attainable, appropriate and measurable'?

THE CONTEXT OF PLANNING

Unlike in the fictional world through which Alice had to make her way, planning in social work takes place in an immensely complex and variable context in which a number of elements may have a bearing on both the planning process and its outcomes. For example, the 'culture' and structure of the agency in which you are working can have a direct bearing on how you approach planning generally. It can be very easy, as Menzies (1970) pointed out in relation to child protection, for example, for any group of professionals to develop relationships, systems of belief (or, more properly, 'systems of disbelief') or particular 'practice cultures' to serve as defences against the anxieties and stresses of the work. These systems of belief can include very firm ideas of 'how we do things here', which may be entirely unproductive as far as service users are concerned. The volume of work you are expected to deal with and the degree of professional support and supervision that you routinely receive are other examples of how agency context can determine your capacity to plan adequately.

Your capacity to plan is also clearly influenced by your own professional skill and knowledge. You cannot plan for what you do not know or, more positively, the more extensive your repertoire of interventive techniques, the more alternatives you might be able to build into your direct work. Of course, the resources at your disposal, including those provided by agencies other than your own, will influence your plans.

Certain planning goals can be subject to particular, or more general, disapproval, depending on the local or national political context in which you work. At times, alternatives to custody for juveniles, for example, have been broadly supported. At others, they have been reviled. The professional credibility of social work and social workers ebbs and flows and certain interventions or risk thresholds are supported at certain times, with certain user groups and in certain places, and at others they are not.

Your plans are made in the context of countless other plans made by other individuals and other organizations, including government. Indeed, one of the liveliest debates over recent years in social work with children and families has been over the way in which central government has become increasingly active in the 'politics of enforcement' and the drive to 'modernize, rationalize, managerialize and order' (Parton 2000, p.461). In part, this shift towards increased 'standardization' is associated with the rise of the 'evidence-based practice' (EBP) movement.

The immediate origins of EBP are usually traced (see Gibbs and Gambrill 2002) to the 'research–practice gap' in medicine; that is to say, to the realization in the United States that medical practitioners did not have access to research findings and consequently their formal knowledge base was commonly out of date and not easily remedied by programmes of continuing professional education. This could lead to the continuing use of interventions/treatments that, at best, had little or no demonstrated efficacy or, at worst, were positively harmful. Possibly the most widely quoted definition of EBP was derived in this context:

> Evidence based practice is the conscientious, explicit and judicious use of current best evidence in making decisions about the care of individual patients, based on skills which allow the doctors to evaluate both personal experience and external evidence in a systematic and objective manner. (Sackett and others 1997, p.2)

In the UK, the development of EBP in social work draws additionally on several different traditions, most notably on behavioural social work (see for example, MacDonald and Sheldon 1992; MacDonald 1994, 1998) and the empirical practice movement (Bloom 1993; Fischer 1993; Reid 1994; McGuire 1995). It has been modified and applied by the Centre for

Evidence-Based Social Care at Exeter University, with the main emphasis being upon seeking the practical goal of 'what works'. The core assumption, as Webb notes, is 'the idea that a formal rationality of practice based upon scientific methods can produce a more effective and economically accountable means of [delivering] social services' (2001, p.58).

Although both the rise of 'managerialism' and EBP are subjects too large to be adequately addressed here, it is important that you are aware that both are controversial. You can continue your own exploration of this important debate through the various professional and academic journals (see web resources at the end of this Unit). We would wish you to do so with perhaps a little more optimism than some (see, for example, Webb 2001; Butler and Pugh 2003). We do not believe that any of the elements that we have described as forming the context of planning are immune from the planning process or that your plans are necessarily entirely determined by external considerations. Even where social workers operate in accordance with 'strict' agency policies, variations do occur. You may think of social work agencies operating as strongly hierarchical organizations with line-management structures organized as a pyramid: the chief officer at the top and you somewhere near the bottom. Such structures are said to have more or less strongly centralized decision- and policy-making structures and procedures. However, as each agency is increasingly composed of professionally trained people who rely on personal judgements, in fact, real executive power and decision-making is dispersed amongst those operating at the 'front line'. Workers on the front line tend to be grouped in units, which are, in fact, dispersed more in the manner of spokes on a wheel rather than as the broad base of a pyramid.

In this way front-line units have considerable scope for recreating and redefining agency policy and practice by the way in which they decide to order priorities, initiate new work and set objectives in their day-to-day work with service users. Front-line units can acquire a high degree of autonomy, both from the centre and from each other – that is to say that, to some degree, the agency's policy is created from the countless small decisions that are taken at the front line rather than being something which is generated at the top and disseminated downwards through the agency. Differing professional thresholds of 'good enough parenting' amongst individual social workers, for example, may more strongly influence the rate at which children are looked after by the local authority than any chief-officer-led strategy to reduce admissions to residential care. In such organizations, the main problem of the organizational parent is one of control and it will usually seek to introduce a variety of regulatory and standardizing procedures (e.g. case conferences). But their effect can be overstated. It is these variations in the context of planning that, in part, account for the enormous variety in social work practice from agency to agency and across the country. It is for you to decide whether such variation is to be welcomed or managed out of the system.

There is one element of the context of planning, however, that has been established explicitly as a unifying set of principles and practices: namely the Children Act 1989. We have seen at several points in this book already how the Act frequently provides the immediate context for practice in this field. As well as the Act itself, the statutory Regulations and Guidance that accompany it can greatly influence the form and content of direct work. (See Footnote 3 in Unit 5 for a description of what is meant by 'Regulations' and 'Guidance'.) Without wishing to influence the plans you have begun to formulate for the Taylor family, we suggest that you may have recognized that you will shortly have to plan for the children being looked after by someone other than Tracy. The following study text is intended to locate your planning with the Taylor family in the context of Guidance and Regulations.

Note: Before you read the following study text you may wish to re-read Study Text 5.2, which deals with the general duties that a local authority has in relation to a child that it is, or is proposing to, look after.

Study Text 8.2: Planning for Children Looked After by the Local Authority

Remember that the full text of all of the Regulations (Statutory Instruments or SIs) can be accessed via the Stationery Office website – see Unit 1. You should note also that in the case of Wales, Northern Ireland and Scotland, separate legislative arrangements for the introduction of Regulations now exist. This often results in the production of separate SIs that, while broadly similar to those introduced for England, may apply differently in the different countries of the UK. Simply for reasons of space, this study text describes the law as it relates to England, except where stated.

THE ARRANGEMENTS FOR PLACEMENT OF CHILDREN (GENERAL) REGULATIONS 1991[1]

These Regulations require the agency proposing to place a child (the 'responsible authority') to make 'immediate and long-term arrangements' ('plans') for the placement and for 'promoting the welfare of the child who is to be placed' (Regulation 3 (1)). This should be done before the placement or as soon as practicable thereafter. The Guidance makes it clear that 'planning is required from the earliest possible time after recognition of need or referral' (Department of Health 1991a, 1991e, para. 2.9). Guidance further notes that planning will achieve its purpose of safeguarding and promoting the child's welfare in so far as 'the drawing up of an individual plan for each child looked after will prevent drift and help to focus work with the family and child' (Department of Health 1991a, 1991e, para. 2.20).

Plans are to be recorded in writing (Regulation 3(5)) and notification made to those with whom the authority consulted before making the placement under s. 22 (4) of the Act. In addition, the relevant health authority, the local education authority and the child's general practitioner (GP) (amongst others – see Regulation 5 (1)) should be notified. Schedule 1 of the Regulations lists matters to be considered by the responsible authority when drawing up its plans. These include:

- the discharge of any existing care order or other change in a child's legal status

- arrangements for contact

- the authority's longer-term plans for the child, which should include a consideration of alternative courses of action and preparation for when the child will no longer be looked after by the authority, and whether plans need to be made to find a permanent substitute family for the child

---

1   SI 1991/890 (as amended SI 1991/2033; 1993/3069; 1995/2015; 1997/649; 2002/546).

- whether an independent visitor should be appointed for the child.

Remember, however, that these considerations are not intended to be exclusive and do not repeat matters already covered in the Act and noted above.

The Regulations also require the authority to arrange for a health assessment (Regulation 7). See Study Text 5.3 for details of what is to be included in a health assessment. In relation to the child's education, the authority must have regard to achieving continuity and identifying and acting upon any educational need that the child may have (again, see Study Text 5.3 for further details).

Additionally, Schedule 4 of the Regulations makes specific provisions for children who are to be accommodated but who are not in care. The Schedule requires a statement of 'any services to be provided for the child' (Sch. 4, para. 1). It also requires clarification of the respective roles of the authority, the child's parents and those with parental responsibility – particularly in relation to any delegation of parental responsibility (Sch. 4, para. 4), decision-making (Sch. 4, para. 5) and contact (Sch. 4, para. 6). The Schedule also requires that the parties consider

> the expected duration of arrangements and the steps which should apply to bring the arrangements to an end, including arrangements for the rehabilitation of the child with the person with whom he was living before the voluntary arrangements were made... (Sch. 4, para. 9)

THE REVIEW OF CHILDREN'S CASES REGULATIONS 1991[2]

These Regulations establish the timing, form and core content of the review of looked after children's cases.

An initial review must take place within four weeks of a child beginning to be looked after by a responsible authority (Regulation 3 (1)). The second review should then be carried out no later than three months after the first, with subsequent reviews carried out at six-monthly intervals

---

2   SI 1991/895 (as amended SI 1991/2033; 1993/3069; 1995/ 2015; 1997/649; 2002/546).

(Regulation 3 (2)). Responsible authorities are required to set out in writing how reviews are to be carried out and to inform the child, his or her parents and anyone else with parental responsibility or who has a relevant interest in the review of the procedures (Regulations 4 and 7). Where 'reasonably practical', the authority should consult and involve in the review those whom it has a duty to inform, including inviting the attendance of 'persons in relation to any particular matter which is to be considered in the course of the review' (Regulation 7 (2)). Guidance makes it clear that 'only in exceptional cases should a parent or child not be invited to a review meeting' (Department of Health 1991a, paras 8 and 10; see also Department of Health 1991e, para. 3.10).

In the review, the responsible authority has to consider all of those matters set out in Schedules 1 and 2 of the Arrangements for the Placement of Children's (General) Regulations (repeated in Schedules 2 and 3 of these Regulations) concerning the child's general and health needs and consider the child's 'educational needs, progress and development' and any special educational needs (Sch. 1, paras 7 and 4). SI 2002/546 has amended the original Regulations to increase the frequency of health reviews for children aged under five to every six months and every 12 months after they have attained the age of five. It should be noted (as per SI 2002/546) that health assessments on placement or review may, but need not necessarily, include a physical examination of the child and that review assessments may be conducted by a registered nurse (or midwife), under the supervision of a GP.

SOCIAL CARE, ENGLAND. CHILDREN AND YOUNG PERSONS, ENGLAND. THE FOSTERING SERVICES REGULATIONS 2002[3]

Although they are largely concerned with the regulation of fostering services provided either by the local authority or by a voluntary or independent provider, the approval of foster carers and the supervision of placements, which are beyond our immediate concern in this Unit, there are certain elements of these Regulations that may have a bearing on planning for the Taylor children.

3   SI 2002/57.

Regulation 33 prevents the placement of a child in a foster home unless the responsible authority is satisfied that this is 'the most suitable way' of performing their duty to safeguard and promote his or her welfare and that 'placement with the particular foster parent is the most suitable placement having regard to all the circumstances'.

Placements cannot be made (except in an emergency – see Regulation 38) without a written agreement between the foster carers and the authority. Matters to be dealt with in such agreements cover such practical issues as the financial support of the child, matters of consent for medical or dental treatment, arrangements for contact and permission to live, even temporarily, away from the foster parent's home, and the arrangements for the child to have contact with his or her parents (Sch. 6, paras 2, 3, 4 and 6). They must also contain a 'statement containing all the information which the authority considers necessary to enable the foster parents to care for the child'. In particular, this statement must contain details of the authority's 'arrangements for the child and the objectives of the placement'. Other information required includes details of the child's personal history, religious persuasion, cultural and linguistic background and racial origin; the child's state of health; the safety needs of the child; the child's educational needs and any needs arising from any disability that the child may have (Sch. 6, para.1).

CHILDREN'S HOMES AND LEAVING CARE

Although not directly relevant to the situation of the Taylor family, there are two other sets of Regulations of which you need to be aware; those dealing with children's homes and those dealing with children leaving care.

The Children's Homes Regulations 2001 (SI 2001/3967) are largely concerned with the management, regulation and inspection of children's homes. Regulation 4 requires each home to have a 'statement of purpose' and a guide for children to the home. The statement must include such matters as an account of the 'underlying ethos and philosophy' of the home (Sch. 1, para. 11); the arrangements for consultation with children on how the home is operated (Sch. 1, para. 15); the arrangements made for child protection and to counter bullying (Sch. 1, para. 17) and a description of the home's policy on anti-discriminatory practice and children's rights (Sch. 1, para. 27).

Children's homes, in consultation with the local authority placing a child, must also draw up and maintain a 'placement plan' (Regulation 12) for each child. This plan must include details of 'how, on a day to day basis, [the child] will be cared for and his welfare safeguarded and promoted by the home' (Regulation 12 (1) (a)) and include details of the arrangements made for the child's health care and education. The plan must also set out the arrangements to be made for contact between the child, his or her parents, relatives and friends (Regulation 12 (1) (c)). (See also Standard 2 of the *NMS for Children's Homes* Department of Health 2002a.)

The Children (Leaving Care) Act 2000 and subsequent Regulations (SI 2001/2874) make substantial amendments to the Children Act 1989 in respect of children and young people formerly looked after by local authorities. The Children (Leaving Care) Act 2000 imposes new duties on local authorities to assess and meet the needs of certain categories of young people aged 16 to 18 who are or were looked after by them; to keep in touch with them until they are at least 21 (and to provide assistance with employment, education and training); to appoint a personal advisor for them and to ensure that every eligible young person in care is to have, when they turn 16, a comprehensive pathway plan mapping out a clear route to independence. Details of what must be included in a pathway plan are set out in Figure 8.1. Further details of how these arrangements are being implemented and some examples of good practice can be found in *Care Leaving Strategies* (Department of Health and others 2002) and via the 'Quality Protects' website (see web resources at the end of this Unit).

Exercise 8.2: Planning for Placement

In the event, the only placement available for the Taylor children is with the Williams family.

1. Review your plans for Alison and Michael and revise as necessary. Your review should include a consideration of all of those matters required by the Children Act 1989 and associated Regulations and Guidance.

2.   Set out the sequence of events that will be necessary to put your plans into effect.

3.   Using the diary sheets (Figure 8.2) construct a timetable to operate alongside the plan that indicates the order in which tasks (including consultations and notifications) will be undertaken.

4.   Prepare a statement for the foster carers, as required by Regulations.

Matters to be dealt with in the pathway plan and review

1.   The nature and level of contact and personal support to be provided, and by whom, to the child or young person.

2.   Details of the accommodation the child or young person is to occupy.

3.   A detailed plan for the education or training of the child or young person.

4.   How the responsible authority will assist the child or young person in relation to employment or other purposeful activity or occupation.

5.   The support to be provided to enable the child or young person to develop and sustain appropriate family and social relationships.

6.   A programme to develop the practical and other skills necessary for the child or young person to live independently.

7.   The financial support to be provided to the child or young person, in particular where it is to be provided to meet his accommodation and maintenance needs.

8.   The health needs, including any mental health needs, of the child or young person, and how they are to be met.

9.   Contingency plans for action to be taken by the responsible authority should the pathway plan for any reason cease to be effective.

Figure 8.1 Pathway plans
Source: Reproduced from The Children (Leaving Care) (England) Regulations 2001 Schedule (Crown copyright).

	Week 1	Week 2	Week 3	Week 4
M				
T				
W				
Th				
F				
Sat				
Sun				

Week 5
Week 6
Week 7
Week 8
Week 9
Week 10
Week 11
Week 12

Month 4
Month 5
Month 6
Month 7
Month 8
Month 9
Month 10
Month 11
Month 12

Figure 8.2 Diary sheets

Points to Consider

1.   What are the specific goals and objectives that your plan sets out to achieve?

2.   What are the main tasks that:

   (a)   the foster carers

   (b)   the parents and

   (c)   the social worker

   need to undertake in order to achieve these goals and objectives?

3.   Is the timescale that you have determined appropriate to those goals and objectives?

4.   What contingency plans have you made and does everyone know what these are?

5.   What help do:

   (a)   the foster carers

   (b)   the parents and

   (c)   the children

   need to prepare for the admission?

6.   Who will be responsible for, and involved in, planning for these children's longer-term future?

PLANNING TOGETHER

We have made several references to the mutuality of the planning (and assessment) process. One way in which a commitment to such forms of practice can be given effect is through the use of written agreements with service users. Often, such agreements are described as 'contracts', although we would suggest that such a term should be avoided as too legalistic and possibly too intimidating for all concerned – it may remind partners of experiences that they would rather forget and be suggestive of an adversarial stance. White (1983) suggests that the intentions behind such arrangements are best conveyed by the term 'agreed planning document'. Sheldon (1980, p.2) defines written agreements as: 'agreements between social workers and their clients for the purpose of giving greater definition or sense of direction to working relationships'. He goes on to say that their usefulness lies in the way that they are able to specify who is to do what and so act as a 'continual reminder of the agreed goals and purposes of the intervention' (p.2).

Written agreements clearly offer the potential for shared work, shared responsibility, common goals and clear expectations. They do not constitute a guarantee of improved practice, however. If they are no more than a set of tasks that the service user has to carry out, with no prior negotiation and no reciprocal commitment and obligations on the social worker, then they are only of negative value. We can begin to explore their potential for positive practice by reference to what it is that families say they want from a written agreement. The following study text begins with such an exploration.

Study Text 8.3: Written Agreements

Based on the work of Atherton and Dowling (1989), we can identify ten pre-conditions for the effective use of written agreements:

1. *The social worker's / agency's motivation must be pro-service user.* Written agreements that are intended to serve other than the explicit purposes of helping the service user to overcome the present difficulties are unlikely to prove effective. For example, a written agreement that deals with the quality of parenting but which is no more than an evidence-gathering device for a forthcoming court appearance is not an agreement in any meaningful sense. This sort of negative attitude simply increases suspicion and sets an unbridgeable gap between the worker and the family. Families need to feel and believe that what is being agreed is being done so in order to help them reach their goals, with your assistance, rather than introduce a series of increasingly difficult obstacles against which to measure almost inevitable failure.

2. *Agreements should be negotiated, not imposed:* Given that we usually find what we are looking for, if you are genuinely committed to negotiating agreement you will be surprised by how often agreement can be reached. If you begin with the expectation that agreement cannot be reached, then of course it will not be. There will be occasions when agreement between the various parties cannot be reached and often it will be you who will be called upon to make a decision. However, the distinction between what is unilaterally decided and what is negotiated must be made. Any blurring of this distinction will do nothing to establish the engagement of the family in the helping process or to establish any form of trust.

3. *All parties can take advice:* In reality, of course, social workers do take advice throughout the process. We are usually less comfortable when service users do the same. This may be interpreted as a threat to the social worker's competence or authority; to the comfortable and comforting illusion that we

know best. You will almost always have access to colleagues and a variety of forms of professional advice. For families, advice may come from a friend or relative or their own solicitor. It is the worker's job to encourage, rather than frustrate, the participation of such advisors in the process and to view their presence positively. The very important principle of confidentiality (see Study Text 6.2) is often used spuriously to discourage the involvement of other family or community members in the helping process. The role of third parties is particularly important if there is a cultural or linguistic gap to bridge.

4. *The family's view is genuinely respected:* There is all the difference in the world between listening to a family's view, and hearing a family's view, and between hearing a family's view and respecting it. Respecting it means giving it value and allowing the possibility that you will be at least as influenced in the direction of the family's view of the problem as you are by your own views. It is at the heart of negotiation and is a process of compromise.

5. *Agency tasks must be clearly defined:* Essentially, this is a further comment on the lack of specificity in most social work interventions consequent upon the absence of planning and any sense of what the purposes of intervention are. Too many written agreements are little more than sets of tasks for the service user to perform, with the expectations of the worker and their agency left largely unarticulated.

6. *The agreement will both be followed and reviewed:* To begin the process of intervention with the written agreement and to see it rapidly confined to the recesses of the case file is to add insult to injury. In jettisoning the agreement unilaterally, you also jettison any expectation you might have of the co-operation of the family.

7. *The agency is willing to reconsider whether both the terms and implementation of the agreement were fair:* Written agreements can never become tablets of stone – the contents of which can never be changed, even if they have demonstrably failed in some way. The agency, as much as the service user, should be prepared to look at its own role in determining the reasons for any particular outcome.

8. *The final written document is agreed by all:* This is a point about checking out that the written agreement is actually the agreement that has been made and that the scribe of the written contract has not subtly, or otherwise, misconstrued or misrepresented the agreement.

9. *It is written in clear unambiguous language:* There is evidence to suggest that when social workers and other professionals are themselves uncertain of what they mean, or they wish to disguise the true content of their communication, they will use professional jargon and other devices to ensure that their status remains unquestioned and, so, unthreatened.

10. *Its contents can be appealed against:* This is clearly related to Point 7 and, in the case of services for children and families, has now been given some statutory force in that each local authority is required to have in place an appropriate complaints and representations procedure (Children Act 1989, s. 26).

It is a salutary lesson to learn that much more recent studies than those on which Atherton and Dowling based their work (e.g. Brandon and others 1999; Thoburn, Wilding and Watson 2000) have reached very similar conclusions in respect of what 'works' in encouraging parental participation in social work intervention. Taking the findings of this research and the points made by Atherton and Dowling together, we can see how a written agreement can provide a basis for open and honest communication between families and social workers and occupy a particular role in relationship to the planning process in that it:

- promotes explicit decision-making on the part of parents, social workers, children and other collaborating persons or agencies
- specifies time-frames for decision-making
- ensures clarity of tasks, goals and objectives for clients, workers and others
- provides the basis of periodic review.

In terms of the kinds of cases in which written agreements might be used, there is no reason why agreements should be considered in only very restricted circumstances or only at particular points in your involvement with the family. Written agreements can, for example, take the form of:

- a preliminary statement focusing on general or broad themes and formulated early in the contact with a family
- a more definitive agreement reached after adequate discussion and review with a family and others who may be involved
- a partial agreement delineating in further detail a section of a more general agreement.

Given the variety of specific and general purposes to which an agreement might be put, it is difficult to generalize about its specific form and content. Each agreement should be seen as a unique document that flows from, and is adapted to, the particular needs and circumstances of the service user. However, there are certain components of an agreement that will be required in most situations:

- participants in the agreement
- a statement of commitment to the agreement
- a time-frame for the agreement
- a statement of the goals and objectives of the plan
- specification of the tasks that will need to be undertaken by the parties to the agreement
- arrangements for periodic review
- appropriate signatures.

And what happens if one party fails to keep to the agreement? This question is often put in terms of 'where are the teeth in a written agreement?' To put this question is often to miss the point altogether. If the agreement is not honoured then it needs to be re-negotiated or, if this is not possible, it may need to be withdrawn and one or other of the parties may need to act independently. The social worker may seek recourse to the court or a family may relinquish their relationship with the agency (if they have a choice), for example.

In so far as written agreements reflect the worker's ethical responsibility to respect the service user's right to self-determination and to regard family members as active rather than passive recipients of services, they provide an effective tool for planning in partnership.

Exercise 8.3: Agreeing the Plan

TASKS

1.   Prepare a draft agreement detailing the plans that you have been making for accommodating Alison and Michael.

2.   Identify the areas of negotiation required.

 Points to Consider

1.   Have you identified those parts of the written agreement that are non-negotiable (e.g. statutory requirements)?

2.   Is the agreement written in such a way that the children will understand it?

3.   Will the children be asked to sign it? Who will advise them on the content of the agreement?

4.   Does the agreement include the foster carers? If not, why not?

5.   Have you made provision for review and possible revision of the agreement?

6.   Are the tasks that fall to you and your agency made as explicit as they can be?

 CONCLUSION

In his book *An Introduction to Social Work Theory*, David Howe (1987) reviews the literature that describes what the users of social work services perceive as effective help. He is in no doubt that service users often feel confused, threatened and angered by the social worker who is vague or uncertain about his or her role and purpose (p.6):

> Both social workers and clients should know where they are and where they would like to go. If you do not know where you are, you will not know in which direction to move. If you do not know where you are going, you will not know when you have arrived. Drift and a lack of purpose in much social work practice suggests that many social workers have little idea of place in their work with clients. Thus a sense of location and a sense of direction should structure practice.

If you are to prevent you and the children and families becoming lost in the wood like poor Alice, never venture far without a plan of where it is you are seeking to go.

 NOTES AND SELF-ASSESSMENT

1. Do you think that social work really is about 'making things happen'?

2. Do you think that planning of the sort described in this Unit might rob social work of its creativity and spontaneity?

3. How 'planned' would you say your life is? What might this suggest about your attitude to planning?

4. Do you believe that, in the 'real world', planning in any kind of detail would prove impossible? What would be the consequences of not planning?

5. Given the statutory basis of much social work in this area, how free to plan are you?

6. How good are you at 'sticking' to a plan?

RECOMMENDED READING

Bell, M. and Wilson, K. (eds) (2003) *The Practitioner's Guide to Working with Families.* Basingstoke: Palgrave/Macmillan.

Gilligan, R. (2001) *Promoting Resilience: A Resource Guide on Working with Children in the Care System.* London: BAAF Adoption and Fostering.

TRAINER'S NOTES

Exercise 8.1: Goal-Setting

A larger group can be subdivided with two groups asked to plan on behalf of each child separately and a third on behalf of both children together. Subsequent discussion should be aimed at reconciling any differences. Once agreed, it is helpful to ask participants to role play presenting the plan in summarized form (i.e. 'bullet points'), either for the purpose of a simulated case conference or for discussion with the children and parents concerned. It is a useful corrective for over-ambitious plans if the trainer consistently asks participants how they will achieve what is being proposed as well as when.

Exercise 8.2: Planning for Placement

For the purposes of Tasks 2 and 3, a larger group can be subdivided in order to provide a contrast between ideal solutions (i.e. unlimited time, no bureaucratic hurdles, etc.) and the practical task of planning in practice. Discussion should focus on the acceptability of the compromises that will have to be made. Task 4 can be undertaken by one group with access to the Regulations and by another without. This provides an opportunity to evaluate what the Act requires and what the various parties to the process might ideally want.

Exercise 8.3: Agreeing the Plan

A larger group can begin by 'quickthinking' all of the areas that such an agreement should cover. Smaller groups can then draw up the details of the agreement and present them to an 'ethics committee' of the whole group which will evaluate the agreement in terms of its tone much more than its content. The group should re-read Study Text 4.3 before establishing its own evaluative criteria.

 WEB RESOURCES

http://www.doh.gov.uk/choiceprotects This is the website for the Department of Health's review of fostering and placement services. The review was launched in March 2002 and aims 'to improve placement choice and placement stability for looked after children'.

http://www.doh.gov.uk/qualityprotects/work_pro/project_10.htm This is the website for the 'Quality Protects Project Team on Placement Choice'. The team's objectives are:

- to increase the supply and quality of placements for looked after children

- to increase the supply of adoption placement options

- to support the National Priorities Guideline objective of 'reducing to no more than 16% the number of children who have three or more placements within one year'.

The site provides access to useful research and access to examples of good practice. You might also like to look at **http://www.doh.gov.uk/qualityprotects/work_pro/project_5.htm** which is the web page for the 'Quality Protects' Team looking at leaving care.

http://www.foyer.net The Foyer Federation. Foyer provide local solutions to address local needs of young people who are in need of accommodation and support services in order to progress out of social exclusion in their chosen life path. By providing, at a minimum, access to affordable accommodation, education, training and employment services and personal support in a holistic, individually-centred package, Foyer empower and enable young people to become active and contributing members of their communities.

The text of the Department of Health guide to good practice in planning leaving care strategies can be found at **http://www.doh.gov.uk/qualityprotects/work _pro/care_strategies.pdf**.

Child Protection

OBJECTIVES

In this Unit you will:

- Explore aspects of awareness and recognition of child abuse.
- Explore aspects of risk assessment in child protection.
- Explore the investigative process as defined by the Children Act 1989.
- Learn how child protection services and systems are organized and administered.

 SOME BASICS

In Unit 6, we explored how the term 'child abuse' and the realities it describes are socially constructed and, in part, subjectively defined. The same can be said for 'child protection'. Consider, for example, the distinction that might be made between being 'protected' and feeling 'safe' that we described in Study Text 7.2. Our present point is not just that 'child protection' can be understood differently depending, for example, on your relationship to the 'facts' of the case but that there is a qualitative dimension to child protection practice just as there is to social work practice with children and families in any other context. The experience of being 'protected' can be made better or worse by the manner in which it is achieved.

You might like to re-read the course text at the beginning of Unit 5 with this in mind.

The point has, perhaps, best, and most famously, been made by Lord Justice Butler-Sloss in her report of the events in Cleveland. Butler-Sloss LJ noted, after criticizing some aspects of professional practice undertaken as part of a child protection intervention, that a 'child is a person and not just an object of concern' (Cleveland Report 1988). A child's longer-term interests, dignity and sense of identity, already made vulnerable by the process of abuse, must be preserved through any process of child 'protection'. The investigation of abuse, for example, can, without proper regard for the rights of the child, itself become abusive – as events in Orkney and Cleveland have been held to demonstrate. As such, child protection practice must be firmly embedded in the context of attitudes, values and best practice in other areas of social work with children and families. Child protection is a *specialist* field but it is not to be understood as a *separate* field of practice.

Hence, this Unit, whilst focusing on child protection processes and practice, will do so in the context of knowledge, skills and values that have a more general application. We have chosen to do this not only because it would be absurd to try and compress a comprehensive account of practice in child protection into a single chapter but also because we believe that there are dangers if social workers and other professionals think about child protection in terms which isolate it from a broader understanding of what social work with children and families means. In working through this Unit, therefore, we do not want you to jettison all that you have thought about in terms of attitudes, values and the essentials of good practice just because you are engaged in 'child protection'. We cannot take you far into an understanding of the complexities of practice in this area (we purposely omit any reference to post-abuse work as this is well beyond the scope of a book such as this) but we do want you to begin your journey with a positive regard for what you know rather than with misgivings about what you have yet to learn.

For example, you will have considered, as part of Units 4 and 5, the local authority's general duty to 'safeguard and promote' the welfare of children (see Children Act 1989, s. 17 (1) and s. 22 (3)). This duty should govern your understanding of work to protect children from harm just as much as it should your work in supporting children and families in other circumstances. You are required to 'safeguard' the welfare of the child – which might imply the sense usually associated with the term 'protect' – but, at the same time, you are required to 'promote' his or her welfare. Neither, on its own, is sufficient. The following exercise, based on developments with the Taylor family, should demonstrate to you what you already know about 'protecting' children.

TAYLOR FAMILY CASE FILE

Despite the careful arrangements that you made for the children, you have had to revise your plans once again. Ron could not bring himself to consent to Alison and Michael being provided with accommodation and decided to exercise his parental responsibility and make arrangements of his own. With Tracy's blessing, and with the informed consent of both Alison and Michael, the older children have gone to live with Ron and his wife and child in Northtown. Supervision by the local social services department has been arranged and you have been invited to monthly review meetings with the children, Ron and the area social worker. The children are to have unrestricted contact with Tracy.

All of this has happened very quickly and the children moved to Northtown on 19 February. Tracy and John continued to live at Mrs Taylor's (senior) house on Old Estate. At first everything seemed to be going along well: the older children had settled down in Northtown and were making good progress in school and at home and Tracy seemed to be getting on well with her mother. Tracy said that she didn't really need your help and your visits declined to no more than once every three weeks.

In early May the local health visitor telephoned to say that she had recently seen John at the GP's request. The GP had noted that John was being brought to the surgery very frequently with a succession of minor childhood ailments. The GP indicated that she thought John 'wasn't being very well cared for' and that 'he looked a bit on the thin side'. You visited the home on 14 May. The house was dirty and very disorganized. Tracy told you that John was 'off his food and had the runs'. When asked about the state of the house, Tracy said that Alun had started to call around and was being very difficult and that the stress she was feeling meant that she had 'let things slide a bit'. Her mother, according to Tracy, 'couldn't be bothered', leaving more for her to do than she could manage. There had been a minor fire in the kitchen recently that made matters look worse than they were, according to Tracy. You arranged for the repair of the kitchen via the local authority's maintenance department and for the temporary re-connection of the gas supply, which had been turned off four months ago because of unpaid bills. You also arranged for a cash payment to enable Tracy to stock up with food. Tracy agreed to attend the local child health clinic on a weekly basis and accepted your offer of referral to the local family centre where John could attend 'toddlers club' and Tracy could meet other women in her position who might be able to offer advice and support.

On 3 June, the health visitor informed you that Tracy had not kept a single appointment at the clinic. On the same day that the health visitor had been in touch, Tracy turned up at your office (while you were out) and left a message to say that she wasn't getting on with the health visitor and asking that you visit her. You tried, on four occasions over the next three weeks, to see Tracy but she was never in at the times at which you had agreed to call. On the last day of June, during evening surgery, Tracy called at the clinic to see the health visitor. The health visitor had left for the day but Tracy was seen briefly by the practice nurse who said she would pass on a message to the health visitor in the morning. There has been no response, as yet, from the family centre to which you had referred Tracy.

In the first week of July, an anonymous caller informs your duty office that a young child had been left unattended in the garden for most of the day. He was crying and there didn't seem to be anyone looking after him. The address given was Mrs Taylor's house in Old Estate. You visit and find Tracy at home. You tell her what you have been told. Tracy explains that she has been away for a few days with Alun and that her mother was supposed to be looking after John. Tracy tells you that Mrs Taylor (senior) has taken John out in his buggy. They both return while you are still there. John is still clearly very distressed. Mrs Taylor explains that 'he must have caught the sun' and that he's just 'hot and bothered'. Tracy accuses her mother of not looking after John. She responds that Tracy shouldn't have gone off and left him like she did and an argument develops between the two. Each accuses the other of failing to look after John properly. Tracy shouts at John that this wouldn't have happened if it wasn't for him. John is sitting silently in his buggy, watching what is going on around him. You intervene in the argument between the two women. You observe that John is sitting in a very dirty nappy and that his buggy is filthy and very smelly.

Neither Tracy nor Mrs Taylor seems prepared to do anything about this. Tracy says that she will see to John after you've gone. You notice that he has a number of what appear to be bruises on his arms with two much darker ones on each arm, just below the shoulder. You ask Tracy how he got them and she explains that Alun had been playing 'aeroplanes' with him. Mrs Taylor (senior) asks Tracy whether Alun had been around the house, as she never wanted to see him again. Tracy says that she hadn't seen Alun and it was the boyfriend of a friend of her's who had been playing with John.

You ask Tracy to meet you at the clinic in the morning. She doesn't keep her appointment but does see the duty doctor later in the day. The doctor is clear that John is underweight for his age and that he is suffering from moderate sunburn and impetigo, aggravated by urine burns. He insists that you visit and 'get this sorted out'.

 Exercise 9.1: Safeguarding and Promoting

Having read the account of developments in the Taylor family, complete the following tasks. Today is 3 August.

1.   Write down what you consider to be John's primary needs at this point.

2.   Assuming that John's needs are as you predicted, identify the ways in which these might be met.

3.   How far does your answer to (2) adequately safeguard and promote John's welfare?

Points to Consider

1. Which of John's needs must be met in order to 'safeguard' his welfare?

2. Which of John's needs must be met in order to 'promote' his welfare?

3. Write short definitions of what you understand by the terms 'safeguard' and 'promote', in order to clarify their meaning for you.

4. Do you consider John to be an abused child? If so, at what point did this case become a 'child protection' one? Be clear about your reasons.

5. Would such a determination make you revise your plans for investigating John's situation further?

6. Would such a determination make you want to revise your plans for meeting John's needs?

RECOGNIZING CHILD ABUSE

It might reasonably be argued that all of the work undertaken so far with the Taylor family is aimed at child protection, in its very broadest sense, in so far as it was intended to 'safeguard and promote' the children's welfare. John's situation is now (probably) an abusive one and your answers to the questions posed by the last exercise, and to the points that you have been asked to consider, should have raised new and more pressing concerns for you. John almost certainly needs a more immediate and direct form of protection now. Even so, in safeguarding John's welfare from this point on, it will be vital to ensure that we also continue consciously and actively to promote it.

As suggested in Unit 6, child abuse rarely presents itself in a dramatic or easily identifiable form. Families where child abuse occurs may not be immediately distinctive from other families with which you are working. Sometimes, especially in the case of neglect, what has been a chronic family situation, such as that described in the Taylor file, may shift catastrophically into some other more easily defined form of abuse. Indeed, in Unit 10, we will see that this is what happens in this case. However, at this stage we clearly will need to investigate John's situation further. We will need to have regard to what predictive and diagnostic indicators of abuse are present and to evaluate the degree of current and potential risk to John. The following study text will describe some of the more frequently used diagnostic indicators that may inform your recognition of abuse.

Study Text 9.1: Recognizing Child Abuse

For present purposes, we will be using a more limited categorization of abuse than that which we used in Unit 6. It is that used by social services departments for recording entries in the child protection register (see Study Text 9.3) and by the Department of Health for statistical purposes. It is taken from *Working Together to Safeguard Children* (Department of Health and others 1999), an important source of guidance for work in this field.

The definitions of abuse offered in *Working Together* (pp.14–15) are:

- *Physical abuse:* May involve hitting, shaking, throwing, poisoning, burning or scalding, drowning, suffocating or otherwise causing physical harm to a child. Munchausen's syndrome by proxy may also constitute physical abuse.

- *Emotional abuse:* Is the persistent emotional ill-treatment of a child such as to cause severe and persistent adverse effects on the child's emotional development. It may involve conveying to children that they are worthless or unloved, inadequate, or valued only in so far as they meet the needs of another person. It may involve causing children frequently to feel frightened or in danger, or the corruption of children.

- *Sexual abuse*: Involves forcing or enticing a child or young person to take part in sexual activities, whether or not the child is aware of what is happening. The activities may involve physical contact, including penetrative or non-penetrative acts. They may include non-contact activities such as involving children in looking at pornographic material or watching sexual activities, or encouraging children to behave in sexually inappropriate ways.

- *Neglect*: Is the persistent failure to meet a child's basic physical and psychological needs likely to result in the serious impairment of the child's health or development. It may involve a parent or carer failing to provide adequate food, shelter and clothing, failing to protect a child from physical harm or danger, or failing to ensure access to appropriate medical care or treatment. It may also included neglect of a child's basic emotional needs.

In this study text, we have chosen to concentrate on neglect. We do so because it is one of the most difficult forms of abuse to detect and because of our belief that social workers, and others, have the greatest difficulty in recognizing and responding to neglect. We will deal with emotional abuse in the context of other forms of abuse.

NEGLECT

In 2000, neglect was the most common reason for children to be placed on the child protection register (ONS 2002, Chart 8.20). This represents a marked change in recording practice (see Creighton 1986) as, historically, children who suffered neglect or emotional abuse were consistently registered in comparatively small numbers. You should not read too much into this in terms of believing this to represent a marked change in the actual incidence of neglect, as the relationship between child abuse registers and the incidence of abuse is problematic (see Creighton 2001). What it may represent is an increased readiness on the part of social workers to recognize neglect and to respond.

Any difficulty in recognition has to be understood against the background of the very broad range of a child's emotional, psychological and physical needs, many of which are age specific. Accordingly, universally reliable indicators of neglect are as elusive as any comprehensive definition of the process itself. Moreover, neglect is about things undone rather than things done, acts of omission rather than commission, and non-events are that much more difficult to observe, of course. Also, neglect, by definition, occurs over a period of time and may proceed almost imperceptibly.

Neglect can only be identified by comparison with the circumstances and development of the non-neglected child. In terms of general development, particularly in the case of infants and children under five, there are recognized standards against which any individual's progress or lack of it can be measured. Where a child's general development is delayed other than for medical reasons (non-organic failure to thrive), although this is usually the province of the health visitor, the social worker still has an important role to play. You should be concerned if a young child suffers repeatedly from chronic diarrhoea, recurrent and persistent infections, voracious appetite or no appetite at all; thrives while away from home and/or has a general delay in acquiring such skills as sitting, crawling, walking and talking.

In behavioural terms, a neglected or emotionally abused child may be unresponsive to social stimulation and avoid eye contact. Such a child may also exhibit excessively 'clingy' behaviour developed through lack of confidence and any sense of emotional or physical security. There may be signs of self-stimulating behaviour, such as head banging or rocking. Most striking of all (and not confined to neglect or emotional abuse) is the child who distances her- or himself from others and observes whatever is happening in an attitude of 'frozen watchfulness', ready to respond to a blow or a threat but not actively engaged with what is going on around him or her.

Older children may appear more obviously dirty and unkempt. They may be smelly and dirty. They may rush around, unable to concentrate on anything for very long and may have great difficulty in playing with other children. They may also be 'touch hungry' and seek physical contact, even from strangers. There may be additional signs of self-stimulating behaviour, including self-harm. At school, there may be apparent signs of learning difficulties and poor peer relationships as well as social and emotional immaturity.

While neglect is a difficult area, both conceptually and definitionally, this is not the most important consideration in relation to child protection practice and the neglect of children. Research has shown that our collective tolerance of the neglect of children can be far too high and that the comparative neglect of neglected children by those professionals whose job it is to protect them needs to be carefully examined (Reder, Duncan and Gray 1993; Minty and Patterson 1994; Department of Health 1995).

It is possible to suggest a number of explanations for the failure to see abuse, even if signs of the neglect are obvious:

- In our work generally, and in child protection specifically, we are too much concerned with the actions and behaviour of adults and too little concerned with the consequences for children. Few of us would tolerate a urine-soaked mattress, infestation or prolonged cold and hunger for ourselves or those close to us for a moment longer than we could avoid, yet child death enquiries would seem to indicate that we will accept excuses from adults for the neglectful treatment of some children.

- We avoid confronting neglect through misplaced cultural relativism. We console ourselves with the thought that 'Children around here all live like that. They may be scruffy, but they're happy!' *All* children have a right to adequate standards of care and a right to our protection.

- We confuse neglect with poverty. It is true that, in the context of structural poverty, the potential for children to lead impoverished lives on a grand scale is disturbingly high. The fact of structural economic inequality and the consequences of poverty provide a bleak background against which to identify particular instances of neglect. Nevertheless, it is a dangerous fallacy to locate the responsibility for neglect other than with a child's carers. Responsibility is not, of course, the same as blame. Minty and Patterson (1994), writing about neglect, are clear that poverty increases the likelihood of neglect and that living in poverty increases the likelihood of being officially labelled as 'neglectful'; poverty attracts the attention of the authorities as parents are forced to ask for financial or other assistance; poverty forces cruel choices on parents and increases the stress of parenting. However, many children and their parents achieve 'good enough' parenting despite the grinding poverty that is the lot of so many parents and children today.

- Linked with this idea is also the 'Fear of the Flood': this is the very real anxiety that were anyone to move the current threshold of tolerance of neglect, personally and organizationally, we would be overwhelmed.

We also avoid neglect through falling in with the general sense of hopelessness that can infuse such cases. This sense of hopelessness arises because of the elusive nature of much neglect, which often leaves the social worker with no specific behaviour or clear circumstances to work with to bring about change. Indeed, long-term interventions may seem wholly unproductive as they attempt to address the personalities of the carers or else rely inappropriately on 'support services' that maintain, rather than reduce, the problem. In other words, neglect cases can seem deeply unsatisfying in professional terms and their hopelessness can easily become ours.

PHYSICAL ABUSE

Distinguishing between a non-accidental injury and an accidental one is no more straightforward than being able to identify neglect, even for skilled forensic paediatricians. All children collect bruises and other signs of injury as part of the routine business of being a child and, although there are patterns of difference between accidental and non-accidental injuries, there are exceptions to almost every rule. The typology in Figure 9.1 is typical of many that you will come across.

Remember that, as well as the physiological signs of physical abuse, the child may also show similar social, emotional and psychological attributes to those described as consequent upon neglect. Remember also that every one of those indicators associated with non-accidental injury can have an accidental cause.

SEXUAL ABUSE

There are a number of physical signs that may be associated with sexual abuse. These are not usually accessible to the social worker and need careful consideration by a paediatrician. They include injury to genital area (these are often minor but inconsistent with accidental injury), vaginal or anal soreness, discharge or bleeding, presence of a sexually transmitted disease, soft tissue injury to breast, buttocks or thighs, love bites and semen stains and/or pubic hair on skin or clothes.

Sign of injury	Non-accidental	Accidental
Bruise:	More numerous; bruises may be at different stages of healing; often found in soft tissue, e.g. ear, cheeks, mouth; often patterned, e.g. finger-and-thumb pinch mark, slap mark or imprint of hard object; may be symmetrical, e.g. grab marks on both arms or ears, two black eyes	Likely to be few and scattered; likely to occur where bone is close to the surface, e.g. forehead, elbow, knee or shins
Burns:	Contact burn likely to show distinct boundary, e.g. hot-plate, cigarette burn; likely to be at unusual site, e.g. palm of hand, top of thigh, buttocks	Likely to be treated, easily explained and minor, e.g. brush with cigarette rather than defined edge
Fractures:	Numerous and not appropriate to age and stage; may include ribs or skull; 'spiral' fractures	Likely to be arms and legs; fractures are rare in babies and young children
Other injuries:	Large bites, fingernail marks, deep cuts, poisoning	Minor and superficial; likely to have been treated

Figure 9.1 Indicators of physical abuse

The social worker is more likely to be alerted to sexual abuse through the behaviour of the child. The interpretation of behaviour is a notoriously imprecise science and the investigation of sexual abuse remains a highly contested area – it is also one that is much better left to more experienced practitioners than those we imagine might read this book. However, there are some indicators that are more useful than others and which may alert you to the need to report any concerns that you may have to others better placed to investigate and evaluate them. These include a preoccupation with sexual matters and compulsive sexual behaviour. Most children are curious about sexual matters but overtly sexualized behaviour, attempts at simulating sexual acts, persistent masturbation in public or anatomically detailed drawings by younger children should be taken as possible causes for concern.

In older and younger children, the stigma and sense of betrayal associated with sexual abuse can produce profound psychological effects, which may manifest themselves in severe depression, self-harm, suicide attempts and severe social isolation. Self-evidently, these indicators, whatever their cause, should be a cause of concern to every social worker (see also Frosh 2001).

RECOGNIZING ABUSE

At several points, we have indicated that almost each and every sign of abuse can have an innocent explanation. Certain medical conditions can produce bruising, skin discolouration and fractures. The most unlikely accidents do happen. None of the indicators, taken in isolation, can ever be considered as conclusive evidence of abuse. Nonetheless, it is important to recognize that the absence of proof in child abuse is not proof of absence and you must always give serious thought and proper consideration to any and every indication of possible abuse.

In particular, your concern should be heightened in those situations where there has been a failure or reluctance to seek appropriate medical advice or assistance, where the account of the injury or other indication is not credible in terms of the child's age and stage of development or where the account changes when closely examined or when carers give inconsistent accounts of the same series of events.

However, the essential uncertainty which remains at the heart of child protection practice need not lead you to over-predict abuse or to fail to recognize it when it is happening. Whether your strategy is an optimistic one (which rushes to find or accept innocent explanations for indications of abuse), whether it is a pessimistic one (which finds evidence of abuse in innocent, if unfortunate, circumstances) (Dingwall 1989) or whether it is a balanced one will be a function of how acute are your observations, how extensive and current is your knowledge base and how far you have consciously developed the capacity to exercise your professional judgement. It is only through the exercise of that judgement that the determination of abuse can be made.

It may be helpful in developing your capacity to exercise that judgement to reflect on the usefulness of the term 'abuse' in relation to child protection practice. A narrow focus on 'abuse' may serve to imply a distinction between children who are the subject of child protection systems and processes and the wider population of children in need. In many ways, this distinction is one that is very difficult to maintain in practice and one that can, in one sense, be unhelpful. Parton (1997) has suggested that the central purposes of the Children Act 1989 have become distorted by this distinction in that child protection has come to dominate the child care agenda to the detriment of other forms of work (p.3):

> Not only are the family support aspirations and sections of the Act being implemented partially and not prioritised, but the child protection system is overloaded and not coping with the increased demands made of it. While child protection is the dominating concern and this is framing child welfare more generally, increasingly it is felt that too many cases are being dragged into the child protection net and that as a consequence the few who might require such interventions are in danger of being missed.

The 're-focusing' debate (a term used to describe the continuing discussion as to where the appropriate balance should be struck between the provision of universalist/preventive services and those aimed more specifically at rescue/remedial work, especially with those who have been abused) remains far from settled, both in practice and in policy terms. The professional tensions and funding issues that lie at opposite ends of this debate are not our immediate concern in this Unit but it is important to recognize that they do not have their origins in the Children Act itself.

You may by now be familiar with those parts of the Act that define 'need' and 'significant harm' (If not, see Study Texts 4.1 and 10.1 where each is explained). For our present purposes, it is sufficient to note that in practice, this legal distinction has, to all intents and purposes, come to differentiate those who have suffered abuse and those who have not. But note that, in the Act, this is a functional distinction, not a categorical one. In other words, the concepts of need and harm are distinguished in order to provide different kinds of mandates for intervention in children's lives, each resting on differing degrees of compulsion. The Act does not require us to think in terms of two distinct 'kinds' of children; those in need and those suffering 'significant harm'. It certainly does not require us to narrowly associate harm with specific instances of abuse. Harm to children may well follow as a consequence of being chronically in need. This is particularly so in situations of chronic neglect, as we have suggested. One might note also that the narrow association of harm, particularly 'significant harm', with abuse implies a rather unhelpful understanding of abuse as an event rather than a process.

Brandon and others' study (1999) noted in child protection case conferences:

> what appeared to be an unconscious avoidance of discussion of the nature of significant harm to the child in question, in favour of discussion of specific acts of abuse or neglect and categories for registration.

Commenting on the Brandon study and others, Aldgate and Statham (2001) concluded that (p.47):

> The shift from an identification of children in need as those at risk of suffering harm to an identification based on the impact of factors on children's development has not yet been achieved.

We regard this as unfortunate, not least because such an approach tends to reinforce a sense which many qualifying and newly qualified workers take into child protection work – that such work is altogether different from other kinds of work with children and their families; that values, principles and forms of practice that they support in one context do not transfer to the other and that their knowledge base is inadequate. We would suggest to you that recognizing abuse cannot be reduced simply to a forensic exercise, based on a defined pathology or set of behavioural or physical markers. These can be helpful and certainly should be part of every qualified social worker's knowledge base, but recognizing abuse also requires a holistic awareness of the needs and rights of children and the careful, reflective and informed exercise of professional judgement on the part of the social worker (and others) involved – as with every other piece of work undertaken with a child or their family.

Exercise 9.2: Signs of Neglect

Read over the case notes for the Taylor family in this Unit and in Units 7 and 8 and then:

1. Write down those indicators of the possible abuse and/or neglect of John that you find in the case notes.

2. Try and construct a completely innocent explanation for each of the indicators you have listed at (1).

3. Make a list of the additional information you might need to verify or refute your suspicions of neglect and/or other forms of abuse.

Points to Consider

1. How confident do you feel now about whether John is being abused?

2. How much additional information would be required to convince you?

3. How confident would you need to feel before you decided that matters should be further investigated or action taken?

4. Do you think that, in the circumstances, what is happening to John was probably inevitable and as such, unavoidable?

5. Who is responsible for the standard of John's care?

6. What might prevent you from seeing evidence of neglect or other forms of abuse?

RISK

There are few incontrovertible indicators of abuse, and no check-lists or simple measures that you can apply to establish the facts easily, but the forensic determination of the 'facts' of abuse is only one dimension to the process. There is also the determination of 'risk'.

Questions of risk are of particular and acute interest to many social scientists today. (For an accessible guide to thinking about risk see Lupton 1999.) They recognize that we are all becoming more aware of, and averse to, risk. Evidence of this can be found, for example, in the development of systems for the careful, hi-tech monitoring of the health of mother and child through pregnancy, which has produced dramatic falls in the rate of infant and maternal mortality since the Second World War. At the same time, these very techno-economic developments make us all more risk prone. The consequences of one major nuclear accident would have a much greater effect on generations of children yet unborn than any progress we might have made in perinatal care over recent years. Consequently, as well as creating risk through social, cultural and technological processes, society is actively engaged in weighing up the potential social benefits of any risk against the potential social costs. In our own field, for example, the social and economic costs of the kind of surveillance that could guarantee the protection of children has to be weighed against the social costs of gross interference by the State with the 'sanctity of the domestic hearth'. The following study text explores risk in the context of child protection.

Study Text 9.2: Risk Evaluation

There is a wide diversity of expert approaches to risk. Engineers, economists and actuaries attempt to predict the probability of hazardous events, such as natural disasters. Lawyers and criminologists have examined the control and regulation of behaviour that serves the maintenance and order of society. Psychologists and sociologists have explored a variety of forms of risk behaviour, including sexual promiscuity and drug misuse. From this diversity of approaches, an important definitional distinction emerges: that between risk and risk evaluation.

Risk has been defined as: 'the probability that a particular adverse event occurs during a stated period of time, or results from a particular challenge' and risk evaluation as: 'the complex process of determining the significance or value of the identified hazards and estimated risks to those concerned with or affected by the decision' (Royal Society 1992).

Risk is a matter of statistical calculation; risk evaluation is a matter of subjective judgement, and the two do not necessarily coincide. For example, researchers in the US (Fischoff, Lichtenstein and Slovic 1981) determined the risk of death from various causes. A large sample of the general public was then told the number of deaths arising from road accidents and asked to estimate the numbers of deaths from other specified causes. Not surprisingly, vivid deaths, such as those arising from botulism or tornadoes, were over-estimated and those arising from less dramatic causes, such as cancer or a stroke, were under-estimated. Clearly, the statistical likelihood of an event occurring and the subjective estimation of that event occurring can vary. This study text will explore risk in child protection by considering what we know about risk calculation and what practitioners can do to optimize the conditions in which to carry out the subjective process of risk evaluation.

RISK EVALUATION

Not all risks can be calculated to precise actuarial standards. Many hazards are cumulative, diffuse, slow-acting and insidious. They have diverse causes and complex mechanisms. There is uncertainty about the nature, scale and timing of possible outcomes and the cost of error in policy and personal terms can be high. Child abuse is one such 'elusive hazard' (Kates 1985).

Faced with an increasingly risk-averse culture and a resurgence of interest in particular scientistic forms of evidence-based practice, this can be a difficult point to pursue. Nigel Parton (1998, p.23; see also Parton 2001) has described how 'systems procedures and organisational frameworks which operate *as if* issues are resolvable in any kind of realist, scientific or calculative/probabilistic sense are in great danger of missing the point'. He goes on to argue:

> We are in a situation where notions of artistic, situated judgements should be valued, and where organisations should concentrate on developing notions of mutual trust and be respectful of different points of view. The rehabilitation of the idea of uncertainty, and the permission to talk about an indeterminacy which is not amenable to or reducible to authoritative definition or measurement, is an important step...for recognising the contemporary complexities of practice. (Parton 1998, p.23)

One of the consequences of failing to recognize that 'notions of ambiguity, complexity and uncertainty are the core of social work' (1998, p.23), according to Parton was, as we have noted, too great an emphasis on narrowly defined child protection work at the expense of preventive strategies, such that 'need itself was ultimately understood in terms of risk' (Parton 2001, p.65). Another potential consequence was a form of defensive practice that might inhibit any attempts to work inclusively, especially with children and young people themselves. In reflecting on evaluating risk, we would hope that you will maintain a realistic appreciation of how far it can be 'managed out' of your practice and consider also what the consequences might be if it were.

With this caution in mind, we should note that in child protection practice there have emerged, at different times and according to particular ways of understanding abuse, several types of risk assessment instruments aimed at identifying when a child is at risk or is likely to be so in the future. These risk assessment instruments are usually produced in the forms of check-lists. A particularly well-known one is that produced by Greenland in 1987 and referred to in Reder and others' (1993) influential book on the non-accidental deaths of children, *Beyond Blame – Child Abuse Tragedies Revisited* (see also Reder and Duncan 1999). Greenland describes risk factors associated with the parents of a child at risk and those of the child itself (Figure 9.2).

Parent

- Was previously abused/neglected as a child
- Has a history of abusive/neglectful parenting
- Has a history of criminal assaultive and/or suicidal behaviour
- Is a single parent, separated or the partner is not the biological parent
- Is socially isolated, including frequent moves and poor housing
- Is poor, unemployed, an unskilled worker or received inadequate education
- Abuses alcohol or drugs
- Is pregnant or in the post-partum period or has a chronic illness

Child

- Was previously abused/neglected, especially when under five years of age
- Was premature or of low birthweight
- Has a birth defect, a chronic illness or developmental lag
- Had prolonged separation from the mother
- Is adopted, fostered or a stepchild
- Is currently underweight
- Cries frequently or is difficult to comfort
- Shows difficulties in feeding or elimination

Figure 9.2 Greenland's check-list

But, despite being well established, Greenland's check-list can be criticized as much for what it omits as for what it includes. For example, as Reder points out, Greenland's check-list does not include the frustration of access to a child as a warning sign, although Greenland's own work would suggest that it is a significant risk indicator. Nor does it recognize how crises elsewhere in the family's life or relationships between parents/partners heighten the risk to the child. From Reder's work, other risk indicators were identified, which included the failure of children to live up to the role expectations carers had for them. The period following a return home from care was particularly dangerous in this respect.

However, the most significant indicator of danger to the child, identified by Reder, and illustrated in the Taylor case, was what he termed 'closure' in the family–professional interaction. Closure manifested itself in families actively reducing contact with the outside world, with few people able to meet or speak with them. Curtains would be kept drawn, children would not play outside or attend nursery, appointments and meetings were missed, etc. The same effect can also be achieved through flight (where parents/carers move from their accommodation) or disguised compliance (where parents appeared to be co-operating with the plans made but rarely actually did) or by popping up in unexpected places, with the effect that suspicion or concern is lowered – that is turning up at the health visitor's, but not at the case review.

The point to be made is that such check-lists, and any commentaries upon them, at best describe broad sets of circumstances that are associated with child abuse. They rarely, if ever, approach being able to give causal accounts or even strong correlations. In fact, almost all of the research that informs the determination of such risk factors is methodologically very weak. As has been pointed out elsewhere (Dingwall 1989; Sargent 1999), these studies are often based on non-representative samples, are retrospective, demonstrate associations rather than causal links or directions, or use broad definitions of child abuse.

Even if one was persuaded not to dwell on the technical deficiencies of the research that informs these risk assessment instruments, in practice such assessment tools have proved generally unhelpful. A particular problem that many of them share is the production of false positives (predicting abuse which then does not occur) and false negatives (failing to predict abuse that does then occur) (Dingwall 1989). We might note

Reder's conclusion that the abuse of children can neither be 'confidently predicted or completely prevented'.

Notwithstanding this, child protection takes place as a professional activity, legitimated and, indeed, required by state and society; and risk assessment still plays a major part in professional practice. Check-lists may prove more or less helpful to you as a way of guiding and structuring your assessment but the process remains one of applying general rules to specific situations and, as such, much more of an art than any kind of science. It remains an exercise in judgement still and neither is it a one-off activity. As MacDonald has noted (2001, p.257):

> On one level it is misleading to identify risk assessment as a discrete phase, since new information can, at any time, signal the need to re-assess a child's safety. In this sense, the assessment of risk should be seen as a thread running throughout child protection case management.

This is a further illustration of the absolute requirement to embrace the necessary uncertainty that surrounds any form of risk assessment. Nevertheless, is there anything that can be done to improve our capacity to exercise that judgement more effectively?

IMPROVING RISK EVALUATION IN CHILD PROTECTION

The work of Maureen Stone (1992) begins from two basic premises derived from a review of risk assessment research in areas other than child protection. First, that the process of risk assessment and decision-making must be an open one where, as far as is possible, the various influences on the person making the assessment are acknowledged and accorded appropriate significance. Second, as assessment and decision-making are human activities, it is essential to consider the human element. In child protection, this means being aware of the potential consequences for the practice of the personal and professional circumstances of the practitioner. Stone goes on to argue that the negative impact of particular circumstances in which the practitioner may be working – such as feeling inadequately supervised or supported, feeling burnt out, experiencing poor inter-agency relationships, working in an organization which is undergoing unsettling change or feeling grossly under-resourced – can add to the level of risk a child faces through indirect means; namely, through having an influence on the type of decisions and responses taken by that practitioner.

The model of risk assessment that Stone develops, as well as taking into account primary risk factors relating to the child and its family and the social, financial and environmental context in which it lives, also takes account of *secondary risk* factors which are related to the context in which the risk assessment takes place. These include (p.26):

- the nature of the child protection organization (e.g. its structure and management and the quality of staff support and supervision)
- human failings (e.g. poor relationships, tiredness and stress)
- deficits and resource problems (e.g. training deficits, poor recording or other skills)
- inter-agency problems (e.g. different professional values, communication difficulties)
- media pressure/fear of ridicule (e.g. 'defensive social work', doing only what is uncontroversial).

The following exercise should help you explore the context of decision-making in your own agency.

 Exercise 9.3: Risk Evaluation

Using Stone's (1992) classification of secondary risk factors, undertake an 'audit' of the decision-making context of the particular work setting or practice placement in which you are located. You should ensure that you can answer at least the following questions:

1.   Your own organization:

   ○   Are lines of accountability clear?

   ○   Are the support services adequate?

   ○   Are records easy to find?

   ○   How long does it take for case notes to be updated?

   ○   Do you have time to think as well as act?

2.   Human failings:

       ○   Do you have strategies for dealing with stress?

       ○   Do you have the skills needed to do your job properly?

       ○   Do you have strong feelings about the people you work with/for?

3.   Deficits and resource problems:

       ○   Can you see the children and families with whom you are working sufficiently often?

       ○   Are the available material and human resources required by your work sufficient?

       ○   Who provides leadership in your work setting?

4.   Inter-agency problems:

       ○   Do you understand what the other agencies you regularly work with are really trying to do?

       ○   How might you check your understanding of other agencies' priorities?

       ○   Do you think that partner agencies understand what your agency is trying to achieve?

5.   Media pressure/fear of ridicule:

       ○   Are there recommendations that you would not dare make in reports?

       ○   Are there people in your organization whom you would never contradict or challenge?

       ○   Are case notes written up with a public inquiry or the editor of the local paper in mind?

 Points to Consider

1.   In your view, how far do these 'secondary risk' factors influence the quality of risk assessment in your agency?

2.   Do you think that your colleagues are aware of the potential effect of such factors?

3.   How can you make them more aware?

4.   What can you do to reduce the impact of any one of these factors on your own, and your agency's, capacity to evaluate risk?

5.   How might your colleagues react to your questioning of risk assessment processes in your agency?

6.   How safe is risk evaluation in your agency?

 ## SOME LIMITATIONS

It is beyond the scope of this book to simulate a credible organizational context and culture for you to explore further, although you are encouraged to pursue some of these issues through the reading that has been recommended at the end of this Unit. In terms of the Taylor family, we have determined that some further investigation is necessary. The following study text explores how the Children Act 1989 and *Working Together to Safeguard Children* (Department of Health and others 1999) inform that investigative process and establish the structure that will decide what happens next.

 ### Study Text 9.3: Investigation, Decision-Making and Review

THE AREA CHILD PROTECTION COMMITTEE

The precise details of the investigative process in any particular local authority area will be part of a published set of child protection procedures. These procedures will have been discussed and agreed by the several agencies involved in child protection in that area. Those agencies will almost always include the social services department, the police, staff of the health service, the probation service and the education service. These agencies, and possibly others such as the NSPCC, will be members of the Area Child Protection Committee (ACPC). The main task of the ACPC is to agree how the different groups will work together to protect children in their area – its specific responsibilities are set out in *Working Together to Safeguard Children* (Department of Health and others 1999) para. 4.2:

- to develop and agree local policies and procedures for inter-agency work to protect children, within the national framework provided

- to audit and evaluate how well local services work together to protect children

- to put into place objectives and performance indicators for child protection, within the framework and objectives set out in Children's Services Plans

- to encourage and help develop good working relationships between different services and professional groups, based on trust and mutual understanding

- to ensure that there is a level of agreement and understanding across agencies about operational definitions and thresholds for intervention

- to improve local ways of working in the light of knowledge gained through national and local experience and research, and to make sure that any lessons learned are shared, understood and acted upon

- to undertake case reviews where a child has died or – in certain circumstances – been seriously harmed and abuse and neglect are confirmed or suspected. To make sure that any lessons from the case are understood and acted upon

- to communicate clearly to individual services and professional groups their shared responsibility for protecting children, and to explain how each can contribute

- to help improve the quality of child protection work and of inter-agency working through specifying needs for inter-agency training and development, and ensuring that training is delivered and

- to raise awareness within the wider community of the need to safeguard children and promote their welfare and to explain how the wider community can contribute to these objectives.

Given that each area will have interpreted the requirements of *Working Together* (Department of Health and others 1999) differently to reflect local needs and service structures, it is of the utmost importance that you familiarize yourself with the procedures determined by the appropriate ACPC for the area in which you work and make yourself fully conversant with the responsibilities attaching to your agency and your post. The Department of Health and others (2003) have published Guidance on the core tasks associated with *Working Together,* including flow charts of the required responses. This is available via the Department of Health's website – see the web resources listed at the end of this Unit. The Department of Health's website also has a section describing the work of ACPCs and providing contact details for every ACPC in England and Wales – see the web resources at the end of this Unit. The remainder of this study text can only provide a schematic account of the investigative and decision -making structures as established by the Children Act 1989 (the Act) and *Working Together,* which does not relieve you of your professional responsibility to read and fully understand your own local procedures and your role within them.

THE INVESTIGATIVE PROCESS

Upon receipt of a referral suggesting concern about a child's welfare, the social services department should decide whether an initial assessment (as defined by the *Framework for the Assessment of Children in Need,* Department of Health and others 2000, and described in Unit 7) is required. This may be very brief if it becomes clear that there is a need for urgent action to safeguard the child concerned.

After the initial assessment, if it is judged that the child is at risk of actual or likely significant harm, then a 'strategy meeting' (which may be conducted over the telephone if necessary) is likely to be convened, involving the social services department, the police and other relevant agencies. This meeting, as well as sharing available information, will decide what further action is needed immediately to safeguard the child and determine whether enquiries under s. 47 of the Act should be initiated.

The local authority has a statutory duty under s. 47 of the Act to investigate whenever it 'has reasonable cause to believe that a child who lives, or is found, in their area is suffering, or is likely to suffer significant harm' (s. 47 (1)(b)) (see Study Text 10.1 for a full definition of 'significant harm'). Section 47 of the Act requires the local authority to determine whether it should apply to the court for an order or exercise any of its powers under the Act, including the provision of services to the child and its family. In order to assist in this determination, Section 47 also requires the local authority to take 'such steps as are reasonably practical' (s. 47 (4)) to obtain access to the child, either directly or through a person authorized by the authority 'unless they are satisfied that they already have sufficient information with respect to [the child]'. If access is frustrated, the local authority must apply to the court for one of a range of orders unless it is satisfied that the child's welfare can be 'satisfactorily safeguarded without their doing so' (s. 47 (6)). In the course of its investigations under s. 47, the local authority can make reasonable requests for information from any local authority, including education and housing authorities.

Based on extensive research, *Working Together* sets out ten of the commonest 'pitfalls' associated with initial assessments and enquiries. These are outlined in Figure 9.3 and reinforce many of the points that we have made already in this Unit and in Unit 7.

The strategy meeting will also decide whether to commence a core assessment (as defined by the *Framework for the Assessment of Children in Need*, Department of Health and others 2000, and described in Unit 7) to run alongside enquiries under s. 47 of the Act. Both the assessment and the s. 47 enquiry may take place in parallel to police investigations into any possible crimes.

THE INITIAL CASE CONFERENCE

Within no more than 15 working days after the start of the investigation, an initial child protection case conference should be called. Local procedures will determine the arrangements for the chairing of case conferences and the provision of support services, including the taking of minutes. The purpose of the case conference is to bring together the family and the professionals involved so that they can analyse the information that has been obtained, to make judgements about the likelihood of a child suffering significant harm in the future and, most important, to decide what

1. Not enough weight is given to information from family, friends and neighbours.

2. Not enough attention is paid to what children say, how they look and how they behave.

3. Attention is focused on the most visible or pressing problems and other warning signs are not appreciated.

4. Pressure from high status referrers, or the press, with fears that a child might die, lead to over-precipitate action.

5. Professionals think that when they have explained something as clearly as they can, the other person will have understood it.

6. Assumptions and pre-judgements about families lead to observations being ignored or misinterpreted.

7. Parents' behaviour, whether co-operative or unco-operative, is often misinterpreted.

8. When the initial enquiry shows that the child is NOT at risk of significant harm, families are seldom referred to other services that they need to prevent longer-term problems.

9. When faced with an aggressive or frightening family, professionals are reluctant to discuss fears for their own safety and ask for help.

10. Information taken at the first enquiry is not adequately recorded, facts are not checked and reasons for decisions are not noted.

Figure 9.3: The pitfalls of initial assessments and enquiries
Source: Adapted from Department of Health and others (1999), p.44 (Crown copyright).

further action is needed to safeguard the child and to form this into an outline child protection plan. The case conference does not need to make a determination that a particular person has committed the abuse. That is a matter for the courts.

Another important decision that the case conference will make is whether or not the child or young person's name should be placed on the child protection register and allocated a key worker accordingly. The role of the key worker is described in paragraph 5.76 of *Working Together*:

> The key worker is responsible for making sure that the outline child protection plan is developed into a more detailed inter-agency plan. S/he should complete the core assessment of the child and family... The key worker is also responsible for acting as lead worker for the inter-agency work with the child and family. S/he should co-ordinate the contribution of family members and other agencies to planning the actions which need to be taken, putting the child protection plan into effect, and reviewing progress against the objectives set out in the plan.

THE CHILD PROTECTION REGISTER

In each local authority area, a child protection register must be maintained. 'The register should list all the children resident in the area who are considered to be at continuing risk of significant harm and for whom there is a child protection plan' (Department of Health and others 1999, para. 5.95).

'Children who are judged to be in need of active safeguarding' (Department of Health and others 1999, para. 5.96) are placed on the register in one of the various registration categories (described in Study Text 9.1). The register provides a mechanism for ensuring the regular review of children for whom there is an inter-agency plan, a speedy point of access to information for professionals who have concerns about a child and useful information for the ACPC and its members on patterns and trends in child protection practice.

THE CHILD PROTECTION REVIEW CONFERENCE

The first child protection review conference should be held within three months of the initial child protection conference and subsequent reviews should take place at no more than six-monthly intervals for as long as the child's name remains on the child protection register (Department of Health and others (1999), para. 5.90ff). The purpose of review conferences is (para.5.90):

to review the safety, health and development of the child against intended outcomes set out in the child protection plan; to ensure that the child continues adequately to be safeguarded; and to consider whether the child protection plan should continue in place or should be changed.

CONCLUSION

We would stress that the account of child protection processes and protocols that we have given in this study text is highly schematic. Matters do not necessarily proceed in the rather linear way that we have described, for example. Nor have we provided you with an account of those actions and formal orders that usually accompany the more urgent cases that come to the attention of social services departments. We are assuming that you are not at the stage in your career when you will have to take a lead role in child protection but, as we pointed out in Unit 6, you may find yourself engaged in a child protection investigation long before you think you are ready.

Perhaps the most useful service we can provide to you at this point in your professional development is to reinforce the point that you must ensure that you have access to the child protection procedures for the area in which you work, or are on placement, at the earliest possible stage of your induction period. Your agency has a professional obligation to provide such access. You have a professional responsibility to make full use of it.

 CONCLUSION

Recognition of abuse, even in apparently 'clear cut' situations, must be preceded by an *awareness* on your part of the potential for abuse. We emphatically do *not* mean by this that every child and family case in which you are involved must be considered as a potential case of child abuse. What we mean is that if you do not have a clear sense of what is meant by 'good enough parenting', the needs and rights of children and a clear sense of your personal and professional thresholds, then you might not be able to recognize abuse even when confronted with an unambiguous instance of it. The same point must be made in your consideration of an appropriate response. Both remain questions of professional judgement. That judgement can be informed by specialist knowledge and improved by the use of lessons learned by research but it must be predicated on a thorough grounding in the essentials of good practice.

We do not want you to feel intimidated by work in child protection. In this Unit, you have already begun the process of making, testing and reflecting on your professional judgement in such cases, albeit only on paper. That judgement is rooted in your existing knowledge, skills and values. It is important to hold on to this thought, not just at the beginning of your career when it should give you confidence to extend your professional competence, but also later in your career when familiarity with abuse can arouse no more than a weary cynicism.

 NOTES AND SELF-ASSESSMENT

1.   Do you want to work in child protection? Can you explain why/why not?

2.   How prepared are you to work in child protection, in terms of knowledge and skills?

3.   How prepared are you emotionally to work in this area?

4.   What personal qualities could you bring to work in child protection?

5.   Do you know what to do when you are confronted with an incident of possible abuse?

6.   Where would you find the ACPC child protection procedures where you work?

RECOMMENDED READING

Department of Health, Home Office and Department for Education and Employment (1999) *Working Together to Safeguard Children*. London: The Stationery Office.

Wilson, K. and James, A. (eds) (2001) *The Child Protection Handbook*. Second edition. London: Baillière Tindall.

TRAINER'S NOTES

Exercise 9.1: Safeguarding and Promoting

Tasks 1, 2 and 3 can be undertaken either in small groups or by 'quickthinking' in a larger group. Material generated can be organized according to the proto-assessment prepared as part of Exercise 7.3. It is important that Task 3 is not carried out with too much emphasis on what a local authority might do at this stage. The emphasis should be on John's needs. Ideas generated here can be reviewed in the light of participants' reading of Study Text 9.3 and compared to the range of options considered as part of Exercise 4.2.

Exercise 9.2: Signs of Neglect

This exercise is best conducted in pairs, with a plenary session to compare notes. Participants should be encouraged to let their imaginations operate freely at Task 2. The plausibility of each explanation can be tested in debate between its proponent(s) and the rest of the group. This usually demonstrates where individuals feature on the pessimistic/optimistic continuum. The kind of information (i.e. doctor's assessments, teacher's observations, etc.) that may be suggested as part of Task 3 must include reference to the participant's own 'observations', notes, records and professional knowledge, etc. as there is sometimes a tendency for workers in child protection to look for 'proof' outside of their own knowledge and expertise.

Exercise 9.3: Risk Evaluation

Participants should be encouraged to prepare five-minute presentations of their audit. Discussion should allow for comparisons to be made and for any patterns relating to an agency's capacity for safe decision-making to emerge (e.g. size of organization, management culture, etc.). The group should be encouraged to draw up an action plan or procedural guidance that they might be able to take back to their agencies for further discussion.

 WEB RESOURCES

http://www.doh.gov.uk/acpc The Department of Health's website on Area Child Protection Committees (ACPCs) provides information about what ACPCs do and full contact details for each ACPC in England and Wales.

http://www.doh.gov.uk/safeguardingchildren/index.htm This section of the Department of Health's website contains a summary of and access to the complete text of *Safeguarding Children: What to do if You're Worried a Child is being Abused. Children's Service Guidance.* There are direct links (at the bottom of the page) to the flow charts referred to in Study Text 9.3.

The NSPCC website, as well as containing access to probably the most comprehensive source of information on child protection in the UK through its 'inform service' (see Unit 6), also has on-line access to advice pages for children (http://www.there4me.com/home/index.asp) and their parents and carers (http://www.nspcc.org.uk/html/Home/Needadvice/advicepages.htm).

UNIT 10

Court Craft

OBJECTIVES

In this Unit you will:

- Rehearse the process for obtaining a care order.
- Learn how to prepare a witness statement.
- Explore some fundamentals of court craft.

 GOING TO COURT

The purpose of going to court is to obtain, vary or discharge an order in respect of a child. For many social workers, even the most experienced, going to court can seem a daunting prospect. We may feel uncertain at finding ourselves on unfamiliar territory where people around us dress differently, use a strange vocabulary and engage in rituals that we do not fully understand. Our apprehension may be increased by our awareness that a great deal depends on the outcome of the court hearing, not only for the child and family most immediately concerned but for us too. We may feel that our own reputation and self-esteem might be threatened, and even that justice might not be done, if we do not play our part fully.

Families, too, can find the experience of going to court intimidating and confusing. Research (see, for example, Freeman and Hunt 1998; Brophy and others 1999) has demonstrated how parents can find themselves ill-prepared both practically and psychologically, anxious about having to speak in public and having to face a great many practical problems in simply attending the hearing. Some parents reported receiving poor-quality legal representation and very restricted access to expert advice of the sort usually available to social workers. Children too may be anxious, having developed wholly inaccurate impressions of what 'going to court' involves; often basing their expectations on what they have seen on television, especially soap operas and American (criminal) court dramas (see Butler and others 2003). Some of these deficiencies could be addressed by better information being made available to parents and children at an early stage in the conduct of proceedings and by a more inclusive approach being adopted by social workers. We do not intend to develop these points here (but see Study Texts 4.3 and 7.2) as our primary focus is on the social worker's role in the court process, but we do not under-estimate their importance and we want you to bear them in mind as you work through this Unit.

As for the social worker, a degree of apprehension, which appropriately reflects the seriousness of the occasion, is certainly preferable to a sense of complacency. If that apprehension provokes us to prepare assiduously and reflect seriously on the case before the court then it will have served a very useful purpose, for there can be no doubt that the courtroom can be a rigorous test of what we do and believe as social workers. We would probably agree that if our work could not bear close scrutiny then its deficiencies should be exposed. On the other hand, if it can withstand a thorough examination then we can proceed strengthened by the knowledge that our work has demonstrable rigour and coherence.

Just how early in your professional career or how frequently you will find yourself in court is very much more dependent on where you work than you might imagine. Although the average number of looked after children per 10,000 of the population under 16 across England is 54, the figures for individual councils range from 18 to 143 (Department of Health 2003b, paras 1.13–1.14). Geography itself is not the issue, of course, even taking into account broad economic and social differences between areas. The rate of applications to the court is in no small measure a function of 'differences in the responses of...individual social services departments in meeting the needs of the children in their area' (Department of Health 2003b, para. 1.13). This means that the kinds of decisions you and your colleagues make about whether or when to go to court and the outcomes you seek to achieve may be as important as the actual circumstances of children and families in determining the use made of compulsory powers.

This Unit aims to provide you with a practical appreciation of the process of going to court. Our particular interest in this Unit is in those public law orders that we may have to consider in relation to the Taylor family and which you are more likely to encounter or make use of in practice. But, before we look in detail at what is involved in applying for a care order, we should catch up with events in the Taylor family.

TAYLOR FAMILY CASE FILE

On 3 August, you called at Mrs Taylor's (senior) house to see why Tracy had not turned up to meet you at the clinic as you had arranged, only to be told that Tracy had moved back in with Alun. Mrs Taylor told you that she and Tracy had had a major row over her various choices of partner. You were not able to visit Tracy in New Estate that day.

At lunchtime on 4 August, you received a telephone call from a very distraught Mrs Taylor (senior). She told you that Tracy had been to see her, with John, and that John had a very big bruise over his eye. Tracy had told her that Alun had hit John and Tracy. Mrs Taylor had told Tracy that 'she had made her bed and so must lie in it' and to go home to Alun. She now very much regrets having said this and wants you to go and 'make sure that Tracy is all right'.

You arrived at Tracy's at around 2 p.m. Upon arrival you found John playing in the front garden. He was digging a hole in the ground with a tin can. There was no gate on the garden, which fronts on to the busy main road. John was only wearing a T-shirt and nappy, despite the fact that it was drizzling and far from warm. There was no immediate sign of Tracy or Alun. As you picked John up you could feel how cold he was. You could also see what appeared to be bruises. There was a dark bruise over John's left eye and his right ear was red and swollen. There were also some yellow/brown marks on his neck; there were three on the left side of his neck and one on the right side. The one on the right side was bigger than the others, about the size of a 50p piece. There was a similar pattern of marks on John's left leg, above the knee; the larger mark was on the inside of his thigh. You took John into the house, the front door was open, and wrapped him in a towel that was lying in the hall at the foot of the stairs. You called out but received no answer.

On entering the front room, you found Alun. He did not respond to your call and appeared to be asleep. On the floor were several cans of 'Special Brew', apparently empty. Alun eventually woke when you touched his arm. He smelled strongly of drink and appeared disorientated. He seemed not to recognize you. His speech was slurred and he had difficulty in rising to his feet. He eventually told you, in reply to your questioning, that Tracy was upstairs. She also appeared to be asleep. She had a black eye and a scratch on her right cheek. You could not rouse her.

Taking John with you, you went to the phone box at the end of the road and called an ambulance and the police. Upon returning to the house you found that Alun had gone back to sleep. The ambulance arrived before the police. Alan woke and started to shout at you and the ambulance crew. John was clearly very distressed and began to cry. This seemed to make Alun even more aggressive and you were relieved when the police arrived. Alun was blocking the doorway as they approached the house, preventing your exit and that of the ambulance crew who were trying to bring Tracy down the stairs. John was very distressed by this stage and Alun tried to take him out of your arms. A police officer tried to hold on to Alun's arm but Alun hit out at him. Alun was arrested.

The police exercised their powers under the Children Act 1989 (Section 46) and escorted you to Southtown General Hospital with John. You were joined at the hospital by a colleague who stayed with John while you went to secure an emergency protection order (EPO), which you successfully did by application to a single magistrate at around 4 p.m.

John was admitted to the paediatric ward at Southtown General that same afternoon, shortly after your return. Upon examination, he was found to weigh just less than 9 kg and, in the opinion of the paediatrician, to be severely developmentally delayed. You were told that the marks that you saw were bruises at different stages of healing and that they were consistent with a sharp blow to the side of the head and to being gripped very tightly around the back of the neck and on the leg. The paediatrician also told you that there were other marks on John's back, consistent with being hit with a strap. He told you that, in his opinion, all of the injuries were consistent with non-accidental injury and that the police should be informed. In the view of the paediatrician, John will need nursing care for at least four to six weeks on an in-patient basis as he has so much weight to gain. John has quietened down and is asleep by the time that you leave the hospital at around 7 p.m.

It transpires that Tracy had taken an overdose of painkillers and was admitted overnight to the same hospital as John. Alun was detained overnight in police cells but was bailed the next morning. He was re-arrested after his appearance in court and was charged with the assault on John. He appeared in court for the second time later in the day and was remanded on bail for a week, despite police objections.

On the next day (5 August), you visited Tracy in hospital. She appeared horrified to hear of the bruises to John and denied all knowledge of them. Tracy says that she intends to return to Alun as soon as she can and will take John with her. She says that she does not want to see you again and that she does not need or want any help from you or your agency. Tracy seems to believe that Alun was attacked by the police and even suggests that the bruises to John may have been caused in the scuffle at the house. The ward sister told you that Tracy is very depressed and that she ought to stay in hospital for a few days. However, Tracy discharged herself later that day. John remained in hospital under the terms of the EPO. Tracy visited her mother to tell her, according to a later conversation you had with Mrs Taylor (senior), that she no longer wanted anything to do with her mother, whom she blamed for 'causing all this trouble'. Tracy returned home to Alun.

The strength of the relationship between John and his mother is acknowledged and the importance of continued contact with her is recognized in allowing her unrestricted access to him in hospital. You want to work in partnership with Tracy and, possibly, even with Alun, to ensure that John's welfare is safeguarded and promoted but decide that the partnership needs to be an unequal one at this stage and that you need to be able to determine how far Tracy and Alun can be involved in parenting John at this point in their lives. Accordingly, with the agreement of an initial child abuse case conference, it is decided to make application for a care order in respect of John. His name is also entered on the child protection register.

Study Text 10.1: The Care Order

The remainder of this Unit will focus on the process of applying for a care order in respect of John. We have chosen to do this not necessarily because we consider this the typical or inevitable outcome of such cases, nor because we believe that a care order has a particular significance above that of other orders, but principally so that we can explore in greater depth what is involved in securing one particular order rather than take a wider, but necessarily more superficial, view of the range of possible outcomes in this case.

The decision to make such an application must never be taken lightly or without proper consideration by a multi-disciplinary case conference. *The Children Act 1989 Guidance and Regulations Volume 1 Court Orders* (Department of Health 1991b, para. 3.10) makes it clear that:

> no decision to initiate proceedings should be taken without clear evidence that provision of services for the child and his family has failed or would be likely to fail to meet the child's needs adequately and that there is no suitable person prepared to take over the care of the child under a residence order.

The question for the local authority must be: 'What will the use of compulsory powers add in safeguarding the child and is the gain sufficient to justify the use of compulsion and the trauma that may result' (Department of Health 1991b, para. 3.11).

In the artificial circumstances of the Taylor case we are not able to judge entirely satisfactorily that the decision to apply for a care order was the only or best alternative. Guidance (Department of Health 1991b, para. 1.12) states that 'where the prognosis for change is reasonable and the parents show a willingness to co-operate with voluntary arrangements, an application for a care order...is unlikely to succeed'. For the purposes of the remainder of this Unit, we will ask you to assume that the prognosis for change is not good, although you will have an opportunity to reflect further on this in Exercise 10.1.

But what precisely is a care order? The remainder of this study text offers an abbreviated account.

EFFECT AND DURATION

When a care order is made with respect to a child it becomes the duty of the local authority named in the order to receive that child into its care (s. 33 (1)) and to accommodate him and maintain him during the currency of the order and to safeguard and promote his welfare (s. 22 (3)). The local authority will assume parental responsibility for the child and acquire the power to determine how far others shall be allowed to exercise their parental responsibility in respect of the child (s. 33 (3)). Any residence order in force before the care order is extinguished. Proceedings for a care order cannot be brought before the birth of a child or after the age of 17 (16 if married) and no care order can last beyond the child's 18th birthday (s. 31 (3)).

THE COURT'S DECISION

The decision of the court to make a care order or not is taken in two stages: first, the court must decide whether the statutory 'threshold' criteria have been satisfied and, second, that the principles contained in Part I of the Act have been applied. The 'threshold' criteria relate to whether the child has suffered, or is likely to suffer, 'significant harm' (see below). The relevant Part I principles are that the child's welfare must be the court's paramount consideration (s. 1 (1)), understood in the light of the 'welfare check-list' (s. 1 (3)) (see Study Text 1.3). This 'check-list' requires the court to consider, for example, the wishes and feelings of the child and the child's physical, emotional and educational needs, and to have regard to the range of powers at its disposal. The court must also determine that making an order will be 'better for the child than making no order at all' (s. 1 (5)). The court will also have regard to arrangements for the child to have contact with parents or others (s. 34 (11)).

THE THRESHOLD CRITERIA

Section 31 (2) of the Act establishes that:

> A court may only make a care order or supervision order if it is satisfied
>
> (a) that the child concerned is suffering, or is likely to suffer, significant harm: and
>
> (b) that the harm, or likelihood of harm is attributable to –
>
>> (i) the care given to the child, or likely to be given to him if the order were not made, not being what it would be reasonable to expect a parent to give to him; or
>>
>> (ii) the child's being beyond parental control.

By 'is suffering' is meant at the point of the hearing, or the point at which the local authority initiated the procedure to protect the child, provided that whatever arrangements were put in place then have remained in place (*Re M* [1994] 3 WLR 558). In the case of John Taylor, assuming that the EPO is still in force and/or an interim care order was made, the time at issue would include the day of your visit to his home. By 'likely to suffer', the House of Lords has ruled (*Re H and Others (Child Sexual Abuse: Standard of Proof)* [1996] 1 All ER, 1, [1996] 1 FLR 80.) that in s. 31 '…likely is being used in the sense of a real possibility, a possibility that cannot sensibly be ignored having regard to the nature and gravity of the feared harm…'. 'Harm' is defined (s. 31 (9)) as meaning 'ill-treatment or the impairment of health or development' including, for example, impairment suffered from seeing or hearing the ill-treatment of another: development means 'physical, intellectual, emotional, social or behavioural development': health means 'physical or mental health' and ill-treatment includes 'sexual abuse and forms of abuse which are not physical'. You should note that ill-treatment without consequent impairment might still constitute harm.

The Act does not offer a gloss on 'significant'. *The Children Act 1989 Guidance and Regulations Volume 1 Court Orders* (Department of Health 1991b) relies on a dictionary definition of 'significant' as meaning 'considerable, noteworthy or important' (para. 3.19). Note that it is the harm that has to be significant, not whatever act caused it. Hence, a sustained series of privations, not individually harmful, as in the case of neglect, could amount to significant harm as far as the child's development was concerned. Not all harm will be significant nor will significant harm in one context necessarily be significant in another. Ultimately, it is a matter for the court to determine whether the harm is significant for the particular child in question. In those circumstances where the harm is said to be to the child's health or development, the court must compare it with what could be reasonably expected of a similar child (s. 31 (10)). A 'similar child' is one with the same attributes, needs and potential of the child in question, taking into account, for example, any particular learning or physical disability.

The harm caused to the child must be attributable to the care given to the child or to its being beyond parental control. The test of what would 'be reasonable to expect a parent to give him' is an objective one and does not depend on the motives or capacity of the carer. A parent may be trying very hard but still not be able to provide an adequate standard of care to meet the needs of the particular child. (You should note that s. 105 of the Act establishes the foregoing as the definition of significant harm for the remaining purposes of the Act, including when used to form the grounds of an application for an EPO or for the purposes of a s. 47 investigation – see Unit 9).

In some cases, it is not possible to directly attribute the harm caused. For example, in *Lancashire County Council* v *B* [2000] 1 FLR 583 a seven-month-old baby had suffered at least two episodes of shaking but it was not clear whether this was at the hands of the mother, father or childminder. The House of Lords ruled that it was sufficient for the court to be satisfied that the harm was caused by one of the child's primary carers.

A series of cases have established a positive duty on local authorities to take action where there are child protection concerns. These cases have arisen from claims of negligence by local authorities and breach of Article 3 of the Human Rights Act (HRA) 1998 for failure to protect children. In *E* v *United Kingdom* (2002) The Times, 4 December, ECHR, the court followed the line established by *X* v *Bedfordshire* [1995] AC 633. The local authority had failed in its duty to protect E and her brothers and sisters and to monitor the behaviour of a known offender who lived with the children and their mother. In the view of the court, damage caused to the children by the offender could have been minimized or avoided had the authority acted properly. As a result of the breach, the children were entitled to an award in damages.

PROCESS

Most public law applications under the Act will be commenced in the Family Proceedings Court (C(AP)(A)O 1994 Art. 3). Figure 10. 1 sets out the court structure for proceedings under the Children Act 1989. The application must be made on the prescribed form. The form is divided into sections and seeks information under the following headings:

- the child – e.g. name, address, representation
- the applicant – as above
- the child's family – e.g. marital status of parents; brothers and sisters
- whether a court-directed investigation has been ordered in the case
- distribution of parental responsibility
- any other applications that affect the child – e.g. if an EPO is in force, details of any pre-existing orders
- the basis of the application itself – e.g. nature of grounds on which application is based and any directions required if an interim order is to be made
- plans for the child if the order is made.

The final section of the form requires the applicant to declare that the information given is 'correct and complete' to the best of his or her knowledge.

Once the form has been received by the court, the court must fix a date either for the hearing of the case or, much more likely, for a directions hearing to be held. The court will then return copies of the forms to the applicant so that one can be served on all of those persons who have standing in the case. A full copy of the application (and the date fixed for the directions or full hearing) must be served on everyone with parental responsibility for the child and the child itself; that is to say to the 'automatic respondents' in the case. Other people can apply to the court and become full respondents and have a voice in proceedings. Certain people are entitled to receive notice of the application and be informed of the date, time and place of the hearing but not to receive details of the application. These include parents without parental responsibility and any person with whom the child was living before the application was begun.

HOUSE OF LORDS

The House of Lords hears appeals from the Court of Appeal and from the High Court.

COURT OF APPEAL (CIVIL DIVISION)

The Court of Appeal hears appeals from the High Court and County Court.

HIGH COURT (FAMILY DIVISION)

The High Court deals with private and public law cases where there are complex points of law involved; applications by children in private law matters; wardship and appeals from the Family Proceedings Court.

COUNTY COURT

Almost all private law applications begin here.
There are three broad catergories of County Court as far as proceedings under the Children Act are concerned:

Divorce Centres, which may determine applications under Parts 1 and II of the Act, apart from contested s8 orders;

Family Hearing Centres, which deal with applications under Parts 1 and II of the Act, including contested s8 orders;

Care Centres, which may determine both private and public law matters, including applications under Part III, IV and V of the Act transferred from the Family Proceedings Court.

FAMILY PROCEEDINGS COURT

Almost all public law cases and some private law matters begin here.

Figure 10.1 Court structure

The directions hearing is a formal procedure designed to minimize delay in such proceedings. It is attended by the applicant, the respondents and/or their representatives, although usually not by the child concerned. Rules (Family Proceedings Courts (Children Act 1989) Rules 1991, r 14 (2)) establish what kind of directions can be given. They include:

- the timetable for proceedings
- the appointment of a Children's Guardian
- arrangements for the submission of evidence. We will return to the submission of evidence in Study Text 10.2
- whether it is necessary to have a split hearing so that factual disputes can be resolved at an early stage.

INTERIM CARE ORDERS

In most cases, interim care orders will be made before the final hearing of the care order application (s. 38). During this time, ongoing assessments may be conducted and the child's wishes and feelings will be ascertained. An interim order will be granted where the local authority can satisfy the court that there are reasonable grounds to believe the threshold criteria apply and for which evidence will be presented at the final hearing. Interim hearings may be contested and provide a forum for challenge of contact arrangements.

THE CHILDREN'S GUARDIAN

The Children's Guardian is part of the Children and Family Court Advisory and Support Service (CAFCASS), which was established in 2001. CAFCASS is a national, non-departmental public body covering England and Wales. It brings together services previously provided by:

- the Family Court Welfare Service
- the Guardian *ad Litem* Services
- the Children's Division of the Official Solicitor.

(You might wish to note that CAFCASS' website provides one of the most useful, user-friendly and most easily understood source of information to parents, children and teenagers that we know of! See the web resources section, below.)

Children's Guardians, who represent the interests of children during cases in which social services have become involved and in contested adoption cases, are one of four kinds of 'officers' managed by CAFCASS. The others are:

- *Children and Family Reporters* – who become involved when parents are divorcing or separating and have not been able to reach agreement on the arrangements for the children.

- *Reporting Officers* – who ensure that parents understand what adoption means for them and their child and whether or not they consent to it.

- *Guardians* ad Litem – who are occasionally employed, usually when there is some particular difficulty with the case, when parents who are divorcing or separating cannot agree on arrangements for the children.

The Children's Guardian will usually, but not necessarily, be a qualified and experienced social worker. She will have been appointed 'as soon as practicable' (The Family Proceedings Courts (Children Act 1989) Rules 1991 r. 10 (1)) in the legal process and will be asked her advice not only on matters relating to the interests of the child but also on such matters as the appropriate forum for the proceedings, the timetable for proceedings and the range of options that might be used to resolve best the matter before the court (Rules 11 (4)(c–f)). In reaching her opinion on how the child's interests might best be served, the Guardian will consult with those whom she or the court see fit (Rules 11(9)(a)), have access to local authority records concerning the child (Children Act s. 42) and obtain such professional advice and assistance as she determines appropriate (Rules 11(9)(c)). She will also consult with the child on a wide range of matters but Guardians are not bound by children's views in forming their opinion on what is in the children's interests. The Guardian will usually appoint a solicitor to represent the child (Rules 11(2)) unless the solicitor is of the opinion, or the court directs, that the child instruct the solicitor on its own behalf. The range of proceedings in which a Guardian may be appointed is extensive (s. 41 (6)) and, to all intents and purposes, will include most of the cases in which you, as a social worker, are likely to be involved. Courts are not obliged to appoint a Guardian in every case where an appointment is permissible but must do so 'unless satisfied that it is not necessary to do so in order to safeguard [the child's] interests' (s. 41 (1)). Where the court does not follow the recommendations of the Guardian, it must give reasons for not doing so (*S* v *Oxfordshire County Council* [1993] 1 FLR 452).

POWERS OF THE COURT

Upon hearing an application for a care order, the court has access to the full range of orders available under the Act. Accordingly, the court may make any of the following orders in addition to a care order:

- parental responsibility order (if applied for)
- appointment (termination) of guardianship order
- care contact order (s. 34).

The court may also, on refusing a care order, make a supervision order or any of the orders listed above or any s. 8 order (see Appendix 1), with or without an application having been made. The influence of the HRA 1998 means that the order which the court ultimately makes must be proportionate in all the circumstances, adopting a preference for the least interventionist stance. In *Re O (Supervision Order; Future Harm)* [2001] 1 FCR 289, the court held that, in the circumstances, a supervision order was more appropriate than a care order in the light of Article 8 of the HRA 1998, the right to respect for private and family life.

OTHER CONSIDERATIONS

As well as having regard to the arrangements for contact with a child subject to a care order, the local authority's plans for the child are also open to detailed scrutiny by the courts. Before making a care order, the court must be satisfied that this is better for the child than making no order at all. The care plan for the child will be highly influential in reaching this determination. As a result of a number of cases which challenged the extent to which the court (and Guardian) could retain any involvement with a case after making an order (and review elements of the care plan), a new provision relating to care plans has been introduced into the Children Act 1989. The court may not make a care order until it has considered a care plan, as provided for in s. 31 of the Act. The local authority must keep the plan under review until the order is made and it will be possible for the courts (and Regulations) to specify issues to be considered in the plan. After the order is made, s. 26 of the Children Act 1989 is also amended so that the care plan will be considered as part of the regular reviews for children in care. It will be possible for a 'prescribed person' to refer the case to a CAFCASS officer who will be able to return the case to court if the care plan is not proceeding. A separate care plan is required for each child who is the subject of care proceedings. (See Harwin and others, forthcoming.)

THE DECISION OF THE COURT

The court will reach its conclusions on matters of fact 'on the balance of probabilities', which means, in Lord Denning's famous dictum (*Miller* v *Ministry of Pensions* [1947] 2 All ER 372), that the court must be satisfied that it is 'more likely than not' that the particular events took place. The burden of proof is on the local authority to satisfy the court that the s. 31 threshold criteria have been met. It is not for a parent to exculpate him- or herself (*Re O 7 N* [2002] EWCA Civ 1271). The court must record the reasons for its decision and any findings of fact. This is essential where there is any prospect of an appeal.

You may find the arrangement of material in this study text a useful template for your study of other orders under the Children Act 1989.

 Exercise 10.1: Establishing the Grounds

This exercise is designed to give you an opportunity to familiarize yourself with the grounds on which a care order is made.

TASKS

1. Examine recent entries in the Taylor Case File and determine whether a reasonable case can be made for the making of a care order in respect of John. You should structure your response as follows:

    ○ Is he suffering harm?

    ○ Is he likely to suffer harm?

    ○ What is the precise nature of the harm he is, or is likely to, suffer?

    ○ Is it ill-treatment?

　　　　　physical

　　　　　sexual

　　　　　mental

　　◦　Is it impairment of health?

　　　　　physical

　　　　　mental

　　◦　Is it impairment of development?

　　　　　physical

　　　　　emotional

　　　　　behavioural

　　　　　intellectual

　　　　　social

　　◦　Is that harm significant?

　　◦　Is it attributable to the standard of care given to him?

　　◦　Is it attributable to the standard of care likely to be given to him?

　　◦　Is it attributable to his being beyond parental control?

2.　Consider whether the use of compulsory powers is justified in this case. In particular, you might consider:

　　◦　How can John's immediate and medium-term needs best be met, such that his welfare is properly safeguarded and protected?

　　◦　What potential for change exists in John's carers' circumstances or capacity to provide for his needs?

　　◦　What services would need to be provided in order to enable John to continue in the care of his parents?

　　◦　What is the likely level of co-operation from Tracy, Alun and Mrs Taylor?

Points to Consider

1. How does the Children Act's concept of 'significant harm' correspond with your definition of abuse? Is it a broader or a narrower definition?

2. Look back at the answers you gave in Exercise 6.2. Would an understanding of 'significant harm' have helped you to make your decisions more easily? Would it have made you make different decisions?

3. Would your understanding of 'significant harm' have helped you to determine more easily whether John was subject to abuse before this recent series of incidents?

4. Given your understanding of secondary risk factors (Study Text 9.2), what factors do you think influence decisions to make use of compulsory powers where you work?

5. Do you think that the threshold for making applications to the court is clearly and appropriately fixed where you work?

6. What does the fact that you have access to compulsory powers in this way tell you about the nature of your role at the boundaries of family, State and the law?

PREPARING FOR THE HEARING

Once the decision is made to make an application for a care order, the procedural, managerial and administrative arrangements required to ensure that the necessary steps are taken, in the right order, will vary from area to area. In some local authorities, the matter will be steered by the authority's legal advisors from a very early point in the process. Some local authorities, for example, arrange for legal advice to be available routinely at case conferences where decisions to make applications to the court are likely to arise. In other areas, social workers will be responsible for obtaining, completing and, in some cases, serving the relevant forms.

Whatever the arrangements, the social worker will have an important part to play in establishing the basis of the application through the evidence that they will offer the court. The following study text and exercise will familiarize you with what is required in the preparation of your evidence.

 Study Text 10.2: Evidence

THE WITNESS STATEMENT

You may have noted that one of the considerations to be made at the directions hearing concerned the submission of evidence (*Family Proceedings Courts* (Children Act 1989) Rules 1991 r. 14(2)(f)). Rule 17 explains that parties to the proceedings (i.e. applicants and respondents) must file with the court, and serve on the remaining parties, 'written statements of the substance of the oral evidence which the party intends to adduce at a hearing…[and]…copies of any documents, including…experts' reports, upon which the party intends to rely…'. That is to say that you will have to prepare, in advance of the hearing and to the timetable established at the directions hearing, a comprehensive account of the evidence you intend to give at the hearing and co-ordinate the submission of any other reports that it is intended to use in pursuit of the application. Paragraph 3 of Rule 17 establishes that you will need the permission of the court to adduce additional evidence or seek to rely on a document that you have not filed with the court and served on the remaining parties. You may not be able to rely on your case notes, for example, unless you have previously filed them with the court or are prepared to have them scrutinized by the other parties' representatives, nor will you be allowed to call a mystery expert at the last dramatic moment. The principle of 'advance disclosure' is an important one in family proceedings.

It is clear just how important your witness statement will be. It will form the basis of the 'evidence in chief' that you will present to the court and on which you will be cross-examined; it will be closely read by the magistrates before the case and by the lawyers representing the respondents, as well as by family members. This study text will provide some guidance on the preparation of your witness statement, but it will be necessary first to make some general points about evidence in civil proceedings.

THE RULES OF EVIDENCE

Rules of evidence differ between civil and criminal cases. The focus here is on evidence relating to care proceedings, which are civil proceedings. It should be borne in mind, however, that the same facts might lead to both civil and criminal proceedings. For example, an alleged case of sexual abuse could give rise to care proceedings in order to protect the child, and to a criminal charge to prosecute the perpetrator.

In order to be taken into account by a court making a decision in any matter before it, evidence must be relevant and admissible. In order to be relevant, the evidence must logically bear on proving or disproving the point at issue. Unless a particular exclusion applies, all relevant evidence is admissible. The general exclusions are hearsay evidence, evidence concerned with opinion and evidence concerned with character. However, in the case of proceedings under the Act, certain qualifications apply to these general exclusions (the rules of evidence relating to character apply largely to criminal proceedings and are not considered here).

HEARSAY EVIDENCE

The general rule is that witnesses should give evidence of that which they have actually observed. Hearsay evidence is 'evidence of a statement made to a witness by a person who is not himself a witness' and is generally inadmissible. However, in order, particularly, to bring the evidence of children before the court in such a way that the child need not be present, The Children (Admissibility of Hearsay Evidence) Order 1993 does allow such evidence where it relates to the upbringing, maintenance or welfare of the child to be admitted. This provision does not apply only to statements made by the child concerned. However, the court, which will always have a preference for the best and most direct evidence, will have to assess what weight to attach to hearsay evidence. Cross-examination of hearsay is likely to focus on the source and reliability of the evidence.

OPINION EVIDENCE

The general rule that witnesses should confine themselves to matters of fact and not offer an opinion does not apply when the opinion offered is that of an expert (in the view of the court) and that the opinion will be of use to the court in determining the matter in question. Expert witnesses, including social workers, will usually give evidence on matters of fact observed by them or interpretations of those or other facts adduced in evidence and offer an opinion on the significance of the facts or interpretation. All expert witnesses, again including social workers, must only offer opinions that they genuinely hold and not just those that favour one or other party to the proceedings. If you need to quote research evidence to support your opinion, do so sparingly and make sure that you are aware of what criticisms have been made of the original research.

PREPARING YOUR STATEMENT

Perhaps the most important point of all to bear in mind when preparing your witness statement is that you cannot make it better than the assessment that informs it or the work that has already gone into the case. You should not now be at the point of reading the case file for the first time or of imposing a structure on your knowledge of the family! You will need to re-read the file and refresh your memory as you compile your statement, of course. As part of this process, you may identify material that you wish to rely on in your evidence, such as a piece of correspondence or a working agreement, which could then be appended to your statement. But, the real preparation for drawing up your statement began when you were first allocated this case and committed yourself to working to the highest professional standards that both families and the court have a right to expect of you.

If it is the case that you cannot make a witness statement better than the thinking and the work that has preceded it, the converse certainly does not hold. It is perfectly possible to prepare a witness statement that makes well thought out and skilfully delivered work seem confused and poorly planned. Witness statements need time to prepare and you will need to rid yourself of as many distractions as you can in order to concentrate on researching, thinking and writing the statement. You should try to 'block out' at least two or three days for the purpose. It is important to seek the advice and support of your lawyer at this stage too.

GENERAL ADVICE

- *Stick to the point.* It is a more demanding task to select relevant material that you wish to present to the court than to include everything you ever knew about the family and the practice of social work. In the Taylor case, it is not relevant to anything that Ron is a mechanic and that so was his brother-in-law! Extraneous material obscures more than it reveals.

- *Differentiate between fact and opinion.* Consider the following sentence: 'When I arrived at the house, John was in danger from the traffic on the main road as he was playing, unattended, in an un-gated garden.' It is a matter of fact that John was playing in the garden with easy access to the main road but it is a matter of opinion as to whether that was potentially dangerous.

- *Make sure that any opinion you offer is within your competence* (i.e. within your observations and professional expertise). Consider this sentence: 'When I entered the living room, Mr Evans, who was drunk, lay asleep on the sofa.' You are not competent to judge Alun Evans' state of intoxication (certainly not when he is asleep!). You are not a doctor nor do you have any knowledge or training that would enable you to determine his state of mental or physical alertness.

- *Wherever possible, let the facts speak for themselves.* Compare the following statement with the one above and decide which is the most helpful to the court in understanding what you saw and what subsequently happened: 'I observed Mr Evans lying on the sofa. There were a number of empty beer cans on the floor around him. Upon my waking him, he appeared disorientated and his speech was slurred.'

- *Clearly distinguish between hearsay and direct evidence.* Compare the following statements:

  1. 'Ms Taylor later denied that Mr Evans had hit John, although previously she had said that Mr Evans was responsible for the bruises to John.'

  2. 'I was informed by Mrs Taylor (senior) that her daughter had told her that Mr Evans had hit Ms Taylor and John. Mrs Taylor reported this conversation to me on 4 August

during the course of a telephone call requesting that I visit her grandson. Mrs Taylor seemed very agitated during the course of the telephone conversation and expressed her concern for the well-being of both Ms Taylor and John. During the course of an interview with Ms Taylor, conducted by me on 6 August while Ms Taylor was still a patient in Southtown General Hospital, Ms Taylor said that she did not know anything about the bruises to John and suggested to me that they may have been caused during the incident which led to the arrest of Mr Evans.'

It is important that the court is fully aware of the circumstances in which hearsay evidence was gathered in order to determine what weight to attach to it.

- *Present a balanced account.* You have a duty to tell the whole truth to the court and not simply to select those 'facts' that fit your case. Consider these versions of the same event:

    1. 'I first became involved with the Taylor family when arrangements for the care of her two older children had reached the point of breakdown.'

    2. 'Ms Taylor referred herself to the social services department, seeking help to manage difficulties that had arisen concerning the upbringing of her two older children.'

- *Avoid jargon.* What does the following actually mean? 'The dysfunctional relationship between the two older siblings and Ms Taylor's former spouse had expressed itself in acting-out behaviour on Michael's part.'

- *Use language that is respectful, authoritative, that you understand and with which you feel comfortable.* You will need to ensure that the importance of your statement is reflected in the tone that you adopt, but resist the temptation to write in your 'telephone voice'. Use family names and polite forms of address and make sure that your grammar and spelling are of the highest order. What might the following tell the court about the author of the statements?

1. 'I implied from what Tracy said to her mum that John had got his bruises from Alun who hit him the previous day when she spoke to me on the phone.'

2. 'I had facilitated access for Tracy and John to the local family treatment resource. This she had not availed herself of.'

Neither of these statements would tell the court very much about the facts of the case.

STRUCTURE OF THE STATEMENT

Your agency may well have a favoured format for witness statements of this sort and may require you to use existing pro formas. If not, the following (adapted from Plotnikoff and Woolfson 1996) may be of use:

1. *Cover sheet and declaration:* This should provide all the identifying detail that will ensure that the statement arrives at the right place at the right time as well as information on how to contact you. You will also have to make a declaration, as required by the Rules, declaring the truth of the statement and your knowledge that it may be placed before the court.

2. *The author's credentials:* A very brief statement of your qualifications and experience.

3. *The statement's provenance:* This should include a brief history of your involvement with this family and the sources that you have consulted in compiling your statement.

4. *A 'cast list':* Compile an index of all of those whose name appears in the statement and a brief identifying description. You might also include at this stage a detailed account of family structure and relationships, possibly using a genogram.

5. *A chronology:* This should be a chronology of key events that have a material bearing on the case. It will probably extend to include details of the births of all three children but need not, at this stage, go back as far as Tracy's own childhood. If it is decided to include a more detailed account of Tracy's past, this is best done within the body of the statement. Include critical incidents and dates of case conferences, planning meetings, etc.

6.   *The substantive case:* This should include a detailed history of your involvement with the family as well as any more recent precipitating events. It is helpful if this section is broken down into subsections dealing, in turn, with the family, the child and the issues giving rise to concern. Information about the parents should include an account of their capacity to look after the child, their response to services and support already offered and their wishes and feelings for the future. Information about the child should include a consideration of all of those matters referred to in the 'welfare check-list' and those matters referred to in s. 22 (5)(c) of the Children Act 1989 requiring a full consideration of the child's racial, cultural, religious and linguistic background.

7.   *Your assessment of risk:* This should include a consideration of possible alternatives to the action that you are now asking the court to allow as well as a thorough account of those primary risk factors that have been demonstrated in the case.

8.   *The care plan:* This should include arrangements for contact and must be described in a way that follows directly from your previous assessment of the child's needs, the capacity of its parents to meet them and your consideration of alternative courses of action. You must demonstrate to the court's satisfaction that what you intend will accord with the court's duty to have the child's welfare as its paramount concern and that this can best be achieved by the making of the order that you seek.

9.   *Conclusion:* This should provide a concise statement of the reasons for the application before the court and demonstrate that your proposed course of action is the most appropriate in this case.

See also: Brammer (2003): Chapter 4 includes guidance on giving evidence effectively and developing good working relations with lawyers.

Exercise 10.2: Writing a Witness Statement

Using the material included in Units 7–10, and the structure recommended in the previous study text, write a full witness statement to support an application for a care order in respect of John Taylor.

Points to Consider

1. Is your conclusion a convincing argument that the making of a care order is necessary to adequately safeguard and promote John's welfare?

2. Do your plans for John reflect the need to exercise compulsory powers?

3. Do you feel confident in the opinions that you offer?

4. Are these opinions based on, and justified by, the facts of the case?

5. Can you ground your opinions in an established body of social work knowledge?

6. Does your statement represent your honest belief that the course of action proposed will allow the court fairly to discharge its burden to have John's welfare as its paramount consideration?

GIVING EVIDENCE

The process of compiling a witness statement is a complex and daunting one. Once you have finished it, however, provided that it is based on competent practice and a well-considered analysis, your confidence in the course of action you are about to undertake should begin to rise. If you are not confident that what you are asking the court to sanction is, in all the circumstances, the best course of action open to you in order to safeguard and promote the welfare of the child concerned, then you must seek professional advice immediately. In any well-considered case there will be some residual uncertainty, of course; but if you are not convinced that what you propose will enable the court to make the order with the child's welfare as its paramount consideration then you should not be asking the court for such a decision.

Your confidence in your plans for the child and its family may not, however, equate to confidence in your own ability as a witness during the course of the hearing. The following study text offers some guidance on giving oral evidence. It begins with a brief account of the procedures likely to be encountered in the courtroom and a description of who else may be present.

 ## Study Text 10.3: In the Box

COURTROOM LAYOUT AND KEY PERSONNEL

Almost invariably, proceedings such as the one we are simulating will commence in the Family Proceedings Court. The physical layout of such courts varies considerably, not least with the age of the court building, but, generally speaking, the 'bench' of magistrates (usually three) will sit together facing the 'well' of the court. It is the magistrates alone who determine matters of fact in proceedings and who decide what order(s), if any, to make. The court clerk, who will be legally qualified, will usually sit in front of the bench but sufficiently close to be able to speak to the bench easily. The court clerk is there to advise the bench on points of law and procedure and quite often will act as 'ringmaster' in the court. S/he is assisted by one or more ushers who will call witnesses, direct them to the witness box and administer the oath or affirmation. Usually facing the bench will sit the lawyers representing the various parties to the proceedings. Sometimes the party from whom they are 'receiving instructions' will sit behind them but it is not uncommon for parties to be excluded at various points in the proceedings. The general public will not be allowed into the courtroom. Usually present throughout will be the Children's Guardian.

PROCEDURE IN THE COURTROOM

The evidence is usually 'adduced' in the following order, although the court can direct otherwise:

- the applicant
- any party with parental responsibility
- other respondents (e.g. unmarried father)
- the Guardian
- the child (if not a party and there is no Guardian).

Closing speeches are usually in the following order:

- other respondents
- any party with parental responsibility
- the applicant
- the Children's Guardian
- the child (if not a party and there is no Guardian).

Once called to give evidence, you will be asked to take an oath or make an affirmation that the evidence you are about to give will be truthful. Your legal representative will then question you on the basis of the written statement you have filed with the court and which will form the basis of your 'evidence in chief'. Even though almost everyone in the room will have read your statement, the evidence it contains will be brought out in the course of this 'examination'. You will then be 'cross-examined' on the evidence you have given by the legal representatives of the other parties to the proceedings. The express purpose of this process is to test your evidence and, where it is weak or open to other interpretations, to make that clear to the court. Your legal representative may then re-examine you. This re-examination is not to adduce fresh evidence but to clarify any possible confusion or misunderstandings that may have arisen as a result of your cross-examination.

GIVING EVIDENCE

One important way in which courts evaluate the credibility and reliability of a piece of evidence is by the reliability and credibility of the witness. In other words, how you are perceived will strongly influence how much weight can be attached to what you have to say. Managing your 'performance' in the witness box is a skill that develops with experience. For present purposes, bearing in mind all of the points made in relation to the presentation of written submissions, we offer the following 'do's' and 'don'ts':

- *Do* think hard about what impression your clothing and demeanour will make on the court. If you arrive breathless, bedraggled and spilling papers on the floor (it has been known!), you will look as disorganized and ill-prepared as you probably are. Courtrooms are probably less formal than they used to be but everyone else will be dressed soberly, recognizing the seriousness of the business in hand. If you turn up in clothes more suited for the beach, you will attract the same kind of opinion as if you turned up for the beach in a dark suit. Remember, the court will only have what they hear and see before them to help them make up their minds about you and what you have to say.

- *Do* address your evidence to the bench. All of your answers are for the benefit of the whole court, not just the questioner. There are a number of things you can do to remind yourself to address the bench. Position your feet facing towards the bench when you enter the witness box. Then, as you begin to respond to questions, even if you have turned to hear what the questioner is asking, your body will naturally return to face in the direction of your feet. Alternatively, you can begin your answers with the words 'Your Worships, I...'. This, again, will have the effect of making you turn towards the bench.

- *Don't* engage the lawyer asking you questions in conversation. Although it is 'natural' to wish to respond directly to the person asking you questions, an experienced advocate will be looking for visual clues from you in order to know when to interrupt. If you have not finished your answer, it is much easier to continue if it is your 'conversation' with the bench that the advocate has interrupted. It is the lawyer who will be disadvantaged if s/he appears to be rude. Engaging the bench, rather than your inquisitor, helps to avoid confrontation too.

- *Do* make sure that you can be heard. You can use the taking of the oath to 'warm up' your voice. Remember also that a great deal of additional information can be imparted through the tone of voice used. An expressive voice will secure greater attention than a flat monotone.

- *Don't* allow yourself to be flustered. Sort your notes out well in advance. Label them if you need to and make liberal use of a text marker. If you need to, ask permission to consult your notes, then do so carefully. If the questioner is pushing you along at too fast a pace or not allowing you to say what you want, try to impose a structure on your answers. One tried and tested technique is to reply: 'Your Worships, there are four points I would like to make in reply to that question...'. If you run out of 'points', either say so or say that you have substantially dealt with them in what you have already said.

- *Do* tell the truth! If you don't know the answer to a question, or cannot remember, say so. If you find yourself saying something that is misleading, untrue or incomplete, or if your questioner creates the impression that you believe something that you do not, then you must say so.

- *Don't* be taken by surprise. You should be able to predict, with a reasonable degree of accuracy, what the difficult questions are likely to be. Why did you not make more frequent visits to the Taylor family after the two older children had left? Why did you not do more to ensure Tracy attended the health centre? What happened to the place at the family centre that you had promised but not delivered?

- *Do* be ready to deal with alternative explanations of events. As an expert witness, you will be allowed to give your opinion on certain matters. This means that you should predict what other inferences could be drawn from the facts and be ready with an account of why your opinion contains the correct interpretation.

There are not many situations in life when the express purpose of the person asking you questions is to cast doubt on everything you say. Of course it is uncomfortable. Quite often, it is meant to be. Remember, however, that you and your evidence are vital to the court's decision-making. However uncomfortable you may feel, you have an important job to do and a perfect right to have your evidence, your professional expertise and personal integrity respected by the court. In one sense, giving evidence is no more than a continuation of professional practice by other means:

> The witness who is regarded as serious, caring, undogmatic, well-informed, fair and reasonable, and who shows respect for the family concerned, will be effective in helping the court to establish what is in the child's best interests... It is not suggested that [these qualities] can be acquired for the limited purpose of giving evidence. (Biggs and Robson 1992, p.13)

 ## CONCLUSION

The decision to proceed to court in furtherance of your duty to safeguard and promote the welfare of children with whom you are working should never be taken lightly or alone. In reaching your decision, you will need to seek and consider the advice of senior colleagues and of specialists in other fields than your own. This can be a testing process whereby your judgement and your expertise may be questioned. We hope that you would not wish it any other way.

Similarly, when invoking the powers of the court is the best and most appropriate route to securing the welfare of a child we would not wish you to shy away from your responsibilities. Going to court is an integral part of social work with children and families. Good social workers are good social workers in the witness box just as much as they are in case conferences, team meetings or in direct work with families. It is only the other kind that need have any concerns.

NOTES AND SELF-ASSESSMENT

1. What might the court process do to your future relationship with the child or family concerned? What can you do to maintain an effective relationship?

2. Who is most/least powerful or influential in the court process, do you think? Who should be?

3. Do you think that a courtroom is the most appropriate place in which to resolve complex family problems?

4. What does 'justice' mean in the context of family proceedings?

5. What impression do you want to make in court?

6. How close is that impression to the reality?

RECOMMENDED READING

Brammer, A. (2003) *Social Work Law*. Harlow: Pearson Education.

NSPCC (2001) *Power Packs*. These are extremely helpful information packs (one for children under ten and one for those over ten) containing a 'jargon buster', information on how the court works and the role of solicitors and Guardians in proceedings and information on children's rights. The packs can be downloaded from the NSPCC's website and permission is given for their use in working with young people. (http://www.nspcc.org.uk then navigate to 'publications'.)

TRAINER'S NOTES

Exercise 10.1: Establishing the Grounds

This exercise can best be undertaken by a group, either as a debate or in the form of a simulated case conference, strategy meeting or professional supervision session. The trainer will need to be able to offer expert advice and allocate roles accordingly. In a simulated case conference, it is sometimes difficult for participants to role-play family members or the child concerned. If this is the case, John's interests can be represented by a Children's Guardian (adjusting the fiction a little so that the meeting takes place after the directions hearing). Other members of the group should observe the interactions and imaginatively recreate what this might signify for Tracy and Alun, without becoming actively involved in the drama. This arrangement is closer to what might usually happen in reality.

Exercise 10.2: Writing a Witness Statement

This is a difficult exercise to manage with a large group. However, the most effective way of testing the witness statement, and the court skills described in Study Text 10.3, is to simulate the hearing itself. If at all possible, such an exercise should take place in a real courtroom. These can be hired (and can be quite expensive!) through your court clerk's office or through the administrator for the county court in your area. It is possible to re-arrange the furniture and simulate a courtroom elsewhere but something of the sense of atmosphere and occasion is lost in the process. The trainer should try to secure the services of an experienced local solicitor specializing in family matters to appear on behalf of Tracy. The trainer can act as the solicitor representing the local authority. It is not necessary to rehearse the whole hearing. The most important element is to provide participants with the opportunity to have their evidence adduced and to be cross-examined by someone with the necessary skills and with whom they have no previous acquaintance. The greater the verisimilitude (including insistence on the appropriate dress code), the more useful participants will find the exercise. Trainers may be surprised by the degree of anxiety demonstrated by participants.

 ## WEB RESOURCES

http://www.cafcass.gov.uk This is the website for the Children and Family Court Advisory and Support Service (CAFCASS). As well as explaining what CAFCASS and its officers do, the site contains some excellent guides for parents, children and teenagers on 'the law about children' (including adoption). If only there were more sites like this one! There is even a Welsh language version, which is easily accessible from the main page.

Carelaw, accessed via the website for the NCH (**http://www.nch.org.uk**). Presented in a slightly different format, but equally useful, this site contains easily navigable question-and-answer sections on different aspects of child care law and on other matters relating to looked after children. The site has been created by NCH with the Solicitors Family Law Association in consultation with many other parties.

Almost all of the web resources to which we have directed you in this book have been 'specialist' in the sense that they have a particular relevance to social work with children and families. We ought just to remind you that there are a great many 'generic' sites as well as a great many more specialisms out there! One simple way to begin exploring these is to explore the links provided by the Social Policy and Social Work – Learning and Teaching Support Network (**http://www. swap.ac.uk**). They list over 1000 social work relevant links.

Orders under the Children Act 1989

The following is a thumbnail description of all of the orders that may be made under the Children Act 1989, except those orders concerning financial provisions.

Order	Section	Description
Parental responsibility order	s. 4	Gives an unmarried father parental responsibility for his child
Appointment of Guardian	s. 5	Appoints a person as a child's Guardian
Termination of appointment of Guardian	s. 6	Terminates the appointment of a child's Guardian
Residence order	s. 8	Settles the arrangements as to with whom a child shall live
Section 8 contact order	s. 8	Directs a child's carer to allow the child contact with another person
Prohibited steps order	s. 8	Prevents a specific step that might be taken in relation to the exercise of parental responsibility
Specific issue order	s. 8	Resolves a specific issue in relation to any aspect of parental responsibility
Family assistance order	s. 16	Requires a probation officer or officer of the local authority to advise, assist and befriend a named person

Order	Section	Description
Secure accomodation order	s. 25	Authorizes the admission of a child to accomodation for the purpose of restricting liberty
Care order	s. 31	Places a child in the care of a named local authority (see Unit 10)
Supervision order	s. 31	Places a child under the supervision of a local authority or probation officer
Care contact order	s. 34	Regulates contact between a child in care and a named person
Education supervision order	s. 36	Places a child under the supervision of a named local education authority
Interim care/supervision order	s. 38	Temporary order made during the course of proceedings
Child assessment order	s. 43	Directs and authorizes an assessment of the child's health, development or the way in which the child is treated
Emergency protection order	s. 44	Directs the protection of the child and authorizes either the removal of the child to suitable accomodation or prevents the removal of the child from the place at which s/he is currently accommodated
Recovery order	s. 50	Provides for the recovery of a child in care or who is subject to an EPO or police protection and who has been abducted or has run away

APPENDIX 2

Index to Exercises

APPENDIX 3

Index to Study Texts

References

Abbott, P. (1989) 'Family lifestyles and structures.' In W.S. Rogers, D. Hevey and E. Ash (eds) *Child Abuse and Neglect – Facing the Challenge*. Milton Keynes: OUP.

Adcock, M. (2001) 'The core assessment process.' In J. Horwath (ed.) *The Child's World: Assessing Children in Need*. London: Jessica Kingsley Publishers.

Ahmad, B. (1992) *Black Perspectives in Social Work*. Birmingham: Venture Press.

Ainsworth, M.D.S., Blehar, M., Aters, E. and Wall, S. (1978) *Patterns of Attachment: A Psychological Study of the Strange Situation*. Hillsdale: NJ: Lawrence Erlbaum.

Aldgate, J. and Bradley, M. (1999) 'The children's story'. In *Supporting Families Through Short Term Fostering*. London: The Stationery Office.

Aldgate, J. and Statham, D. (2001) *The Children Act Now: Messages from Research*. London: The Stationery Office.

Aldgate, J. and Tunstill, J. (1995) *Making Sense of Section 17: Implementing Services for Children in Need within the 1989 Children Act*. London: HMSO.

Allan, G. and Crow, G. (2001) *Families, Households and Society*. Basingstoke: Palgrave/Macmillan.

Anderson, S. (1984) 'Goal setting in social work practice.' In B.R. Compton and B. Galaway (eds) *Social Work Processes*. Chicago: Dorsey Press.

Archard, D. (1993) *Children – Rights and Childhood*. London: Routledge.

Archard, D. (2001) 'Philosophical perspectives on childhood.' In J. Fionda (ed.) *Legal Concepts of Childhood*. Oxford: Hart Publishing.

Aries, P. (1960) *L'Enfant et la Vie Familiale sous l'Ancien Regime*. Paris: Libraire Plon. Translated by R. Baldick as *Centuries of Childhood* (1962). London: Jonathan Cape.

Armstrong, C. and Hill, M. (2001) 'Support services for vulnerable families with young children.' *Child and Family Social Work 6*, 351–8.

Arnstein, R.A. (1972) 'Power to the people: An assessment of the community action and model cities experience.' *Public Administration Review 32*, 377–89.

Atherton, C. and Dowling, P. (1989) 'Using written agreements: The family's point of view.' In J. Aldgate (ed.) *Using Written Agreements with Children and Families*. London: FRG.

Bannister, A. (2001) 'Entering the child's world: communicating with children to assess their needs.' In J. Horwath (ed.) *The Child's World: Assessing Children in Need.* London: Jessica Kingsley Publishers.

Bell, M. and Wilson, K. (eds) (2003) *The Practitioner's Guide to Working with Families.* Basingstoke: Palgrave/Macmillan.

Beresford, P. (1994) *Positively Parents: Caring for a Severely Disabled Child.* York: Social Policy Research Unit.

Berridge, D. and Brodie, I. (1998) 'Children's homes revisited.' In Department of Health (ed.) *Caring for Children Away from Home: Messages from Research.* Chichester: John Wiley and Sons.

Berridge, D., Brodie, I., Ayre, P., Barratt, D., Henderson, B. and Wenman, H. (1996) *Hello – Is Anyone Listening? The Education of Young People in Residential Care.* Luton: Luton University.

Berthoud, R. (1998) *Incomes of Ethnic Minorities.* Swindon: ESRC.

Biggs, V. and Robson, J. (1992) *Developing Your Court Skills.* London: BAAF.

Bloom, M. (1993) *Single System Designs in the Social Services: Issues and Options for the 1990s.* New York: Haworth.

Bowlby, J. (1970) *Attachment.* New York: Basic Books.

Bowlby, J. (1973) *Attachment and Loss, Vol. II: Separation, Anxiety and Anger.* London: Hogarth Press.

Bowlby, J. (1980) *Attachment and Loss, Vol. III: Loss, Sadness and Depression.* London: Hogarth Press.

Brammer, A. (2003) *Social Work Law.* Harlow: Pearson Education.

Brandon, M., Thoburn, J., Lewis, A. and Way, A. (1999) *Safeguarding Children with the Children Act 1989.* London: The Stationery Office.

Braye, S. and Preston-Shoot, M. (1997) *Practising Social Work Law.* Second edition. London: Macmillan.

Brayne, H., Martin, G. and Carr, H. (2001) *Law for Social Workers.* Seventh edition. Oxford: Oxford University Press.

Brook, E. and Davis, A. (eds) (1985) *Women, The Family and Social Work.* London: Tavistock.

Brophy, J. with Bates, P., Brown, L., Cohen, S., Radcliffe, P. and Wale, C.J. (1999) *Safeguarding Children with the Children Act 1989.* London: The Stationery Office.

Bryer, M. (1988) *Planning in Child Care.* London: BAAF.

Bullock, R., Little, M. and Milham, S. (1993) *Residential Care for Children – A Review of the Research.* London: HMSO.

Burden, D.S. and Gottlieb, N. (eds) (1987) *The Woman Client.* London: Tavistock.

Buss, A.H. and Plomin, R.A. (1984) *Temperament Theory of Personality Development.* New York: Wiley–Interscience.

Butler, I. (1996a) 'Children and the sociology of childhood.' In I. Butler and I. Shaw (eds) *A Case of Neglect? Children's Experiences and the Sociology of Childhood.* Aldershot: Avebury.

Butler, I. (1996b) 'Safe? Involving children in child protection.' In I. Butler and I. Shaw (eds) *A Case of Neglect? Children's Experiences and the Sociology of Childhood.* Aldershot: Avebury.

Butler, I. (2000) 'Child abuse.' In M. Davies (ed.) *The Blackwell Encyclopaedia of Social Work.* Oxford: Blackwell Publishers.

Butler, I. (2001) 'Abuse in institutional settings.' In K. Wilson and A. James (eds) *The Child Protection Handbook.* Second Edition. London: Baillière Tindall.

Butler, I. and Drakeford, M. (2001) 'Which Blair Project?: Communitarianism, social authoritarianism and social work.' *Journal of Social Work 1,* 1, 7– 20.

Butler, I. and Drakeford, M. (2003) *Social Policy, Social Welfare and Scandal: How British Public Policy is Made.* London: Palgrave/Macmillan.

Butler, I., Noaks, L., Douglas, G., Lowe, N. and Pithouse, A. (1993) 'The Children Act and the issue of delay.' *Family Law 23,* 412–14.

Butler, I. and Payne, H. (1997) 'The health of children looked after by the local authority.' *Adoption and Fostering 21,* 28–35.

Butler, I. and Pugh, R. (2003) 'The politics of social research.' In R. Lovelock, J. Powell and K. Lyons (eds) *Reflecting on Social Work.* Aldershot: Ashgate.

Butler, I., Scanlan, L., Robinson, M., Douglas, G. and Murch, M. (2003) *Divorcing Children: Children's Experience of their Parents' Divorce.* London: Jessica Kingsley Publishers.

Butler, I. and Williamson, H. (1994) *Children Speak: Children, Trauma and Social Work.* London: Longman.

Bynner, J. (2001) 'Childhood risks and protective factors in social exclusion.' *Children and Society 15,* 285–301.

Cheal, D. (1991) *Family and the State of Theory.* Hemel Hempstead: Harvester Wheatsheaf.

Cheetham, J. (1986) 'Introduction.' In S. Ahmed, J. Cheetham and J. Small (eds) *Social Work with Black Children and their Families.* London: Batsford.

Cleaver, H., Unell, I. and Aldgate, J. (1999) *Children's Needs – Parenting Capacity: The Impact of Parental Mental Illness, Problem Alcohol and Drug Use, and Domestic Violence on Children's Development.* London: The Stationery Office.

Cleaver, H., Watton, C. and Cawson, P. (1998) *Assessing Risk in Child Protection.* London: NSPCC.

Clement Brown, S. (1947) 'Foreword.' In D.M. Dyson, *The Foster Home and the Boarded Out Child*. London: George, Allen and Unwin.

Cleveland Report (1988) *Report of the Inquiry into Child Abuse in Cleveland*. London: HMSO.

Clyde Report (1992) *Report of the Inquiry into the Removal of Children from Orkney in February 1991*. Edinburgh: HMSO.

Coit, K. (1978) 'Local action not citizen participation.' In W. Tabb and L. Sawers (eds) *Marxism and the Metropolis*. New York: Oxford University Press.

Cooper, C. (1985) 'Good-enough, border line and bad-enough parenting.' In M. Adcock and R. White (eds) *Good Enough Parenting: A Framework for Assessment*. London: BAAF.

Corby, B. (2000a) 'Child protection.' In M. Davies (ed.) *The Blackwell Encyclopaedia of Social Work*. Oxford: Blackwell Publishers.

Corby, B. (2000b) *Towards a Knowledge Base*. Second edition. Buckingham: Open University Press.

Corob, A. (1987) *Working with Depressed Women*. Aldershot: Gower.

Coulshed, V. (1988) *Social Work Practice – An Introduction*. Basingstoke: Macmillan.

Cournoyer, B. (1991) *The Social Work Skills Workbook*. Belmont, CA: Wadsworth.

Cox, D. and Parish, A. (1989) *Working in Partnership*. Barkingside: Barnardos.

Creighton, S.J. (1986) *Child Abuse in 1985, Initial Findings from NSPCC Register Research*. London: NSPCC.

Creighton, S.J. (2001) 'Patterns and outcomes.' In K. Wilson and A. James (eds) *The Child Protection Handbook*. Second edition. London: Baillière Tindall.

Daniel, B., Wassell, S. and Gilligan, R. (1999) *Child Development for Child Care and Protection Workers*. London: Jessica Kingsley Publishers.

Davies, M. (1994) *The Essential Social Worker – A Guide to Positive Practice*. Third edition. Aldershot: Gower.

Davis, A., Llewellyn, S. and Parry, G. (1985) 'Women and mental health.' In E. Brook and A. Davis (eds) *Women, The Family and Social Work*. London: Tavistock.

de Mause, L. (1976) *The History of Childhood*. London: Souvenir Press.

Department for Education and Employment (2000a) *Sex and Relationship Education Guidance*. Nottingham: DFEE Publications.

Department for Education and Employment (2000b) *Guidance on the Education of Young People in Care*. London: The Stationery Office.

Department for Education and Employment (2001) *Learning to Listen: Care Principles for the Involvement of Children and Young People*. London: The Stationery Office.

Department of Health (1989) *An Introduction to the Children Act 1989*. London HMSO.

Department of Health (1990) *The Care of Children – Principles and Practice in Regulations and Guidance*. London: HMSO.

Department of Health (1991a) *The Children Act 1989 Guidance and Regulations Volume 3 Family Placements*. London: HMSO.

Department of Health (1991b) *The Children Act 1989 Guidance and Regulations Volume 1 Court Orders*. London: HMSO.

Department of Health (1991c) *The Children Act 1989 Guidance and Regulations Volume 2 Family Support, Day Care and Educational Provision for Young Children*. London: HMSO.

Department of Health (1991d) *Patterns and Outcomes in Child Placement – Messages from Current Research and their Implications*. London: HMSO.

Department of Health (1991e) *The Children Act 1989 Guidance and Regulations Volume 4 Residential Care*. London: HMSO.

Department of Health (1995) *Child Protection – Messages from Research*. London: HMSO.

Department of Health (1996) *Children Looked After by Local Authorities Year Ending 31 March 1994, England*. London: DOH/Government Statistical Service.

Department of Health (1998a) *Caring for Children Away from Home: Messages from Research*. Chichester: John Wiley and Sons.

Department of Health (1998b) *Modernising Social Services*. Cm 4169. London: The Stationery Office.

Department of Health (1999) *The Government's Objectives for Children's Social Services*. London: The Stationery Office.

Department of Health (2000) *Excellence Not Excuses: Inspection of Services for Ethnic Minority Children and Families*. London: The Stationery Office.

Department of Health (2001a) *Children Act Report 2000*. London: The Stationery Office.

Department of Health (2001b) *Transforming Social Services: An Evaluation of Local Responses to the Quality Protects Programme, Year 3*. London: Department of Health.

Department of Health (2002a) *Children's Homes National Minimum Standards Children's Homes Regulations*. London: The Stationery Office.

Department of Health (2002b) *Promoting The Health of Looked After Children*. London: Department of Health.

Department of Health (2002c) *Fostering Services: National Minimum Standards Fostering Services Regulations*. London: The Stationery Office.

Department of Health (2003a) *Personal Social Services Performance Assessment Framework*. Module 4, Version 5, March 2003. London: Department of Health.

Department of Health (2003b) *Children Looked After by Local Authorities. Year Ending 31 March 2002. England. Volume 1: Commentary and National Tables.* London: Department of Health.

Department of Health and Social Security (1985) *Social Work Decisions in Child Care – Recent Research Findings and their Implications.* London: HMSO.

Department of Health, Department for Education and Employment and Home Office (2000) *Framework for the Assessment of Children in Need and their Families.* London: The Stationery Office.

Department of Health, Home Office and Department for Education and Employment (1999) *Working Together to Safeguard Children.* London: The Stationery Office.

Department of Health, Home Office, Department for Education and Skills, Department for Culture Media and Sport, Office of the Prime Minister, Lord Chancellor (2003) *What to Do if You're Worried A Child Is Being Abused.* London: Department of Health Publications.

Department of Health, Office for National Statistics (2000) *Children in Need in England: First Results of a Survey of Activity and Expenditure as Reported by Local Authority Social Services' Children and Family Teams for a Survey Week in February 2000.* London: The Stationery Office.

Department of Health; Department of Transport, Local Government and the Regions; Centrepoint (2002) *Care Leaving Strategies.* London: DTLR.

Dingwall, R. (1989) 'Some problems about predicting child abuse and neglect.' In O. Stevenson (ed.) *Child Abuse: Public Policy and Professional Practice.* Hemel Hempstead: Harvester Wheatsheaf.

Directors of Social Work in Scotland (1992) *Child Protection: Policy Practice and Procedure.* Edinburgh: HMSO.

Dominelli, L. (1997) *Anti-Racist Social Work.* London: Macmillan/BASW.

Dominelli, L. and Mcleod, E. (1989) *Feminist Social Work.* London: Macmillan.

Donnison, D.V. (1954) *The Neglected Child and the Social Services.* Manchester: Manchester University Press.

Drakeford, M. (2000) *Privatisation and Social Policy.* Harlow: Longman.

Eekelaar, J. (1991) *Regulating Divorce.* London: OUP.

Eekelaar, J. and Dingwall, R. (1990) *The Reform of Child Care Law: A Practical Guide to the Children Act 1989.* London: Routledge.

Elias, N. (1939) *Über den Prozes der Zivilisation* ('The Civilising Process'). Basel: Falken.

Elliot, F.R. (1986) *The Family – Change or Continuity?* London: Allen and Unwin.

European Network on Childcare (1996) *A Review of Childcare Services for Young Children in the EU 1990–1995.* Brussels: Equal Opportunities Unit.

Fahlberg, V. (1985) 'Checklists on attachment.' In M. Adcock and R. White (eds) *Good Enough Parenting: A Framework for Assessment.* London: BAAF.

Fahlberg, V. (1988) *Fitting the Pieces Together.* London: BAAF.

Fahlberg, V. (1994) *A Child's Journey through Placement.* London: BAAF.

Firestone, S. (1979) 'Childhood is hell.' In M. Hoyles (ed.) *Changing Childhood.* London: Writers and Readers Publishing Co-operative.

Firth, H. and Horrocks, H. (1996) 'No home, no school, no future: Exclusions and children who are looked after.' In E. Blyth and J. Milner (eds) *Exclusion from School: Interprofessional Issues for Policy and Practice.* London: Routledge.

Fischer, J. (1993) 'Empirically based practice: The end of ideology?' In M. Bloom (ed.) *Single System Designs in the Social Services: Issues and Options for the 1990s.* New York: Haworth.

Fischoff, B., Lichtenstein, S. and Slovic, P. (1981) *Acceptable Risk.* Cambridge: Cambridge University Press.

Foley, P., Roche, J. and Tucker, S. (2001) *Children in Society.* Basingstoke: Palgrave (in association with the Open University).

Fortin, J. (1998) *Children's Rights and the Developing Law.* London: Butterworths.

Frankenburg, S. (1946) *Common Sense in the Nursery.* London: Penguin.

Franklin, B. (ed.) (1995) *The Handbook of Children's Rights – Comparative Policy and Practice.* London: Routledge.

Freeman, P. and Hunt, J. (1998) *Parental Perspectives on Care Proceedings.* London: The Stationery Office.

FRG (Family Rights Group) (1989) *Using Written Agreements with Children and Families.* London: FRG.

Frosh, S. (2001) 'Characteristics of sexual abusers.' In K. Wilson and A. James (eds) *The Child Protection Handbook.* Second edition. London: Baillière Tindall.

Fry, S. (1993) 'The family curse.' In *Paperweight.* London: Mandarin.

Gambe, D., Gomes, J., Kapur, V., Rangel, M. and Stubbs, P. (1992) *Improving Practice with Children and Families.* Leeds: CCETSW.

Garrett, P.M. (1999) 'Mapping child-care social work in the final years of the twentieth century: A critical response to the "looking after children" system.' *British Journal of Social Work 29,* 27–47.

Ghate, D. and Hazel, N. (2002) *Parenting in Poor Environments: Stress, Support and Coping.* London: Jessica Kingsley Publishers.

Gibbons, J., Thorpe, S. and Wilkinson, P. (1990) *Family Support and Prevention: Studies in Local Areas.* London: NISW.

Gibbs, L. and Gambrill, E. (2002) 'Evidence-based practice: Counterarguments to objections.' *Research on Social Work Practice 12*, 3, 452–76.

Gilligan, R. (2001) *Promoting Resilience: A Resource Guide on Working with Children in the Care System.* London: BAAF Adoption and Fostering.

Goddard, J. (2000) 'The education of looked after children.' *Child and Family Social Work 5*, 79–86.

Goldman, L. (1994) *Life and Loss: A Guide to Helping Grieving Children.* Brighton: Brunner/Routledge.

Grant, L. (1997) *Moyenda: Black Families Talking – Family Survival Strategies.* London: Exploring Parenthood.

Greenland, C. (1987) *Preventing CAN Deaths: An International Study of Deaths Due to Child Abuse and Neglect.* London: Tavistock.

Grimshaw, R. and Sinclair, I. (1997) *Planning to Care: Procedure and Practice under the Children Act 1989.* London: National Children's Bureau.

Hale, J. (1983) 'Feminism and social work practice.' In B. Jordan and N. Parton (eds) *The Political Dimensions of Social Work.* Oxford: Blackwell.

Hanmer, J. and Statham, D. (1988) *Women and Social Work – Towards a Woman Centred Practice.* London: Macmillan.

Harris, C.C. (1984) *The Family and Industrial Society.* London: Allen and Unwin.

Harwin, J., Owen, M., Locke, R. and Forrester, D. (forthcoming) *Making Care Orders Work: A Study of Care Plans and their Implementation.* London: The Stationery Office.

Hayden, C., Goddard, J., Gorin, S. and Van Der Spek, N. (1999) *State Child Care: Looking After Children.* London: Jessica Kingsley Publishers.

Hendrick, H. (1994) *Child Welfare England 1872–1989.* London: Routledge.

Heptinstall, E., Bhopal, K. and Brannen, J. (2001) 'Adjusting to a foster family: Children's perspectives.' *Adoption and Fostering 25*, 4, 6–16.

Hepworth, D.H. and Larsen, J.A. (1982) *Direct Social Work Practice: Theory and Skills.* Chicago, IL: Dorsey Press.

Holman, R. (1975) 'The place of fostering in social work.' *British Journal of Social Work 5*, 1, 3–29.

Holman, R. (1988) *Putting Families First.* Basingstoke: Macmillan.

Holt, J. (1975) *Escape from Childhood – The Needs and Rights of Children.* London: Penguin.

Horwath, J. (ed.) (2001) *The Child's World: Assessing Children in Need.* London: Jessica Kingsley Publishers.

Howe, D. (1987) *An Introduction to Social Work Theory.* Aldershot: Wildwood House.

Howe, D. (2001) 'Attachment.' In J. Horwath (ed.) *The Child's World: Assessing Children in Need.* London: Jessica Kingsley Publishers.

Humphrey, J.C. (2002) 'Joint reviews: Retracing the trajectory, defining the terms.' *British Journal of Social Work 32,* 463–76.

Humphrey, J.C. (2003) 'Joint reviews: The methodology in action.' *British Journal of Social Work 33,* 177–90.

Jackson, S. (1989) 'Residential care and education.' *Children and Society 4,* 335–50.

Jackson, S. (1998) 'Looking after children: A new approach or just an exercise in formfilling? A response to Knight and Caveney.' *British Journal of Social Work 28,* 45–56.

James, A. and James, A. (2003) *Childhood: Theory, Policy and Practice.* Basingstoke: Palgrave/Macmillan.

James, A. and Prout, A. (1997) 'A new paradigm for the sociology of childhood? Provenance, promise and problems.' In A. James and A. Prout (eds) *Constructing and Reconstructing Childhood: Contemporary Issues in the Sociological Study of Childhood.* London: The Falmer Press.

James, A.N. (1998) 'Supporting families of origin: An exploration of the influence of the Children Act 1948.' *Child and Family Social Work 3,* 173–81.

Jensen, A.-M. and McKee, L. (2003) *Children and the Changing Family: Between Transformation and Negotiation.* London: Routledge/Falmer.

Jewett, C. (1984) *Helping Children Cope with Separation and Loss.* London: BAAF.

Johnson, T. (1972) *Professions and Power.* London: Macmillan.

Jones, D. (2001) 'The assessment of parental capacity.' In J. Horwath (ed.) *The Child's World: Assessing Children in Need.* London: Jessica Kingsley Publishers.

Jordan, B. (1981) 'Prevention.' *Adoption and Fostering 5,* 3, 20–2.

Joshi, H. (1992) 'The cost of caring.' In C. Glendinning and J. Millar (eds) *Women and Poverty in Britain in the 1990s.* Hemel Hempstead: Harvester Wheatsheaf.

Kates, V. (1985) 'Success, strain and surprise.' *Issues in Science and Technology 2,* 46–58.

Kellmer Pringle, M.L. (1974) *The Needs of Children.* London: Hutchinson.

Knight, T. and Caveney, S. (1998) 'Assessment and action records: Will they promote good parenting?' *British Journal of Social Work 28,* 29–43.

Lorde, A. (1984) *Sister Outsider.* New York: Crossing Press.

Lupton, D. (1999) *Risk (Key Ideas).* London: Routledge.

MacDonald, G. (1994) 'Developing empirically-based practice in probation.' *British Journal of Social Work 24,* 4, 405–27.

MacDonald, G. (1998) 'Promoting evidence-based practice in child protection.' *Clinical Child Psychiatry and Psychology 3,* 1, 71–85.

MacDonald, G. (2001) *Effective Intervention for Child Abuse and Neglect: An Evidence Based Approach to Planning and Evaluating Intervention*. Chichester: John Wiley.

MacDonald, G. and Sheldon, B. (1992) 'Contemporary studies in the effectiveness of social work.' *British Journal of Social Work 22*, 5, 615–43.

Macdonald, S. (1991) *All Equal Under the Act?* London: REU/NISW.

MacFarlane, A. (1986) *Marriage and Love in England: Modes of Reproduction*. Oxford: Blackwell.

MacPherson, W. (1999) *The Stephen Lawrence Inquiry: Report of an Inquiry by Sir William MacPherson of Cluny*. Cm 4262–1. London: The Stationary Office.

Madge, N. (2001) *Understanding Difference: The Meaning of Ethnicity for Young Lives*. London: National Children's Bureau.

McCarthy, M. (1989) 'Personal social services.' In M. McCarthy (ed.) *The New Politics of Welfare: An Agenda for the 1990s?* London: Macmillan.

McGuire, J. (1995) *What Works? – Reducing Reoffending*. Chichester: Wiley.

Menzies, I.E.P. (1970) *The Functioning of Social Systems as a Defence Against Anxiety*. Tavistock Pamphlet No.3. London: Tavistock Institute of Human Relations.

Meyer, D.J. (ed.) (1995) *Uncommon Fathers: Reflections on Raising a Child with a Disability*. Bethesda, MD: Woodbine House.

Minty, B. and Patterson, G. (1994) 'The nature of child neglect.' *British Journal of Social Work 24*, 734–47.

Munro, E. (2001) 'Empowering looked after children.' *Child and Family Social Work 6*, 129–37.

National Commission of Inquiry into the Prevention of Child Abuse (1996) *Childhood Matters*. London: The Stationery Office.

NCH (1999) *Factfile*. London: NCH Action for Children.

Newell, P. (1993) *The UN Convention and Children's Rights in the UK*. London: NCB.

NSPCC (National Society for the Prevention of Cruelty to Children) (1997) *Turning Points: A Resource Pack for Communicating with Children*. London: NSPCC Publications.

O'Hagan, K. and Dillenburger, K. (1995) *The Abuse of Women Within Childcare Work*. Buckingham: Open University Press.

Oakley, A. (1982) *Subject Women*. London: Fontana.

ONS (Office for National Statistics) (2001) *Social Trends No.31*. London: The Stationery Office.

ONS (Office for National Statistics) (2002) *Social Trends No.32*. London: The Stationery Office.

Packman, J. and Jordan, B. (1991) 'The Children Act: Looking forward, looking back.' *British Journal of Social Work 21*, 2, 315–27.

Parker, R., Ward, H., Jackson, S., Aldgate, J. and Wedge, P. (1991) *Assessing Outcomes in Child Care.* London: HMSO.

Parton, N. (1985) *The Politics of Child Abuse.* Basingstoke: Macmillan.

Parton, N. (1997) *Child Protection and Family Support: Tensions, Contradictions and Possibilities.* London: Routledge.

Parton, N. (1998) 'Risk, advanced literalism and child welfare: No need to rediscover uncertainty and ambiguity.' *British Journal of Social Work 28*, 1, 5–27.

Parton, N. (2000) 'Some thoughts on the relationship between theory and practice in and for social work.' *British Journal of Social Work 30*, 4, 449–64.

Parton, N. (2001) 'Risk and professional judgement.' In L. Cull and J. Roche (eds) *The Law and Social Work.* Basingstoke: Open University Press.

Phillipson, J. (1992) *Practising Equality – Women, Men and Social Work.* London: CCETSW.

Pinchbeck, I. and Hewitt, M. (1973) *Children in English Society.* London: Routledge and Kegan Paul.

Plotnikoff, J. and Woolfson, R. (1996) *Reporting to Court under the Children Act.* London: HMSO.

Pollock, L.H. (1983) *Forgotten Children: Parent–Child Relations from 1500 to 1900.* Cambridge: Cambridge University Press.

Quinton, D. (1994) 'Cultural and community influences.' In M. Rutter and D.F. Hay (eds) *Development Through Life: A Handbook for Clinicians.* Oxford: Blackwell Scientific Publications.

Qureshi, T., Berridge, D. and Wenman, H. (2000) *Where to Turn? Family Support for South Asian Communities.* London: National Children's Bureau.

Rashid, S.P. (1996) 'Attachment reviewed through a cultural lens.' In D. Howe (ed.) *Attachment and Loss in Child and Family Social Work.* Aldershot: Avebury.

Reder, P. and Duncan, S. (1999) *Lost Innocents – A Follow Up Study of Fatal Child Abuse.* London: Routledge.

Reder, P., Duncan, S. and Gray, M. (1993) *Beyond Blame – Child Abuse Tragedies Revisited.* London: Routledge.

Reid, W. (1994) 'Reframing the epistemological debate.' In E. Sherman and W. Reid (eds) *Qualitative Research in Social Work.* New York: Catholic University Press.

Richards, A. and Ince, L. (2000) *Looked After Children: Quality Services for Black and Minority Ethnic Children and their Families.* London: Family Rights Group.

Rogers, C.M. and Wrightsman, L.S. (1978) 'Attitudes towards children's rights: Nurturance or self determination.' *Journal of Social Issues 34*, 2, 59–68.

Rose, W. (2001) 'Assessing children in need and their families: An overview of the framework.' In J. Horwath (ed.) *The Child's World: Assessing Children in Need.* London: Jessica Kingsley Publishers.

Royal Society (1992) *Risk Analysis, Perception and Management: Report of a Royal Society Study Group.* London: The Royal Society.

Sackett, D.L., Richardson, W.S., Rosenberg, W.S. and Haynes, R.B. (1997) *Evidence-based Medicine: How to Practice and Teach EBP.* New York: Churchill Livingstone.

Sargent, K (1999) 'Assessing risk for children.' In P. Parsloe (ed.) *Risk Assessment in Social Care and Social Work.* London: Jessica Kingsley Publishers.

Schwehr, B. (2001) 'Human rights and social services.' In L. Cull and J. Roche (eds) *The Law and Social Work.* Basingstoke: Palgrave.

Scourfield, J (2003) *Gender and Child Protection.* Basingstoke: Palgrave/Macmillan.

Seden, J. (2001) 'Assessment of children in need and their families: A literature review.' In Department of Health *Studies Informing the Framework for the Assessment of Children in Need and their Families.* London: The Stationery Office.

Seden, J., Sinclair, R., Robbins, D. and Pont, C. (2001) *Studies Informing the Framework for the Assessment of Children in Need and their Families.* London: The Stationery Office.

Shaw, M. (1989) 'Social work and children's rights.' Paper presented at a conference at the University of Leicester School of Medical Sciences, 19 April.

Sheldon, B. (1980) *The Use of Contracts in Social Work.* Practice Notes Series No.1. Birmingham: BASW.

Shemmings, Y. and Shemmings, D. (2001) 'Empowering children and family members to participate in the assessment process.' In J. Horwath (ed.) *The Child's World: Assessing Children in Need.* London: Jessica Kingsley Publishers.

Short Report (1984) *Second Report from the Social Services Committee: Children in Care.* Volume One. London: HMSO.

Shorter, E. (1976) *The Making of the Modern Family.* London: Collins.

Solomos, J. (2003) *Race and Racism in Britain.* Third edition. Basingstoke: Palgrave/Macmillan.

Stein, M. (1994) 'Leaving care: Education and career trajectories.' *Oxford Review of Education 20*, 348–60.

Stone, L. (1977) *The Family, Sex and Marriage in England 1500–1800.* London: Weidenfeld and Nicholson.

Stone, M. (1992) *Child Protection: A Model for Risk Assessment in Physical Abuse/Neglect.* Thames Ditton: Surrey County Council.

Stoppard, M. (1983) *The Baby Care Book.* London: Dorling Kindersley.

Thoburn, J. (1999) 'Trends in foster care and adoption.' In O. Stevenson (ed.) *Child Welfare in the UK.* Oxford: Blackwell Science.

Thoburn, J., Wilding, J. and Watson, J. (2000) *Services for Children in Need: From Policy to Practice.* London: The Stationery Office.

Thomas, N. and O'Kane, C. (1999) 'Children's participation in reviews and planning meetings when they are looked after in middle childhood.' *Child and Family Social Work 4*, 221–30.

Timms, N. and Timms, R. (1982) *Dictionary of Social Welfare.* London: RKP.

TOPSS (Training Organisation for the Personal Social Services) (England) (2002) *The National Occupational Standards for Social Work.* Leeds: TOPSS.

Tunstill, J. (1996) 'Family support.' *Child and Family Social Work 3*, 151–8.

Tunstill, J. and Aldgate, J. (2000) *Services for Children in Need: From Policy to Practice.* London: The Stationery Office.

UNICEF (2000) *The State of the World's Children.* New York: UNICEF.

Utting, W. (1991) *Children in the Public Care – A Review of Residential Care.* London: SSI/HMSO.

Utting, W., Department of Health, Welsh Office (1997) *People Like Us – A Report of the Review of Safeguards for Children Living Away from Home.* London: The Stationery Office.

Van Bueren, G. (1995) *The International Law on the Rights of the Child.* Dordrecht and London: Martinus Nijhoff Publishers.

Van Every, J. (1992) 'Who is the family? The assumptions of British social policy.' *Critical Social Policy 33*, 62–75.

Webb, S.A. (2001) 'Some considerations on the validity of evidence-based practice in social work.' *British Journal of Social Work 31*, 1, 57–80.

White, R. (1983) 'Written agreements with families.' *Adoption and Fostering 7*, 4, 24–8.

Wilson, K. and James, A. (eds) (2001) *The Child Protection Handbook.* Second edition. London: Baillière Tindall.

Winnicott, D.W. (1965) *The Maturational Processes and the Facilitating Environment: Studies in the Theory of Emotional Development.* London: Hogarth.

Wise, S. (1985) *Becoming a Feminist Social Worker.* Manchester: Department of Sociology, University of Manchester.

Subject Index

Author Index